Criminal Procedure in Scotland and France

A comparative study, with particular emphasis
on the role of the public prosecutor

A. V. Sheehan, M.A., LL.B.

Procurator Fiscal Service
Scotland

EDINBURGH
HER MAJESTY'S STATIONERY OFFICE

ISBN 0 11 491329 3

Acknowledgements

I wish to acknowledge my grateful thanks to the Leverhulme Trust Fund for the award of a Leverhulme Fellowship in 1971–72 without which this book could not have been written.

I also wish to acknowledge my indebtedness to the following persons for their invaluable assistance and kindness:

Mr. S. Bowen, the Crown Agent, Edinburgh;
Mr. W. G. Chalmers, Deputy Crown Agent;
Miss M. D. Selby, the Crown Office.

Mr. H. Herron, procurator fiscal, Glasgow;
Mr. D. B. Copeland, procurator fiscal, Hamilton;
My colleagues in the procurator fiscal service.

The Rt. Hon. Baron Wilson of Langside, Q.C., Director, the Scottish Courts Administration.

Professor J. D. B. Mitchell, the Centre of European Governmental Studies, the University of Edinburgh, and his most helpful staff.

Professor G. H. Gordon, Dean of the Faculty of Law, the University of Edinburgh, and other members of the Law Faculty.

Professor A. E. Anton, Department of Jurisprudence, the University of Glasgow.

Mr. P. A. Pageaud, procureur de la République, près le Tribunal de Grande Instance de Paris.

Mr. J. P. Cochard and Mr. Y. Roux, Sécrétaire Général du Parquet de Paris.

Mr. G. Chavanon, procureur général près le Cour d'Appel de Paris.

Mr. M. Viennois, Chef du Bureau du Droit Criminel International et Européen, Ministère de la Justice, Paris, and his colleagues and staff.

Mr. J. Y. Bertrand-Cadi, Maître de Conférences, L'École Nationale de la Magistrature.

Mr. F. G. Marx, the French Embassy (Service culturel), London.

Mr. Le Baron Louis de Cabrol, and his staff at the Consulat General de France, Edinburgh.

Miss T. Cullis, the British Consul, Paris, and the staff of the British Embassy, Paris.

L'Institut Français Culturel, Glasgow.

Mr. G. L. Birch, the Director, Her Majesty's Stationery Office, and his most helpful staff.

The many procureurs, juges, juges d'instruction and other 'magistrats', and members of the various police forces too numerous to mention individually for their unfailing kindness, courtesy and co-operation.

ALBERT V. SHEEHAN

Glasgow, December 1972

Contents

Preface

Introduction

FRANCE

Chapter 5. General Principles of French Criminal Procedure Page

Chapter 6. Institution of Criminal Proceedings

Chapter 7. Proceedings in Court—Trials

Chapter 8. Penalties

Chapter 9. Appeals

SCOTLAND

Chapter 6. Institution of Criminal Proceedings

Chapter 7. Proceedings in court—Trials

Solemn Procedure—

Summary Procedure—

Chapter 8. Penalties

Chapter 9. Appeals

Appendices

Preface

By the Right Honourable Ronald King Murray, QC, MP,
Her Majesty's Advocate

The law is always changing—and the criminal law of Scotland is no exception. If some part of our procedure appears to need alteration, it is extremely helpful to be able to see what happens in other countries. And which other country could provide a better comparison than the other half of the Auld Alliance—France, where procedures in criminal investigations and prosecutions are in some ways so similar to those of Scotland yet in many respects are very dissimilar?

Mr. Sheehan has, of course, considerable experience in the Procurator Fiscal Service in Scotland, but during the year which he spent in France he clearly comprehended the intricacies of the system there, and he appreciates its merits; with the result that his book is a well-balanced comparison of the two sets of procedure.

Jurists not only of France and Scotland but also of other countries are indebted to Mr. Sheehan, and to the Leverhulme Trust, who financed him, for this valuable contribution to our legal literature.

CP-B

Introduction

Modern jurisprudence makes a general distinction between the legal systems of the Anglo-American countries and those of the Continent of Europe. In the realms of criminal law, there is a further difference in that the system practised by the former is described as accusatorial and the latter as inquisitorial. Scots criminal law, which is basically accusatorial, has much in common with the continental countries and in many ways represents a mixture of both systems.

It is often widely assumed that English law applies to the entire United Kingdom, but when the parliaments of Scotland and England were united to form the parliament of Great Britain by the Treaty of Union in 1707, a condition of the Treaty stipulated that Scots law was to retain its separate identity. To this day, Scotland still has its own legal system completely independent of that practised in England and often differing widely therefrom. This difference is very material in the realms of criminal law and applies not only to the law itself, but to legal procedure, the courts, and the persons entrusted with administering and enforcing the law. Since the eighteenth century, Scots law has been influenced by English legal thought and tradition rather than continental, but Scotland has long historical associations with France.

In the fifteenth century it was common practice for Scottish law students to obtain their legal education by attending such French universities as Paris, Bourges, Orleans, Poitiers and Louvain, a practice that lasted until the seventeenth or eighteenth century. During this period, the works of French jurists could be quoted as authority in Scottish courts. Apart from any effect this may have had on the moulding of modern law, certain vestiges from these times are still apparent in Scotland. A Scottish barrister is known as an advocate, as compared with the French 'avocat'; the Scottish term 'solicitor' is derived from the French 'solliciteur' (a term no longer used in modern France). The institution of counsel for the poor introduced in France in 1400 and 1414 (and still in existence today) was adopted by Scotland in 1424 and lasted until a few years ago when a scheme for legal aid in criminal causes was put into practice. The French public prosecutor is called a 'procureur' corresponding to the procurator fiscal, the public prosecutor in Scotland. The concept of pre-trial inquiries being made by the prosecutor or other judicial authority in France has much in common with Scotland where such enquiries are made by the procurator fiscal (and formerly by the Sheriff). It is thus true to say that while Scots law is 'largely indigenous having grown and developed naturally' it has 'strong connections and logical affinities with the legal systems of, and derived from Continental Europe.'[1]

To make a detailed comparison of modern Scots law with that of several con-

---

[1] Walker on the Scottish Legal System.

tinental countries is too great a work to be undertaken here, but since French law set the pattern for much of the continent, and excellent comparative studies exist between French and other European systems, the comparison has been restricted to France, and in particular French criminal procedure. The basic rules and the application thereof will be considered, but a comparative work of this nature can not claim to give exhaustive detail of either system. Any examination of legal procedure based purely on books of law and statute will only provide the theory of how the law should be applied, which often differs from the actual practice. Indeed one modern jurist states that any attempt to define the law is merely an attempt to predict what the courts will do. The exigencies of the moment, the need to adapt to a rapidly changing society, the slowness of legislative machinery, or the impractical nature of the law as it stands all pose problems which the lawyer must overcome as best he may, by interpretation of the law, by mutual agreement between the parties to the case, or by compromise. This book attempts to set forth the law as it is actually practised from day to day in the courts.

In all systems of government, a balance must be drawn between the interests of society and the rights of the individual. If the bringing of criminal proceedings is not to be left in the hands of the private individual, the State must decide how it should intervene to ensure that the interests of society are protected and the laws passed by the legislature are enforced in the courts. Where there is an independent judiciary, the intervention of the State is personified by the public prosecutor. The powers given to him and the restrictions binding him frequently indicate where the balance lies between the State and the individual. The public prosecutor thus becomes an important figure in the machinery of government.

In Scotland, as in France the office of public prosecutor has long existed and forms an integral part of the administration of justice. A comparison of the French and Scottish prosecutors is of interest as an illustration of the attitudes of the respective States to the private citizen. It is however of greater practical value to compare the role of the public prosecutor as an essential figure in the administration of the two countries which share a common legal heritage subsequently developed independently.

At the present time there is a general atmosphere of change and desire for reform in the legal world. In Scotland, a committee recently recommended changes in criminal procedure[2] and legislation embodied some of the suggested reforms. Further legislation may be forth-coming. In 1969 a government committee was constituted under the chairmanship of Lord Thomson to consider Scottish criminal procedure with the following remit—'To examine trial and pre-trial procedures in Scotland (including appeal procedures) for the prosecution of persons accused of crimes and offences, and to report whether having regard to the prevention of crime on the one hand and the need for fairness to accused persons on the other hand, any changes of law or practice are required.'

In England, the organisation of the criminal courts was radically altered in 1972.[3] Furthermore there is a considerable body of opinion in England that the time has come for changes to be made and that a system of public prosecution broadly following the lines of the Scottish system should be introduced.[4] This

[2] Report by the Grant Committee—H.M.S.O. Cmnd. 3248/67.

[3] Courts Act 1971.

[4] Report by Justice (The British Section of the International Commission of Jurists) on the Prosecution Process in England and Wales, 1970.

opinion is gaining ground with the present trend for English police forces to amalgamate into larger units each employing a full-time lawyer to conduct prosecutions on behalf of the police.

In France, although criminal procedure is constantly being reviewed and new laws effect changes each year, there is a widespread feeling that the time has now come for drastic revision to reduce the delays, the formalities and the cumbersome nature of French procedure and to make it better adapted to meet the needs of a modern society. There are many outspoken critics in France, not the least being the judges, prosecutors and lawyers, all desirous of change, and while this may vary between the two extremes of replacing the entire system with a new one on the one hand, and merely making one or two minor amendments on the other, the general attitude does not appear to be one of complacency.

While the entry of Britain into the Common Market does not directly affect the criminal law of any of the member states, the closer relationship and co-operation between the Community countries will entail a greater exchange of ideas and information, inevitably including some aspects of criminal procedure. Greater freedom of movement and travel results in more crimes being committed by foreign nationals and crime itself undoubtedly becomes more international, as has been proved by experience. Such a problem existed among the original Common Market countries and led to greater co-operation between the law enforcement authorities in these countries. With the entry of Britain, the involvement of the British authorities with those of the other member countries is certain.

Finally, since crime itself knows no boundaries, the problems caused thereby are not unique to one country and are frequently common to all. By gaining an insight into how another country uses its legal procedure to combat such problems, it is possible to appraise one's own system in a different light and learn from the experience of others.

France

1. Historical and Political Background[1]

The Legislature

1 Montesquieu stated 'Il y a dans chaque état trois sortes de pouvoirs—la puissance legislative, la puissance executrice . . . et . . . la puissance de juger.' In order to appreciate the role played by criminal law in the general machinery of government, it is advisable to make a very brief examination of its historical and political context.

Since the French Revolution less than two hundred years ago, France has experienced two empires, three monarchies and five republics. The present Fifth Republic, which is based on a written constitution consists of the President de la République, and two legislative assemblies, L'Assemblée Nationale (also known as la Chambre des Deputés) and the Conseil de la République (more commonly called le Senat). The prime minister is formally appointed by the President de la République after receiving a vote of confidence in L'Assemblée Nationale and thereafter forms his government, one of the Ministers being the Minister of Justice. Legislative measures are passed by L'Assemblée Nationale then sent to the Senat and finally the President for approval. While both have powers to delay legislation, neither can ultimately prevent its coming into effect. Such a measure is known as a 'loi'.

Great use has also been made of delegated legislation, usually called a 'decret loi', 'ordonnance' or 'arrêté'. The reason is due partly to the sheer volume of legislation which can not all be considered by L'Assemblée Nationale, and partly to long periods of legislative inactivity due to changes in the constitution or government[2]. Delegated legislation is usually effected by means of statutory powers given to a member of the government for a limited period to make laws on a particular subject without the approval of L'Assemblée Nationale. Many measures amending or reforming existing laws are passed in this way, and a striking example is the Constitution of 1958 which allows all criminal offences classed as 'contraventions'[3] to be dealt with by means of delegated legislation.

The Minister of Justice

2 The Minister of Justice, whose formal title is 'Garde des Sceaux' (Keeper of the Seals) plays an important role in the administration of criminal justice. He is a politician who is a member of L'Assemblée Nationale or of the Senat. He rarely has any form of legal training but may rely on advice from the full-time civil

---

[1] For Scotland, see para 109.

[2] France and 125 Prime Ministers in the 82 years between 1875 and 1957.

[3] See para 7.

servants in the Ministry of Justice, some of whom are 'magistrats' and others have legal qualifications. He has many administrative duties which include the appointment of judges and prosecutors, and overall control of and responsibility for the prosecution of crime. He has numerous other responsibilities, not the least being the drafting of legislation.

Local Government

3　In addition to its central government, France also has a very detailed system of local government which basically follows the pattern laid down by Napoleon. France is divided into 95 'départements' each of which has a 'préfet' who is appointed by and responsible to the central government. In addition to the 'préfet', each 'departement' has an elected council ('conseil général'). A 'département' is divided into 'arrondissements', each of which has a 'sous-préfet' responsible to the 'préfet'. An 'arrondissement' is subdivided into 'cantons' which often serve to form the territorial jurisdiction of courts. Finally, each 'arrondissement' is divided into 'communes', being the smallest unit of local government. A 'commune' has an elected council from whom a mayor is appointed, and although in theory he is independent, in practice, he is subject to the control of the 'sous-préfet'. It thus follows that the central government exerts a great deal of authority over local administration. Certain units of local government have the power to make local byelaws, breach of which may be punishable in the criminal courts.

The French Legal System

4　With regard to French law, it may clearly be divided into different sections—criminal, civil, administrative, commercial, tax, industrial, rent etc. As each section of the law has its own courts to administer justice, this leads to a proliferation of different courts each specialising in one branch of the law. One of the criminal courts which should be mentioned here, as it will not be dealt with later, is the Haute Cour de Justice which was specifically created to try the President de la République should he be charged with treason, or government ministers charged with committing criminal offences in the course of their duties[4]. Should a dispute arise as to which court has jurisdiction to deal with a particular case, the matter is remitted to the 'Tribunal des conflits' to settle the question of jurisdiction.

[4] Proceedings are instituted by means of a majority vote in both L'Assemblée Nationale and the Senat.

2. Sources of Criminal Law[1]

Legislation

5 The main source of French criminal law is legislation, most of which has been codified. The first attempt to codify criminal law was in 1791, but this was short-lived and replaced in 1810 by the present Code pénal,[2] which embodied and reformed the existing law, adding some of the doctrines of the French Revolution. This Code is one the oldest in Europe and is still in force today. Since 1810 it has been frequently amended by statute or delegated legislation such amendments becoming more frequent in recent years.[3] Numerous supplements have also been embodied into the original code, such as the present Road Traffic law which is governed by an 'ordonnance' of 1958, which itself has since been amended, and in 1970 contained 296 sections. As a result, despite frequent changes, some parts of the original code are still in force today and are often not acceptable to modern society. The Code defines criminal responsibility, circumstances which may act as aggravating or mitigating factors, legal defences and what constitutes criminal offences for which both the minimum and maximum penalties are fixed. For example, in dealing with theft, the Code states:

Article 379. 'Any person who fraudulently takes away anything which does not belong to him is guilty of theft.'

Article 380. 'The taking away of anything by one spouse from another . . . shall only give rise to a civil action . . . '

Article 381. 'The penalty for carrying weapons while committing a theft, whether such weapons were concealed or not . . . is death.'

And the same penalty shall apply if a weapon was kept in a motor vehicle used to convey the thief to the scene of the crime or to flee from it.

'Any person convicted of theft, shall be sentenced to life imprisonment if any four of the following conditions apply:

—the theft was committed at night

—two or more persons were involved

—the theft was committed in an inhabited . . . house . . . after entrance had been gained by breaking in, using false keys . . .

—violence was used

—a motor vehicle was used to facilitate the theft or subsequent flight.'

---

[1] For Scotland see para 113 et seq.

[2] For citation purposes this is referred to as 'C.P.'.

[3] Between 1810 and 1910 there were 54 measures amending or affecting the original Code; between 1960 and 1970 there were approximately 184 such measures.

Article 382. 'A sentence of imprisonment of not less than ten years and not more than twenty years shall be imposed on any person who uses violence in the furtherance of theft. If such violence results in injury, the penalty shall be imprisonment for life.'

Article 383. 'Theft committed on a public road, or in passenger trains . . . where two of the conditions mentioned in Article 381 apply, shall be punishable with imprisonment for life . . . '

Article 386. 'A penalty of imprisonment for not less than five years, and not more than ten years shall be pronounced on anyone convicted of theft accompanied by any one of the following conditions:

—if the theft was committed by night and by two or more persons, or with one of these conditions but in an inhabited place . . . '

—if the theft was committed by a servant . . . '[4].

While the Code pénal is the main source of criminal law, it is not the exclusive statutory source. A few statutes which were passed before 1810 and cover offences not included in the Code, are still effective—for example, in 1923 in a case concerning a strike by butchers, it was held that an edict of 1776 was still applicable. Furthermore the Code pénal does not include byelaws and other administrative regulations which are enforced in the criminal courts.

The Code pénal does not deal with procedural matters which are regulated by the Code de procédure pénale,[5] which was passed on 31 December 1957. Since coming into effect, the Code de procédure pénale had been amended or supplemented by approximately 86 measures by 1970, the most important being in 1960, 1963, 1964, 1967 and 1970.

Both the Code pénal and the Code de procédure pénale are supplemented by certain traditional and unwritten rules. Furthermore both are frequently adapted by means of interpretation, the use of discretion or agreement between the parties to the case.

Case-law

6 No French court may make a decision binding future cases.[6] The only decision which is binding is when an appeal is taken to the Cour de Cassation sitting in full bench which is then final quoad the case to which the appeal relates—but not to other cases. However, although decisions are not binding, case law (for which the French term is 'jurisprudence') should not be discounted as a source of law, as it may have a strong persuasive effect and is particularly valuable when interpreting statute law, or making good any defects in statute law. It is of special importance when dealing with procedure in the criminal courts.

Text books

Text books are not binding on the courts, but are useful in so far as they set forth statute law in an orderly manner.

Custom

Custom no longer exists as a source of criminal law in France.

---

[4] The above excerpts from the Code pénal are given as an illustration only; the Code itself should be consulted for full details.

[5] For citation purposes referred to as C.P.P.

[6] Code civile Art. 5.

3. Organisation of Courts of Criminal Jurisdiction[1]

7 In France, there are three separate courts of first instance[2] and two appellate courts. The courts of first instance are the *Tribunal de police, the Tribunal correctionnel* and the *Cour D'assises*. Each court deals with a different range of criminal offences, and for this purpose all criminal offences are divided into three categories according to penalty.[3] Since the Code pénal specifies the minimum[4] and maximum penalty for each offence, there is little difficulty in ascertaining into which category an offence falls. The categories of offences are:

(a) '*Contraventions*'—offences where the penalty is imprisonment for not less than one day and not more than two months (60 days) or a fine not less than 3 Francs and not more than 2000 Francs.

(b) '*Délits*'—offences where the penalty is imprisonment for not less than two months and one day and not more than five years (and in certain cases ten or twenty years) or a fine in excess of 2000 Francs.

(c) '*Crimes*'—offences carrying penalties more serious than the above mentioned, which include death, solitary confinement for life, life imprisonment etc.[5]

Tribunal de police
8 The lowest court in France is the tribunal d'instance which deals with civil matters. When dealing with criminal cases it is called the tribunal de police. In Lyons and Marseilles there is a tribunal de police in its own right dealing exclusively with criminal cases, and distinct from the tribunal d'instance. Paris has 23 such tribunaux de police.

The tribunal de police has a single full time professional judge and deals only with offences classed as 'contraventions'.

---

[1] For comparison with Scotland—see para 118 et seq.

[2] This does not include the Haute Cour de Justice (see para 1) which has a very limited function, nor does it include juvenile courts. Children aged between 13–18 years are dealt with in the Tribunal des Enfants unless for juveniles aged 16–18 years accused of offences classed as 'crimes' who are brought before the Cour d'assises des mineurs.

[3] This classification is a general rule only. There are minor exceptions of offences which do not fall into any particular category in particular offences relating to Customs and Excise, poaching and tax.

[4] The court is not bound to impose the minimum penalty, and in certain circumstances may award a penalty reduced below the minimum according to statutory limits—see C.P.P. 463.

[5] For full details of the range of penalties available to French courts see para 97 et seq.

Tribunal correctionnel

9 The court immediately superior to the tribunal d'instance is the tribunal de grande instance. When dealing with criminal cases it is called the tribunal correctionnel. There are 173 tribunaux correctionnels in France. This court has a bench of three full time professional judges of whom one is the president and the other two are called 'assesseurs'. The reason for having three judges on the bench is to ensure impartiality and a fear that a single judge may ocassionally be affected by personal prejudice.[6] Decisions are unanimous, dissenting opinions not being allowed.

The tribunal correctionnel deals only with offences classed as 'délits'. However, it also deals with some offences which strictly speaking should be classed as 'crimes', but which are treated as 'délits' by means of a process known as 'correctionnalisation'. The Code pénal rigidly defines the penalties for each offence, hence for example while the penalty for simple theft allows this offence to be classified as a 'délit', if the theft was committed by a servant or employee, the statutory penalty is such, that the offence is classed as a 'crime'. Since such a qualification is of little import today, it is felt inadvisable to allow theft by a servant to be classed as a 'crime' either because it does not warrant the cumbersome and expensive process of a jury trail in the cour d'assises, or because a jury, knowing of the obligatory penalty which must follow a conviction, will prefer to give an acquittal rather than allow the accused to suffer a penalty which seems harsh by modern standards. There are numerous such examples due to the antiquated nature of the Code pénal, and in fact, the vast majority of 'crimes' are now treated as 'délits' and taken in the tribunal correctionnel. In order to do this a legal fiction is employed—in the above example, the prosecution would exclude from the libel the qualification that the accused was a servant. The use of legal fictions allowing the process of 'correctionnalisation' is not covered by any statutory provision and is in effect an illegal practice. It is, however, widely used and actively encouraged in certain instances by circulars from the Ministry of Justice. Before this process can operate, the court and all parties to the case must consent (If the court failed to do so, it would refuse to try the case on the grounds of competency, as by failing to recognise the 'correctionnalisation', the offence would be classed as a 'crime' and only competent in the cour d'assises).

The suggestion that an offence be treated in this way usually emanates from the procureur de la République, the public prosecutor in the tribunal correctionnel. He usually does so for the motives above narrated, or because of some mitigating factor of which the Code pénal takes no cognisance. If the case has been the subject of judicial pre-trial inquiries ('information') by a juge d'instruction[7] the suggestion may be made by the juge d'instruction with the consent of the procureur de la République. Should the latter fail to consent, the offence must be treated as a 'crime'; but on the contrary, a juge d'instruction is not bound to accept the view of the procureur if the procureur wishes the offence to be treated as a 'délit', while the juge d'instruction insists it is a 'crime'—in practice such a situation would seldom arise.

While the consent of the accused is also necessary, in most cases it is a formality, as failure to consent would entail the case being tried in the cour d'assises with a

---

[6] As from 1st January 1973, a single judge is empowered to try a limited range of cases if the accused so agrees.

[7] See para 52 et seq.

much severer penalty on conviction. The victim ('partie civile')[8] must agree to the 'correctionalisation,' but again this is usually a formality.

It therefore follows that since the court, the accused and the 'partie civile' will not normally object to this practice, the discretion as to whether or not it should be adopted lies with the procureur de la République. Furthermore since taking the case in the tribunal correctionnel limits the penalty to less than that properly prescribed by law for the offence, the procureur de la République can control the application of the criminal law contrary to the provisions of the Code pénal.

Cour d'assises

10 This is the highest criminal court in France and it deals exclusively with criminal cases. In theory each 'département'[9] has a cour d'assises—there being 95 'departements' in continental France but because of reorganisation in the Paris region, there are only 92 cours d'assises. The cour d'assises has 3 judges (a president and two 'assesseurs') and a jury of 9 laymen. The president is nominated for each session from among the judges of the cour d'appel[10] and the 'assesseurs' are chosen from the judges of the cour d'appel or from the judges of the tribunal correctionnel, hence all are full time professional judges.

The cour d'assises can only deal with cases classified as 'crimes'. Before a case can be heard, it must be remitted to the cour d'assises by the chambre d'accusation.[11] Since this remit confers jurisdiction, if the cour d'assises held that the offence should have been classified as a 'délit', it still has competence to try the offence by reason of the remit.

At the conclusion of the evidence, the jury, who sit on the bench beside the judges, retire with the judges to consider both verdict and sentence.[12]

Cour d'appel[13]

11 The cour d'appel deals with appeals based on fact and law from the tribunal correctionnel and restricted cases from the tribunal de police. There is no appeal against a decision of the cour d'assises, which gives rise to much criticism.

The court consists of three judges—a president and two 'conseilleurs' and there are twenty-eight cours d'appel, each having jurisdiction over a different geographical region (plus nine overseas courts). Any party to the case can lodge an appeal, and the court may consider the whole aspect of the case. If desired, it can re-hear the accused and witnesses.

Cour de cassation[14]

12 This is the highest appellate court in France being situated in Paris, and deals exclusively with appeals based on law. Appeals may be taken to the Cour de

---

[8] See para 26—the victim of a criminal offence has the right to join his civil claim to the criminal action.

[9] See para 3.

[10] See para 11.

[11] See para 13.

[12] For a note re the evolution of the French jury system and the arguments for and against it see Appendix I.

[13] See para 105 for full details of the function, etc. of the Cour d'Appel.

[14] See para 106 for full details of the function, etc. of the Cour de Cassation.

Cassation only when all other means of appeal have been exhausted. The Cour de Cassation is divided into six chambers, one of which deals with appeals in criminal cases. The normal bench consists of nine judges, but if the issue is important, the bench may consist of fifteen judges (assemblée plenière); should such a point be appealed for a second time, a final desicion may be given by a bench of thirty-five judges (chambres réuniés). If the appeal is successful, the case is remitted for re-trial.

Chambre d'accusation[15]

13 This is not a court in the proper sense, in that it does not decide the issues of the case. It is a section of the cour d'appel whose basic function is to decide whether or not a case should be remitted to the cour d'assises for trial. It also deals with appeals against the rulings of the juge d'instruction.

It consists of three judges—a president and two 'conseilleurs', selected from the judges of the cour d'appel. Any judge so selected may not act as a judge at the cour d'assises, lest he would be required to judge a case of which he already had cognisance.

All hearings are in private.

---

[15] See paras 72–74 for full details of the function, etc. of the Chambre d'Accusation.

4. Persons Responsible for the Administration of Justice[1]

The Legal Profession—the Judiciary—the Prosecutor—the Police

Legal Education

14 Prior to entering University, the student must have obtained his 'baccalaureat' at school. This examination consists of a series of comprehensive tests in philosophy, languages, literature natural sciences and mathematics, great emphasis being laid on oral expression. As an alternative to the baccalaureat, the student may obtain a 'capacité en droit' at centres of part time education. On entering University, the student will undergo a four year course in predominantly legal subjects, both theoretical and practical, before obtaining a law degree ('licence en droit'). Many students then take post graduate degrees, but in any event, whichever branch of the legal profession is selected, further training is required.

The Legal Profession

15 The main branches of the legal profession are 'avocat', 'avoué', 'notaire' and 'magistrat'.

An 'avocat' is responsible for pleading in court. He is instructed directly by the client (and not by a solicitor as in Scotland). 'Avocats' are attached to the courts in different areas.[2] To become an 'avocat', the student undergoes a period of training ('stage') either during his last year at university or after obtaining his 'licence en droit'. The length of the training period, during which he is attached to a practising 'avocat', is not specified except that it must exceed twelve months. During the first year of his training the 'avocat stagaire' has no right of audience in the courts, but thereafter he may represent clients in court in his own right. The fees paid to an 'avocat stagaire' are lower than those paid to an 'avocat', hence a 'stage' might last as long as five years or until the 'stagaire' feels he has sufficient experience, reputation and clients to justify becoming an 'avocat' and charging the higher rate of fees.

Since in French criminal trials the parties do not present their cases, nor are the witnesses subjected to detailed cross examination by the parties, the role of an 'avocat' in a criminal trial is to interpret the evidence in the way most favourable to his client.

The 'avocat' has been described as 'an accepted channel of persuasion within a procedural framework which otherwise affords no such opportunity.'

---

[1] For Scotland see para 123 et seq.

[2] In Paris alone there were 3,374 avocats in 1971–1972 of whom approximately 23% were women; of the 3,374 avocats, 784 were 'stagaires'. All avocats are attached to a particular court, the 'Faculté des'avocats' in Paris being the largest faculty.

9

An 'avoué' is responsible for the preparation of civil litigation, including the drafting of written pleadings. He does not appear in court, but will instruct an 'avocat' for the court appearances. 'Avoués' were formerly attached to all the civil courts, but the profession was drastically reduced by a law passed in September 1972 which abolished the profession of 'avoué', merging it with that of 'avocat' in all courts except the cour d'appel and the Cour de Cassation. To become an 'avoué', it is necessary to have a 'licence en droit' and thereafter to serve an apprenticeship with a practising 'avoué'. The duration of the apprenticeship in theory is two or three years, but in practice it usually extends to six years, the apprentice commencing as a clerk and terminating as principle assistant to his employer. He may attend classes at L'École du Droit et Procédure, and at the end of his apprenticeship, he is required to undergo a professional examination. The number of 'avoués' attached to the Cour de Cassation and the various cours d'appel is strictly limited by law, and to obtain a practice, it is necessary to purchase the practice of a retiring 'avoué' (the price usually being four or five times the average of the net profits of the previous five years).

A 'notaire' is a lawyer dealing with non litigous business especially matters such as conveyancing of property, wills, marriage contracts etc.

There was formerly a branch of the legal profession known as an 'agrée' dealing with commercial litigation, but this profession was merged with that of 'avocat' in September 1972.

In addition to the above, there are various persons who style themselves as 'agents d'affaires', 'conseils juridiques', 'jurisconsultes', 'contentieux juridiques'—who are all prepared to give legal advice. Such persons are not members of the legal profession and may not even be legally qualified.

Legal aid

16 Before turning to consider the profession of 'magistrat', it is perhaps appropriate at this point to give some details of legal aid in criminal cases. As noted in the introduction, such a scheme has operated since 1414. Any accused appearing before a criminal court is entitled to ask for legal representation, and if necessary the hearing will be adjourned to allow him to obtain this. If the accused is unable to pay for the services of an 'avocat', either the president of the court will ask any lawyer present if he is prepared to represent the accused, or an official ('batonnier') of the local Faculté des avocats will appoint someone to act on behalf of the accused. The accused must accept the 'avocat' who is appointed to act for him.

The 'avocat' will provide his services without fee and will not be re-imbursed from other sources. In many instances the person appointed to act will be an 'avocat stagaire', or an 'avocat' who is not too encumbered with hisown clients, but in complicated cases an experienced 'avocat' will usually act. In very exceptional instances, if a case is liable to attract much publicity, some 'avocat' might indicate he is willing to act on behalf of the accused, but this would be most unusual and not in accordance with the attitude of the vast majority of 'avocats' who undertake to represent accused persons without means out of a sense of public service and duty.

If the case is being investigated by a juge d'instruction, and the accused is unable to pay for an 'avocat', one will be appointed to act for him as above. In such proceedings it is essential to have an 'avocat', as the accused in person has no right of access to the 'dossier'[3] recording the results of the investigation. Should the case be remitted for trial, the accused must apply again at the trial for the services of an 'avocat' and in such a case he may or may not be given the same 'avocat' who represented him during the pre-trail inquiries.

While such a system ensures that the accused is legally represented, its failing is that the accused is given no choice of lawyer. It therefore follows that especially in important cases, an accused will go to great efforts to afford the necessary fees and thus obtain an 'avocat' of his choice.

The 'Magistrature'
17 The French term 'magistrat' embraces both the judiciary and the public prosecutor. The judiciary is known as the 'magistrature assise' or 'magistrature en siège'; the prosecutor is known as the 'Ministère public' or the 'magistrature debout' or more commonly 'le parquet'.[4] The judiciary and the public prosecutor have equal privileges, status and salary. Interchange between the two branches is simple and not uncommon. In France, a judge or public prosecutor regards himself as being first and foremost a 'magistrat' (as opposed to a 'fonctionnaire'—civil servant), the particular duties whether they be on the bench or prosecuting being of secondary importance and not conferring any rank or privilege over the other. The prosecutor does not regard himself (nor is he so regarded by the judge) as being inferior to the judge; on the converse, the judge, being equal in status to the prosecutor is independent of him and need not follow his demands. As a visible example of their equality, while the prosecutor will stand when addressing the Court, both sit on the same level and wear similar robes. The 'avocat' for the defence speaks from the well of the Court.

Because French courts have a bench of three judges, it follows that there are approximately three times as many judges as prosecutors. Some 'magistrats' are employed on other duties such as in an administrative capacity in the Ministry of Justice; in L'École Nationale de la Magistrature; as juges d'instruction[5]; as juges de l'application des peines[6]; and attached to the Cour de Justice des Communautés européenes at Luxembourg.

Entry to the 'magistrature'
18 There are two methods of becoming a 'magistrat', either by entering L'École Nationale de la Magistrature or by direct entry, the former method being the more common.

(a) L'École Nationale
L'École Nationale, or to give it its proper title 'le Centre Nationale d'Études Judiciares' was established in Bordeaux in 1958 to place the 'magistrat' on a similar footing with other branches of public service, such as the diplomatic corps, which have long had similar establishments. L'École was a success from the outset and now 75% to 80% of 'magistrats' qualify in this way.

To obtain entry, the candidate must possess a 'licence en droit' and many have

[3] See paras 56 and 60.
[4] The French word 'parquet' literally means 'floor'. The prosecutor is the 'magistrat' who speaks from the floor, and not from the bench.
[5] See para 57.
[6] See para 99.

post-graduate degrees. The maximum age is 27 years, although exceptions may be made. Before entry, the candidate if he wishes, may undergo a preparatory course run by the 'Instituts d'études judiciares' during the 3rd year of his university studies at any of fifteen universities, but this preparatory course is not compulsory. Candidates with the basic entry qualifications sit a competitive examination (in 1971 there were 750 candidates for 180 places in L'École).[7] The number of places at L'École is limited to the number of students that can be handled, and not the number of vacancies in the 'magistrature', which are approximately 230 per annum.

The entry examination is part written and part oral. The written part consists of several five or six-hour papers on civil law, criminal law, a translation from a foreign language, and a general subject of social, economic or political importance. The oral part is conducted by a board composed of a president of the Cour de Cassation, two law professors, a member of the Conseil d'Etat, a serving 'magistrat' and sometimes the head of a department in the Ministry of Justice. The candidate is examined on various legal subjects, including a legal paper he is given thirty minutes before the interview. At the conclusion, the candidate may be asked questions of a general nature to see how he responds under stress. In certain cases, older, well qualified candidates may be admitted without such examinations.

A successful candidate is called an 'auditeur de justice', which carries certain rights and privileges. The magisterial oath is taken, and the 'auditeur' is subject to the control of the Minister of Justice from whom he receives a salary[8] and other financial allowances, including the cost of his robes etc. At L'École, the 'auditeur' undergoes a course lasting twenty-eight months designed to fit him for his magisterial duties by giving him specialist training and by broadening his general experience and outlook. During the first six weeks, the 'auditeur' will be attached to an 'avocat', a 'notaire', the police and either a prison or juvenile detention centre anywhere in France. Thereafter the 'auditeur' attends L'École for detailed studies which include legal procedure and other legal topics of current interest and importance, covering a wide field—the Common Market, drugs, labour relations, forensic medicine, psychiatry etc. This can be undertaken by means of private study, visits, seminars, discussion groups and lectures by experts. The courses vary from year to year, but two months are always spent attached to the court at Bordeaux examining the functions of a 'magistrat'. At the conclusion of this study period, the 'auditeur' then spends sixteen months obtaining practical experience, spending three months attached to a procureur de la République, three months with a judge, two months with a juge d'instruction, and one month with a juge des enfants. In the course of these periods of attachment, the 'auditeur' will perform most of the functions of the 'magistrat', such as conducting simple criminal trials, sitting on the bench as one of the three judges, etc. In addition to this legal training, the 'auditeur' must spend fifteen days working as a labourer in a factory, in a bank, and in local government—all designed to give him a personal insight into the problems and activities of the everyday world. The final stage of the course lasts two months, and is spent in Paris where the 'auditeur' will visit various French Institutions such as the Ministry of Justice, L'Assemblée Nationale,

[7] The standard aimed at is five candidates for every place. In 1971, 34% of the successful candidates were women. In 1972, there were 980 candidates for 175 places.

[8] Approximately £1,500 per annum in 1971.

le Senat. As a general rule the 'auditeur' is asked to select one of a limited number of specified subjects of topical interest such as drugs or road accidents, and will examine all aspects of the problem—for example if he chooses drug trafficking he will visit psychiatric hospitals, accompany the police, assist in the drafting of any new legislation, attend parliamentary debates, and participate in any conferences on the subject.

At the end of the course at L'École, the 'auditeur' undergoes written and oral examinations of a very practical nature, where actual processes from the courts are used. The failure rate is approximately 1 %, but candidates are listed in order of merit. A list of all the vacancies for 'magistrats' is prepared, and given to the 'auditeurs' in order of merit. It therefore follows that those 'auditeurs' who are highest on the list of merit have the widest choice of vacancies. After the 'auditeur' has selected his post, his appointment is confirmed by the Minister of Justice, and the 'auditeur' then receives a magisterial commission signed by the President de la République. He is then attached for a further two months to a 'magistrat' of the branch he has selected, after which he commences his duties as a 'magistrat'.[9]

In general, the above system ensures that before taking up his duties, the 'magistrat' has a wide knowledge of the duties and responsibilities of a 'magistrat', the organisation and administration of justice and most facets of social conditions in France. One criticism of the system is that it tends to produce stereotype 'magistrats' with little scope for individuality. There does not seem to be much ground for this criticism, but even if true, it would also presumably ensure a more uniform application of justice.

(b) *Direct entry*

An 'avocat' with ten years experience may apply for entry to the 'magistrature', and such applications are considered by a commission. Direct entry is viewed as a desirable alternative to entry from L'École (which in any event can not produce a sufficient number of candidates) since it allows a widening of the spectrum of candidates to the magistrature. By tradition, certain magisterial posts have always been given to distinguished men of law, and one of the foremost professors of law is, by custom, always appointed as a judge in the Cour de Cassation.

Career structure of the magistrature

19 The salary and status given to a 'magistrat' depend on his grading, and not on whether he is on the bench or acting as prosecutor, for example the salary and status given to the senior president of the tribunal de grande instance (tribunal correctionnel) are identical to those given to the procureur de la République in the same court. Apart from some very senior posts (mostly in Paris), all 'magistrats' are placed on one of two grades. The first grade, which is the higher, has seven salary scales, and includes the senior judges, procureurs de la République and 'magistrats' in the cours d'appel in most of the more populous areas of France (Paris having special grades). The second grade, which has nine salary scales, includes the juges d'instruction, the judges and procureurs de la République in country districts, and the 'substituts' (depute) procureurs de la République.

A newly appointed 'magistrat' will start on the lowest salary scale of the second

[9] If he has chosen to be a prosecutor, he will first be appointed as a 'substitut' (depute) to a procureur de la République; if he has selected the bench, he will serve as an 'assesseur'—i.e. one of 3 judges.

grade and move to the next highest scale each year, so that even without promotion he will reach the top scale on the second grade; in due course, he will automatically be placed on the first grade and after 23 years of service he may reach the salary scale third from the top of the first grade, which is the highest he may go without promotion.[10]

A personal 'dossier' is kept on every 'magistrat', starting with his entry to L'École Nationale. At that point, information is obtained from the candidate's family, school, university and police to ascertain if there is anything to indicate he might be unsuited to the magistracy. Thereafter the 'dossier' records the 'auditeur's' progress through L'École and is given to his superior when he first takes up office. A similar 'dossier' is compiled for direct entry 'magistrats'. Each year the 'magistrat' is assessed by his superior (the 'substitut' by the procureur de la République; the judge by the president of the Court).[11] The assessment relates to specific items such as knowledge of the law, relations with the public, ability to organise, and marks are given on a sliding scale. No 'magistrat' has access to his personal dossier, but he is shown a copy of his annual assessment and may comment thereon.

With regard to promotion, when a vacancy arises, it is not circulated, but any 'magistrat' interested may apply. Alternatively a 'magistrat' wishing promotion or transfer to a particular sphere or area may notify the Minister of Justice of his wishes and ask to be considered for any future vacancy. Promotion depends partly on years of service, but mostly on ability—about 25% of 'magistrats' may expect promotion, which is not normal if the 'magistrat' is aged 60 years or over. In the Ministère public (prosecuting service) the senior appointments such as procureur de la République and procureur général are made by the Minister of Justice. The lower posts are decided by the person in whose office the vacancy occurs (e.g. the procureur de la République may suggest which 'substitut' should be promoted to 'premier substitut') but these promotions are also subject to confirmation by the Minister of Justice. If there are several candidates for a vacancy, the choice is made after examining the personal 'dossier' of each candidate, interviews being most uncommon.

Retiral from the magistracy is optional at age 60, and compulsory at the age of 67 (except for the Cour de Cassation where the compulsory age is 70 years). A pension is given according to years of service, the maximum being 75% of the salary earned in the year prior to retirement. Annual leave consists of thirty days plus public holidays.

A 'magistrat' may not stand in parliamentary or local elections in the area covered by his jurisdiction, but is free to so do elsewhere,[12] nor may he act as a 'magistrat' in any area where he has held political office in the preceding five years. The question of political activity by 'magistrats' is debated from time to time. The 'magistrats' themselves seem equally divided between those who think that a 'magistrat' should remain aloof from politics and those who think that by denying the 'magistrat' the right to enter into politics, he is being deprived of the ordinary

[10] In addition to salary, various financial allowances are given.

[11] Until recently, a procureur de la République could insert informal notes in the personal 'dossier' of a juge d'instruction giving his views as to how the latter performed his duties. This practice has now virtually died out.

[12] At least two 'magistrats' were members of L'Assemblée Nationale in 1972.

political rights of the individual. It is accepted that a 'magistrat' should not demonstrate any hostility to the government, but in a recent case where a 'magistrat' wrote a very critical article condemning two members of the government, he was merely censured, despite an outcry for his dismissal.[13]

A 'magistrat' may not hold any other professional or salaried post, although he may take part in scientific, artistic or literary works. If given express permission, he may take part in other activities provided the same does not 'detract from the dignity or independence of the post of 'magistrat'.' From time to time, a 'magistrat' may be officially appointed to take part in fact-finding commissions. A 'magistrat' can not be appointed in a district in which during the preceding five years he has practised as an 'avocat' or 'avoué or 'notaire'.

A 'magistrat' is expected to live within his jurisdiction, but this rule is not closely observed.

The Judiciary

20 All judicial posts are full time and filled by professional 'magistrats'. There are no part-time posts or lay 'magistrats'. Except for the chambre criminelle de la Cour de Cassation, most judges act in both the civil and criminal courts. Once appointed, a judge can not be removed from office (and can not even be compelled to take promotion) unless he commits a serious offence or breach of duty, or becomes infirm. Breaches of discipline are considered by the 'Conseil superieur de la magistrature' of which the president is the President de la République, and the vice-president is the Minister of Justice. The 'conseil' has nine other members, of whom seven are senior 'magistrats'.

The role of the judge in court is to elicit all the evidence by examining the accused and the witnesses (this is not done by the parties to the case); to decide any legal issues; to decide on the verdict and sentence (except in jury trials in the cour d'assises).[14]

The Public Prosecutor

21 About the time of the fourteenth century, the kings of France began to employ 'procureurs' in the principal courts for the purpose of protecting the king's interests, enforcing penalties and collecting fines (the money going to the Royal Treasury). As the king's authority extended, the powers of the procureur correspondingly increased, so that the procureur had the responsibility of investigating criminal offences and instituting proceedings. It was at this time, by reason of the powers of investigation of the procureur du Roi, that the inquisitorial system replaced the accusatorial under which the responsibility for instituting proceedings lay with the victim of the offence. With this development, the procureur du Roi became known as the 'Ministère public'. The French Revolution did not abolish the 'Ministère public' but dispossessed it of some of its powers which were given to another magistrate called 'l'accusateur public'. This innovation proved to be undesirable and at the end of the Revolution, the 'Ministère public' was restored to its former status, which is virtually the same today. The right to investigate and prosecute was given to the 'procureur Imperial' today known as the procureur de la République. The 'Ministère public' is responsible for undertaking all

---

[13] M. Casamayor writing on the 'Ben Barka' affair.

[14] For greater detail see 'Proceedings in Court'—para 76 et seq.

prosecutions on behalf of the state;[15] he must appear in all criminal courts and all decisions of a criminal court must be made in his presence; he thereafter ensures that the court's decision is enforced.

The organisation of the public prosecutors in the various criminal courts is as follows:

Cour de Cassation—Le parquet près de la Cour de Cassation, consisting of the procureur général and seventeen 'avocats generaux.'

Cour d'Appel—Le parquet près de la cour d'appel, consisting of a procureur général, 'avocats generaux' (for court appearances) and 'avocats deputes' (for administration).

Cour d'Assises—if this court is situated in the same town as a cour d'appel, the prosecutor is the procureur général de la cour d'appel; if this court is situated elsewhere, the prosecution is usually left in the hands of the procureur de la République, but in exceptional cases, the procureur général from the nearest cour d'appel may conduct the prosecution.

Tribunal correctionnel—the procureur de la République, who may have deputes ('substituts') depending on the size of the court.[16]

Tribunal de police—the procureur de la République if the offence carries a penalty in excess of ten days imprisonment or a fine of 400 Francs; otherwise the prosecution is conducted by a senior police officer (commissaire)[17] specially designated for this task by the procureur général. Where prosecutions are conducted by a commissaire, he is subject to the control, supervision and intervention of the procureur de la République.[18]

Control and Administration of the Public Prosecutor

22 The whole service is responsible to and subject to the control of the Minister of Justice who issues instructions concerning administration, the general conduct of prosecutions, or specific instructions concerning a particular case. Such instructions must be obeyed. As a general rule, however, the Minister of Justice being a politician with no legal training will pay great attention to the advice and suggestions of the procureur, regarding him as an expert in this field. It would be most unusual for a Minister of Justice to disregard such advice and issue an instruction contrary to it, especially in view of any political consequences, should

[15] CPP Arts 1, 31.

[16] In Paris, the procureur de la République has 90 'substituts', some of whom are graded as 'premiers substituts'. They are divided into 3 divisions each headed by a 'procureur adjoint'. Each division is subdivided into sections, each section having a specialised function—e.g. financial cases, sex offences, etc. The administration is controlled by a 'secretariat' which has 2 substituts and a 'premier substitut'. In addition there is a clerical and secretarial staff of approximately 200. Specialisation is necessary in Paris because of the volume and complexity of the cases. It has not been thought advisable to divide Paris into different courts because some complex cases require specialist knowledge and because uniformity of control is essential, as is uniformity in the application of the law. No 'substitut' will be appointed to the Paris office unless he has at least 10 years' service elsewhere.

[17] In Paris, such commissaires have legal qualifications; elsewhere this task is merely undertaken as part of normal police duties.

[18] See para 87 dealing with the Tribunal de Police.

affairs turn out badly. In practice he issues circulars through the Ministry of Justice advising how particular types of cases should be handled—for example instructing that no proceedings be taken in sex cases where the victim has subsequently married the potential accused. He will also take an interest in cases of major importance, such as large scale frauds affecting the savings of thousands of investors, or in cases of political significance such as criminal actions by strikers where an untimely prosecution might exacerbate the situation.

The Minister of Justice can not compel a procureur de la République to prosecute or refrain from prosecuting a particular individual, nor can he remove from office a procureur refusing to obey such an order. If a procureur took proceedings in defiance of an order from the Minister, the proceedings would still be valid, but the prosecutor would be liable for disciplinary proceedings, when the reasons for his failure to obey the order would be examined. If it were shown that the procureur had improperly disobeyed the order, he would then be disciplined; if on the other hand, his refusal were justified, and it was established that the Minister had acted improperly, the latter would doubtless require to answer for his conduct in l'Assemblée Nationale, or elsewhere.

Apart from the above somewhat theoretical instance, the procureur is required to obey the written instructions of his superior, just as the 'substitut' is required to obey those of the procureur. But such obedience is only required in so far as any written demands are made by the procureur—in court he is free to say what he wants and may express his own views orally,[19] regardless of what he has formally requested the court to do in writing. In this way, no prosecutor in court is compelled to speak against his personal conviction.

Any prosecutor guilty of misconduct or wilful disobedience can be downgraded or dismissed. The offence would be investigated by a commission consisting of two 'avocats generaux' and a judge of Cour de Cassation, the most senior director (head of department) at the Ministry of Justice and three colleagues of equal rank. The Commission, which would be presided by the procureur général of the Cour de Cassation, having investigated the offence, would make a recommendation to the Minister of Justice, who is not bound to follow the commission's advice. If however, he proposes to deal with the matter in a more serious way than that proposed by the Commission, the Minister must give the Commission advance not ice of his intended action and the reasons therefor.

A 'magistrat' of the 'Ministère public' can not be sued by any person whom he is prosecuting, nor can he be found liable for damages or legal expenses.[20] In theory if a prosecutor is guilty of dereliction of duty he can subsequently be pursued by a method known as 'prise à partie'[21] but there are so many difficulties in this course of action, that in practice it is academic. The 'Ministère public' is regarded as indivisible, so that the actions and words of one 'magistrat' are presumed to represent the views of all the 'magistrats' in the same 'parquet' (office).

The general attitude of the 'magistrats' of the 'Ministère public' is that they are performing a duty to the public, and have not entered the service for gain or reward.[22] In their investigations and actions in court, they display an impartiality

---

[19] 'La plume est serve, mais la parole est libre'. It has been suggested however, that no procureur mindful of his career would disobey a written instruction even in this way.
[20] Code Civile Article 381.
[21] C.P.P. 136.
[22] While the salaries are adequate, they can not compare favourably with the earnings of some of the 'avocats'.

and lack of animus in seeking out the truth. Should the defence suggest some line of evidence, this will invariably be pursued and all assistance is given to ensure the accused receives a fair trial.

Powers and Duties of the Procureur de la République

23 The whole system of public prosecution hinges upon the procureur de la République. He has the following responsibilities:

(a) He receives all the complaints concerning alleged criminal offences from the police and from members of the public.[23]

(b) He takes all necessary steps to investigate alleged offences, sudden or suspicious deaths, explosions, fires, train accidents and any other matter requiring investigation; in order to perform these duties, he not only has the power to direct the police, but has himself all the powers of the police.[24]

(c) Having investigated an offence, he has wide powers of discretion to decide what future action should be taken including taking no proceedings, treating a 'crime' as a 'délit' by means of 'correctionnalisation', deciding whether or not a juge d'instruction should be asked to investigate the offence (except for 'crimes' where this is compulsory).

(d) He conducts in person all proceedings in the tribunal correctionnel and is responsible for all prosecutions in the tribunal de police. In the course of the trial, he has great freedom to state his personal views, or to drop proceedings. Although the court may continue the case despite the wishes of the procureur, in practice it will never do so. He also gives his views as to the appropriate sentence.

(e) If the accused is convicted, the procureur has the responsibility of enforcing the sentence.[25]

(f) After the trial, he has a discretion as to whether or not to appeal.

(g) He has a general power which can only loosely be described as ensuring that law and order is maintained in his district. To this end he must keep himself informed of what is happening, usually by means of regular reports from the police. In particular he receives reports of all crimes committed in his area, and all events likely to give rise to future trouble.

(h) He also has numerous duties not connected with criminal law. These include taking an interest in any civil law case concerning legal status, the management of affairs on behalf of minors or other persons suffering from legal incapacity, or any other civil law case where the court itself decides that the views of the procureur should be obtained. He has a supervisory role over 'avocats' and can report any breaches of discipline to the local faculty. He assists in the award of legal aid in civil cases. He has some supervisory duties in connection with mental institutions. He deals with requests for changes of name, and permission to marry under age or without parental consent.

[23] CPP Art. 40.
[24] CPP Art. 41.
[25] This is done by the procureur général for cases in the cour d'assises.

The above is not an exhaustive list of such duties, but merely illustrative of the principal ones.

(i) As an independent 'magistrat' he can protect the public against any over-zealous activity of the police; similarly by judicious use of his decision to take proceedings, he ensures that the courts are not over-burdened with cases unworthy of pursuit.

The Police

24 There are various police forces in France, each independent of the other. The Sûreté nationale is ultimately responsible to the Minister of the Interior; the Gendarmerie is controlled by the Minister of Defence; municipal police are controlled by local authorities; the Compagnie Républicaine de Securité is responsible to the Minister of the Interior.

In all police forces the members are divided into two classes, the 'police judiciaire' and the 'police administrative'. The 'police judiciaire' are charged with determining whether or not a criminal offence has been committed, collecting evidence and tracing the person responsible.[26] They are subject to the control of the procureur de la République, unless pre-trial inquiries are being made by a juge d'instruction, in which case they come under the control of the latter, acting under his orders, and with powers delegated by him. The 'police administrative' are responsible for maintaining law and order and come under the control of the administrative authorities, namely the 'maire' or the 'préfet' in the first instance. The division between the two types of police is not absolutely rigid and a member of the 'police administrative' seeing a criminal offence being committed would proceed to deal with the matter as if he were a member of the 'police judiciaire.[27]

In the 'police judiciaire', a distinction must be drawn between 'officiers' and ordinary members ('agents'). 'Officiers' have much greater powers which include reporting direct to the procureur de la République, instituting enquiries on their own initiative, receiving delegated powers from a juge d'instruction and in certain urgent cases, commencing formal judicial enquiries prior to the arrival of the procureur de la République or juge d'instruction.[28] Various officials who are not members of the police force have the powers of 'officiers' of the 'police judicaire'—these include the 'maire', forestry officials, the procureur de la République and numerous others. The ordinary members ('agents') of the 'police judiciaire' merely have the power to decide whether an offence has been committed, take statements and report through their superior officers to the procureur de la République.

Relationship of the Police to the Prosecutor

25 The procureur de la République can not issue direct orders to the police, he merely gives advice, directions and instructions, but failure to follow such

[26] CPP Art. 14.

[27] In Paris, the 'police judiciaire' are organised into geographical units, each 'arrondissement' containing 3 or 4 'commissariots' each headed by a 'commissaire' who is an officer of the 'police judiciaire'. The Parisien 'police judiciaire' also have several specialist sections for financial affairs, offences concerning minors, etc. and a 'Brigade Territorial', composed of experts, for dealing with very serious or complex cases. Depending on the circumstances of each case, the investigation may be made either by the local 'police judiciaire', or a specialist section, or the 'Brigade Territorial'.

[28] CPP Arts. 17, 18, 19.

instructions would probably lead to disciplinary action against the officer or member concerned. The procureur is 'on call' permanently and will usually attend the locus of any serious crime of which he must be notified by the police as soon as it is discovered. He normally supervises the police work closely, including checking some of their records.[29] While the attitude of individual procureurs may vary, most insist that the police report all criminal offences to them, whether or not the person responsible can be identified or traced. The police are thus deprived of the power to decide that no proceedings should be taken because of lack of evidence. The procureur maintains a personal 'dossier' on each 'officier' of the 'police judiciaire' in which he assesses the 'officier's' ability and any other pertinent information.

The police are also subject to the control of their superior officers and through them the control of the 'maire', 'préfet' and government minister. The 'préfet' also maintains a 'dossier' on each 'officier', which for promotion purposes, is probably more important than the dossier compiled by the procureur. This control by the administrative authorities has many critics, who would prefer that complete control should be given to the criminal authorities, and in particular to the procureur and the juge d'instruction. A further criticism is levelled against the multiplicity of police forces which can result in members from different forces all investigating the same affair at the same time independently of each other.

The 'Partie civile'

26 While the 'partie civile' is not directly concerned with the administration of justice, it is appropriate that mention should be made here of his position in criminal proceedings.

Any person who has sustained damage or loss as the result of a criminal offence has a choice of three courses of action—raising a separate civil action, or entering appearance in the criminal action (which will then settle the civil issues) or instituting criminal proceedings against the accused (the procureur subsequently taking responsibility for the prosecution, leaving the victim to pursue his civil claim which will be decided in the course of the criminal proceedings[30]).

These rights are partly the vestiges of an accusational system where the victim (and not the public prosecutor) had the responsibility of seeking justice in the courts and partly a remedy against inaction on the part of the public prosecutor.

The following persons may act as 'partie civile'—the victim (who has an option to proceed, not to proceed or settle); the heirs of the victim (in their own right if the offence caused the death of the victim, otherwise only quoad any rights appertaining to the victim); anyone other than the victim who has suffered consequential loss (such as the dependents of the victim); any other person to whom the victim has assigned his rights of action. Although the general rule is that only persons who have personally and directly suffered loss (and the Cour de Cassation tends to interpret this rule strictly when judging on the competence of civil claims), there are various exceptions, notably—fire insurance companies acting on behalf of the victim of a fire; accident insurance companies, in certain cases, where the victim has suffered loss due to homicide, assault or negligence; motor insurance

---

[29] In particular, he scrutinises the record kept by the police of all persons detained by them under 'garde à vue'—see para 45.

[0] CPP Arts. 2, 3, 85.

companies;[31] and other statutory exceptions including the social security ministry which may sue the accused in respect of any injury benefits paid to the victim as a result of incapacity following on the criminal offence.

The right to recover damages from an accused person is not without point. If the accused is sent to prison, the payment of any damages awarded against him may be enforced on his release; if he is not sent to prison, the award may be enforced immediately. The decision to enforce payment of an award of damages, how payment should be made, and whether partial settlement should be accepted is left to the 'partie civile', but the remedies at his disposal include arrestment of the accused's wages.

The grounds on which a 'partie civile' may claim damages can be material or moral, but courts tend to disallow claims if the damage is too remote, or if the state protects the same interests.[32]

Choices of action available to the 'partie civile'

27 With regard to the choices of action available to the victim of a criminal offence, the raising of a separate civil action is usually avoided where possible, since apart from the fact that it will be sisted until the criminal case is settled, civil procedure in France tends to be lengthy, cumbersome and expensive.[33] As a result, most victims prefer to join their civil claim to the criminal action, by entering appearance as 'partie civile' after criminal proceedings have been instituted. Such appearance may be entered before the trial, with the juge d'instruction if he is making pre-trial inquiries, or at the trial itself. The victim thus benefits from the criminal action, having a right of audience at the trial which will settle any civil issues. To this extent the victim, as pursuer in the civil aspect of the case, acts as an additional prosecutor.[34]

Institution of Criminal Proceedings by the 'partie civile'

28 As an alternative to entering appearance in the criminal action, if no such action has already been opened, or if the procureur de la République refuses to prosecute, the victim may himself institute criminal procceedings. Once proceedings have been opened in this way, the procureur must take over the conduct of the prosecution, regardless of his views thereon and even if he had previously decided not to prosecute. If the offence is classed as a 'contravention' or a 'délit', the 'partie civile' will cite the accused to attend court, having first applied to the procureur for a date for the appearance. The procureur will normally obtain any record of the accused's previous convictions, background information, and any

[31] This is allowed by a law dated 23 September 1958. The majority of motor accident civil cases are settled by the insurance company entering appearance as 'partie civile' in the criminal action. As a result, many accused at the trial have two 'avocats', one defending him on the criminal action, and one defending the civil suit.

[32] See the case of Vigne, 1954—the accused was charged with fraud in connection with butcher meat. The court held that the Union of Family Associations of the Departement of Herault had no locus standi in entering a civil claim since the state is responsible for protecting public health.

[33] In a recent opinion poll 66% of the persons interviewed gave the view that civil procedure was virtually unefficacious.

[34] In the Parisien courts, approximately 20% of the criminal actions have civil actions joined thereto.

police report that happens to exist. If no such police information exists the procureur will normally rely on the case prepared by the 'partie civile'. At the trial diet, while the procureur is technically responsible for the conduct of the prosecution, he will normally leave it to the 'partie civile' to conduct the case, restricting his part in the proceedings to commenting on the case. In the course of the trial, should it appear that further investigations are necessary, or should the procureur decide to take a more active part, he may suggest that the court adjourn the case part-heard to a later date, having made it plain that he was not responsible for the initial institution of the proceedings.[35] If the offence is classified as a 'crime' the 'partie civile' can not cite the accused to court, but must appear before a juge d'instruction and enter a formal complaint known as a 'plainte avec constitution de partie civile'. The juge will order intimation of this to the procureur and the juge must then proceed to investigate the complaint unless he thinks it is incompetent to do so.[36] The 'partie civile' has the option of pursuing this course if the offence is classed as a 'délit'. At the conclusion of his enquiries, and after obtaining the views of the procureur, the juge d'instruction will decide what further action to take. If the case is remitted for trial, it will proceed in the same way as if the procureur had instituted the proceedings; should he order no further proceedings, the 'partie civile' may appeal this decision to the chambre d'accusation whose ruling he must accept.[37]

The raising of the criminal action by the 'partie civile' prevents the same accused from being subsequently prosecuted for the same offence by the procureur, even if fresh evidence comes to light, but once proceedings have been instituted by the 'partie civile', he loses all control over the course thereof, even should he later wish them dropped.[38]

As a general rule, before instituting criminal proceedings himself, the 'partie civile' will either enquire of the procureur if the latter contemplates proceedings, or will make a complaint ('plainte') to the procureur in the hope that this will cause the procureur to institute such proceedings, thus allowing the 'partie civile' to enter subsequent appearance in regard to the civil claim.[39]

Rights of the 'partie civile'

29 Regardless of whether he enters appearance in the criminal action, or institutes the criminal proceedings himself, the 'partie civile' has the following rights at the trial:[40] to be legally represented; to suggest questions to be put to the accused or witnesses; to cite witnesses; to give evidence without taking the oath; to submit a case which the court must answer; at the conclusion of the evidence, to give his views thereon (his 'summing up' being before that of the prosecution and defence); in the cour d'assises, to address the court on the civil issues outwith the presence

---

[35] See paras 83 and 85.

[36] For further details see para 53.

[37] The 'partie civile' bringing the matter before a juge d'instruction must lodge caution against the expenses of the action, which may be forfeit if the investigation shows there is no case to answer, or if the accused is acquitted.

[38] In 1970 in Paris, about 2 out of every 1,000 criminal prosecutions were instituted by a 'partie civile'.

[39] See also para 39 dealing with 'plaintes'.

[40] For more detail, see para 76 et seq. (Proceedings in Court).

of the jury—i.e. after the criminal aspect of the case has been decided. If the case is investigated by a juge d'instruction, the 'partie civile' may refuse to be questioned except in the presence of his lawyer (who has a right of access to the 'dossier' recording the juge's investigations); comment on a request by the accused to be released from pre-trial custody; ask for expert evidence to be obtained; appeal certain decisions of the juge d'instruction, of which he must be given notice and finally he has the right of audience before the chambre d'accusation when such appeals are being considered, and when the chambre is deciding on the question of committal for trial.[41]

Effect of intervention by the 'partie civile'

30 The effect of intervention by a 'partie civile' in a criminal action is to bar subsequent civil proceedings on the grounds of res judicata. It thus prevents the duplication of a criminal and civil action based on the same facts,[42] and allows the victim of a criminal offence to benefit from the speed, available resources, powers of investigation and psychological advantage of criminal proceedings.

There are, nonetheless, serious disadvantages in allowing a civil action to be joined to the criminal. Although as mentioned earlier, only certain interested parties may enter appearance, in some instances, several parties have this right. In the case of Jacques Fesch (1956) the accused was charged with the murder of a policeman in an attempt to escape apprehension for assault and robbery. The following 'parties civiles' were held to have a locus standi and all moved for a conviction—the relatives of the deceased policeman, the independent Trade Union of Municipal Police, the Christian Police Trade Union, the Association for the Defence of the Professional Interests of the Police, and the Federation of Trade Unions of the Staff of the Prefecture de Police. To counteract this proliferation of 'parties civiles', French courts are becoming increasingly strict in their interpretation of who may act as a 'partie civile', but this strict interpretation itself poses problems. In a case decided in Lyons in 1972, it was held that an association formed to represent the relatives of a number of teenagers who had died in a fire, could not enter as 'partie civile' as the association had been formed after the offence was committed—however, while refusing to admit this united approach by the relatives, it was held that there was nothing to prevent each relative entering appearance individually.

A further disadvantage is that the victim of an offence who is prevented from raising an action in the civil court because it is incompetent,[43] or who lacks evidence to pursue a civil claim, may attempt to institute enquiries by the procureur or juge d'instruction in the hope that action will be taken, or at least sufficient evidence discovered to justify pursuit of a civil claim. In order to prevent such abuses, an award of expenses may be made against a civil claimant if his actings are judged to be ill-founded and in certain instances the person accused by the claimant will be entitled to seek damages from him.

As a result of these disadvantages, there is a strong movement in France supporting the view that the rights of the 'partie civile' should be severely curtailed.[44]

[41] For more detail, see para 52 et seq.
[42] For a detailed illustration see para 87.
[43] Tribunal de conflits—6 July 1957.
[44] See the article by V. Grannier in Rev. Sc. Crim. 1958, page 1.

5. General Principles of French Criminal Procedure[1]

The Inquisitorial System

31 The basic principle underlying French criminal procedure is that all the facts concerning both the offence and the person alleged to have committed it be placed before the court in order that it may judge the person so accused. This aim is achieved by making detailed pre-trial inquiries; by examining the personality of the accused; and by placing the onus of eliciting the evidence at the trial on the judge rather than on the parties to the case.

Great emphasis is laid on the pre-trial inquiries which allow an investigation into anything that may have a bearing on the case. In serious cases, these inquiries will be made by an independent 'magistrat' known as the juge d'instruction. The accused may also be examined together with any evidence in his favour or witnesses he wishes to call,[2] and while he can not be compelled to answer any questions or reveal his defence, it is in the obvious interest of an innocent person to allow the facts in his favour to be fully investigated. Any unjustifiable attempt by an accused to reserve his defence until the trial while finding out the strength of the case against him in advance, is liable to be looked on with suspicion. It is claimed that an exhaustive investigation into the evidence before the trial not only ensures that all facts both against the accused and in his favour are made known, but also lessens the risk of an innocent person being sent to trial. A court of law, restricted to trial proceedings is by necessity more restricted in the type and scope of the inquiries it can make. By making the facts the subject of prior investigation, the issues between the parties are clearly defined, and there is less risk of one party manipulating the evidence by producing new evidence at the trial, thus placing his opponent either without an opportunity to reply, or to produce existing contradictory evidence. The inquiries, while thorough, in no way pre-judge the case. While an attempt is made to resolve any conflict in the evidence, or at least ascertain where the difference lies, the trial court alone has the right to interpret the evidence and decide on issues of credibility. Pre-trial inquiries are made in private, and it is only at the trial that the evidence is examined in public and made the subject of comment. The inquiries merely establish whether or not there is sufficient evidence, which if believed, would constitute a case for the accused to answer, and if there is such a case, that it be sent for trial in the appropriate court. To that extent only, they resemble English committal proceedings. It can, of course, be argued, that committal for trial only after detailed inquiries will produce a presumption of the accused's guilt. The answer usually

---

[1] For comparison with Scotland, see para 145 et seq.

[2] This does not mean that the rights given to the defence are not jealously safeguarded.

given to this argument is that the pre-trial inquiries do not seek to pre-judge the case, being solely designed to ensure that the full facts of the case are made available to the trial court which alone has the right to interpret and assess the evidence and thus decide on the question of guilt or innocence.[3]

The purpose of a French criminal trial is to judge the accused—'on juge l'homme, pas les faits.' Hence the court does not concentrate on the evidence, leaving it to the accused to take the initiative in regard to his defence. The accused is actively examined in relation to the evidence and it is the accused who is on trial rather than an objective assessment as to whether or not the prosecution has proved its case against him. It is therefore considered essential to have a proper understanding of the accused in order to interpret his actions, judge his credibility and if convicted, determine his degree of guilt when deciding on sentence (which is considered as an integral part of a guilty verdict). Although penalties are fixed with certain limits, the French attitude is that the punishment should fit the criminal, not the crime.[4] All the facts concerning the background and personal life history of the accused (including any previous convictions) are made known to the court before it reaches its judgement. Bad character should not however be considered as a factor when deciding on the issue of guilt. In cases where the pre-trial inquiry has been conducted by a juge d'instruction, especially if the offence is a 'crime', the accused's background is very fully investigated; otherwise such information is provided by the police and by the accused himself.[5]

The results of the pre-trial inquiries—both into the facts and into the personality of the accused—are compiled into a 'dossier'. It is essential that all parties to the case be kept informed of the progress of the inquiries, therefore all parties have access to the 'dossier' to study the contents thereof. This is an additional reason why the accused must be examined before the trial, for otherwise the 'dossier' would provide an unbalanced version of the evidence, containing only the prosecution case. Moreover, an unscrupulous accused, if not subject to prior examination and having learned the full details of the case against him, could wait until the trial to produce false evidence consistent both with the prosecution case and his innocence, such evidence not having been subjected to the same pre-trial scrutiny and verification.

The 'dossier' is given to the president of the court prior to the trial, and while the evidence at the trial is not restricted to the facts contained in the 'dossier', if the pre-trial inquiries have been properly made, the evidence will more or less follow what is contained in the 'dossier'.[6] The duty of eliciting the evidence at the trial is given to the judge, rather than leaving the presentation of the evidence in

[3] With regard to the effect on a jury, the vast majority of cases are taken in the tribunal correctionnel where there is no jury. The acquittal rate in the tribunal correctionnel is in the region of 5%, but since some of these are due to legal reasons (e.g. prescription, amnesty, etc.) the proportion of convictions is exceedingly high. This may prove the efficiency of pre-trial inquiries in ensuring that no innocent person is wrongly sent for trial, or alternatively it may be taken to prove that such inquiries do effectively pre-judge the case. See also para 32 re 'Presumption of innocence'.

[4] Unfortunately a rising crime rate often gives rise to exemplary sentences in the hope of deterring others.

[5] See also paras 80 and 82 for further detail re the tribunal correctionnel.

[6] At the cour d'assises, the jury does not have access to the 'dossier', and can only rely on the evidence presented orally in the court.

25

the hands of parties who have an interest in the outcome of the case. The judge thus plays a predominant role in French criminal trials, examining the accused and the witnesses (although the parties may suggest questions) and taking all other steps which he deems necessary to find the truth. To prevent any evidence being withheld from the court by virtue of some legal provision, virtually no evidence other than hearsay is excluded as inadmissable on the grounds of incompetency or irrelevancy.[7]

By these means, French criminal procedure attempts to ensure that 'the truth, the whole truth and nothing but the truth' is sought and ascertained before and during the trial by means of detailed impartial inquiries. Hence the system is described as inquisitorial, rather than accusatorial where it is left to the prosecution to accuse an individual, producing evidence to justify its accusation, while the individual has the sole responsibility of deciding how to answer the charge.[8] French lawyers tend to criticise the accusatorial system in that it leaves the pre-trial investigations, and more important, the presentation of the case in court in the hands of the parties to the case. This leaves the way open to suppression of the evidence by one of the parties (either because certain evidence is unfavourable to his case, or does not seem worthwhile pursuing) and to manipulation of the evidence and distortion of the truth by the way in which it is presented in court (in that each party emphasises the points in its own favour). To overcome this difficulty complete intellectual honesty is required from both the prosecution and the defence, which is difficult to obtain in view of their opposing roles. In France the judge is regarded as impartial, as he advocates neither the prosecution nor the defence view.

Onus of proof: confessions

32 Under French procedure, no accused person can plead guilty when the case calls in court, so it follows that all court proceedings are trials. A French court will only reach its decision after an examination of all the facts regardless of the attitude of the accused.[9] In practice the accused can always indicate that he does not dispute the evidence against him, and while the evidence will still be examined, the examination will be of a much more cursory nature, great use being made of leading questions and statements given by witnesses prior to the trial.[10] The trial itself will be shorter, and there will be no sense of animus or dispute. Since, however, the accused may not plead guilty, all accused persons are presumed innocent until found guilty.[11] In the tribunal de police and tribunal correctionnel, the presumption of innocence may sometimes be more theoretical than practical since the president of the court, having read the 'dossier' (or police report) in advance of the trial, must in many cases find it most difficult not to prejudge the case. In the cour d'assises the knowledge that the accused has only been committed for trial after exhaustive pre-trial inquiries, must occasionally influence some of the jurors, making it difficult for them to

[7] See para 34.

[8] As is done in Scotland.

[9] Although in the tribunal de police, when dealing with minor cases, the court merely asks the accused if he admits the facts, and if he do so, the court proceeds to penalty, without any examination of the evidence.

[10] See para 34 'oral evidence'.

[11] An exception to this rule is when the accused is charged with certain offences classed as 'contraventions', when he will be assumed to be guilty until he proves his innocence—see para 87; CPP 537.

presume his innocence.[12] Another factor impinging on the presumption of innocence is the pre-trial publicity in the newspapers.[13] The clearest examples demonstrating the presumption of innocence are—if an accused is charged with attempting to commit an offence, the attempt being consistent with various types of offence, it is assumed that the accused attempted to commit the least serious one; in the cour d'assises, when they jury are voting on verdict, any vote that is not clearly expressed against the accused is taken in his favour.

The onus of proving the accused's guilt, thereby overcoming the presumption of innocence lies on the prosecutor. While making his pre-trial inquiries the prosecutor will therefore tend to approach the case with an open, impartial mind, accepting the accused's innocence until the contrary is proved to his satisfaction, or at least until there is a reasonable case for the accused to answer. Once he has instituted trial proceedings, it is his responsibility to prove the accused's guilt. At the trial, however, his duties in relation to presentation of the evidence are very limited. The presiding judge, having studied the 'dossier' in advance, commences proceedings by examining the accused firstly as to his background[14] and then in regard to the evidence. Thereafter the judge examines the witnesses called by the parties to the case, and if he wishes, may adjourn the trial either to allow further witnesses to be called on his instructions, or to instruct further inquiries. The judge thus effectively controls the presentation of the evidence at the trial. In discharging the burden of proof, the prosecutor initially decides what witnesses should be cited;[15] he has the right to suggest questions for the judge to put to the accused or witnesses (and the judge may even allow the prosecutor to put the questions direct)—but whether or not such questions are put lies with the discretion of the judge; at the conclusion of the evidence, he may comment thereon, suggesting how it should be interpreted—i.e. he 'sums up' for the prosecution.

The onus of proof on the prosecution is not discharged by a confession of guilt by the accused. According to French procedure, the police, the procureur, the juge d'instruction and the court all have the power to examine the accused, who may not be legally represented when being questioned by the police or the procureur.[16] During such examinations it is illegal to use threats, force, ruses or other improper means to obtain a confession. Furthermore, the accused is entitled to refuse to answer any question put to him and can not be compelled to do so. Accused persons frequently avail themselves of this right when being examined by the police. Courts tend to regard confessions obtained by the police with a certain reserve, especially if such confessions are subsequently retracted when the accused appears before a juge d'instruction or at the trial. It is accepted that false confessions can be obtained due to mental illness, the desire for notoriety, an attempt to protect some other person, improper pressure by the police, or a simple misunderstanding of a question or answer. A confession is therefore regarded merely as part of the evi-

[12] See para 31 Supra, footnote 3.

[13] See para 35.

[14] Any disclosure of bad character or previous convictions should be ignored as a factor when deciding on the accused's guilt. While a professional judge may be able to do this, a jury may have more difficulty in so doing.

[15] But he has a duty of ensuring that all the known facts are given to the court, whether or not they favour the prosecution case.

[16] Nor on his first appearance before a juge d'instruction, when normally the examination is of a formal nature, the facts of the case not being discussed.

dence, which may or may not be supported by other facts. The judge has complete freedom as to what value he wishes to place on a confession—he may consider it enough by itself to convict the accused, or he may accept only part of it, or he may reject it in its entirety.[17]

In theory, the prosecution also has the onus of proving the absence of any factors affording a complete defence to the charge, hence of disproving any special defence. In practice, however, the onus frequently shifts to the defence. The main special defences are: insanity (when each case is judged on its merits with the assistance of experts); compulsion (physical or psychological force of a nature making it impossible for the accused to obey the law, provided that the situation in which the accused found himself had not arisen from his own actings—'passion' does not amount to 'compulsion');[18] self defence, or defence of another person, or in certain restricted cases, defence of property (there must be a defence against an illegal attack, and the measures taken must relate to the degree of violence used in the attack); necessity (voluntary actions taken to avoid a threat to oneself or another, such as to save life or health, it being essential to prove the necessity of the action was its sole motivation, and that no other factor such as gain, was involved. 'Necessity' differs from 'compulsion' since in the latter case the person is compelled to act contrary to his own wishes).

Standard of Proof

33 Having discussed the onus of proof, it is necessary to mention the standard of proof that is required to demonstrate the guilt of the accused. After considering all the evidence the judge must ask himself if he is thoroughly convinced[19] (of the accused's guilt). In the cour d'assises, the jury are told before retiring 'The law does not require judges to account for the means by which they are convinced, nor does it prescribe rules by which they must assess the sufficiency of evidence; the law only requires that they ask themselves in silence, in reflection and with a sincere conscience what impression the evidence brought against the accused and his defence thereto have made upon them. The law only asks them one question which encompasses their entire duties "Are you thoroughly convinced?" ' ('Avez vous une intime conviction')[20]. It therefore follows that it is the quality of the evidence rather than its quantity which is important. There is no need to have corroborated evidence; a conviction may be based on the testimony of a single witness, even if the remainder of the evidence is contradictory, if such testimony makes the judge thoroughly convinced of the accused's guilt.

Admissibility of evidence

34 Since the purpose of a French criminal trial is to discover the truth by placing all the available information before the court, leaving it to the court alone to assess its value, the general rule is that all types of evidence are admissible for consideration by the court.[21]

There are few exceptions to this rule. Hearsay evidence is not admissible. With regard to evidence obtained irregularly, such as by the ultra vires actions of a police

17 CPP Art. 428.
18 For a note on the 'crime passionnel', see Appendix 2.
19 Le juge decide d'après son intime conviction'—CPP Art. 427.
20 CPP Art. 353.
21 Les infractions peuvent être établies par tout mode de preuve'—CPP Art. 427.

officer, there are no fixed rules, each case being decided on the merits, but in general, the trend is to admit such evidence. If, however, a judge were to act on information secretly disclosed to him by a party to the case and not disclosed to the other parties, such an irregularity would not be accepted.[22] The court will not admit evidence obtained unfairly or improperly. An 'ordonnance' dated 22nd December 1958 states—'Every disregard by a "magistrat" of the duties and standards dictated by his status, honour or dignity will be considered as a breach of discipline.' Hence evidence will not be admitted if it has been obtained by hypnosis, truth drugs, impersonation or other improper means. Tape recorded conversations will only be admitted if the court is satisfied as to the accuracy of the recording process.

The prosecution, defence and 'partie civile' all have equal rights to cite witnesses, and all persons cited are competent to give evidence (although not all do so under oath).[23] All witnesses may be compelled to give evidence except the accused and his spouse who may refuse to answer questions, the court being free to comment on their silence and draw any conclusions therefrom which it pleases.[24] Another exception concerns witnesses such as doctors who are required by law to observe professional secrecy. One authority states that even if a witness in this class agreed to give evidence in violation of the law of professional secrecy, such evidence would be inadmissible. The rule of secrecy does not apply to journalists who can be compelled to reveal their sources. Any witness refusing to give evidence is liable to be fined.[25] A witness who has been specifically paid for giving evidence may only be heard if none of the parties to the case objects.

In theory all evidence should be given verbally at the trial,[26] but in practice this rule only applies to the cour d'assises, and even there the rule is not always strictly enforced. In the tribunal de police and the tribunal correctionnel the court will hear any witnesses who have been cited, supplementing such evidence with information contained in the 'dossier' or the police report.[27] In some trials in these courts there are no witnesses, and the accused is questioned and the evidence evaluated on the contents of the 'dossier', the relevant parts being read aloud by the presiding judge.

Activities of the Press—Publicity

35 Since justice must not only be done, but be seen to be done, the public is admitted to all French trials and may only be excluded in very restricted cases, namely where the evidence is liable to provoke disorder or is of an indecent nature,[28] and even in such cases the verdict and sentence must be given in public. As the public is admitted, the press may report full details of any trial, except details of the jury's deliberations which are secret.[29] Prior to the verdict, it is a criminal

---

[22] The 'Dreyfus' affair.

[23] Juveniles, persons with an interest in the case, etc., do not take the oath. For full details see para 83.

[24] The court may also consider earlier statements made by the accused to the police or to a juge d'instruction.

[25] CPP 326 and 109—the fine being not less than 400 Francs and not more than 1,000 Francs.

[26] For appeals—see para 105.

[27] For more detail see para 83.

[28] CPP Art. 400.

[29] There are special rules for juvenile cases, and trials involving defamation, abortion, etc.

offence to publish comments which could influence the witnesses or the decision of the court.[30] But this does not prevent the newspapers publishing full details of the facts of the case prior to the trial, and since an accused's background is disclosed at the trial, the press may publish full details thereof in advance. If the accused is subsequently acquitted, such publicity can be most unfortunate. Similarly, since the journalists do not have access to the full information contained in the pre-trial inquiries, the facts that are published may give the public a distorted view of the case.[31]

[30] CP 224–227, modified by 'ordonnance' 23/12/1958.
[31] See also para 55 and for Scotland para 154.

6. Institution of Criminal Proceedings[1]

As a general rule, all criminal proceedings are instituted by the procureur de la République.

36 The main exceptions to this rule constitute a very small proportion of criminal trials, and need only be considered briefly. They are:

(a) Criminal proceedings instituted directly by a 'partie civile'[2] (in which cases the procureur takes over the conduct of the prosecution).

(b) Criminal proceedings instituted directly by customs officials, forestry officials and the like who are authorised by statute so to do[3] (in most of which cases the procureur is in no way involved either in the institution or conduct of the prosecution).

(c) In certain circumstances, offences committed in the court itself which disturb the orderly conduct of the trial, may be dealt with on the spot by the court. Such offences may be classed as a 'contravention' or a 'délit'. If the offence occurs in the tribunal de police and is treated as a 'contravention', the court may proceed to deal with the offender, but if the court decides that the offence is of sufficient gravity that it should be classed as a 'délit', the court may only report the matter to the procureur, leaving it to him to institute proceedings in the tribunal correctionnel. If the offence itself occurs during proceedings in the tribunal correctionnel, the court may deal with the offender on the spot.[4] Should the offence constitute a 'crime' (such as committing a serious assault on a 'magistrat' during the conduct of the trial proceedings) the court may order the immediate arrest of the offender, then send a report to the procureur, giving him the responsibility of reporting the offence to a juge d'instruction.

(d) In certain extremely exceptional cases it is believed the police on detecting a serious offence may occasionally report the matter direct to a juge d'instruction without first notifying the procureur (who will be subsequently informed).[5]

(e) In the tribunal de police where the offence carries a penalty of less than ten days imprisonment or a fine of 400 Francs and is prosecuted by a police commissaire, the procureur, while carrying the responsibility for the prosecution,

---

[1] For comparison with Scotland see para 155 et seq.

[2] See para 28.

[3] CPP Art. 1.

[4] CPP Arts. 321, 404, 535, 676, 677, 678.

[5] See para 52 et seq. 'l'information judiciaire'. This would only happen if the police were already investigating an offence on the instructions of the juge d'instruction, in the course of which a further offence came to light.

usually performs a supervisory role, acting personally only where he thinks it necessary.

Informing the Procureur

There is no restriction on the means by which a procureur de la République may learn of the commission of a criminal offence, but the usual channels are the court, a public official, a private individual and the police, the last two, especially the police, being by far the most common.

The court

37 Apart from any instances of offences committed during the trial itself (as mentioned above) the court will also report to the procureur any case of perjury. The court may also formally report to him any facts which constitute a criminal offence and which come to light during the trial for another offence of which the accused is acquitted.

Public officials

38 Any public official or official body learning of the commission of a criminal offence must report the same to the procureur without delay.[6] Thus a registrar dealing with a birth and learning that the mother of the child was under 15 years, would report the facts. Similarly, the procureur receives reports from government departments and similar institutions concerning the commission of criminal offences, such as contravention of the Social Security regulations etc. Reports of this nature are usually called 'dénonciations', and on receiving them, the procureur will frequently instruct the police to verify the facts before taking proceedings.

Private individuals—'plaintes'

39 A report by a private individual may be a 'dénonciation' or a complaint ('plainte'). Any person learning of an attempt against the life or property of another, or against the security of the State, must denounce the same to the procureur. Such occurrences are rare and usually take the form of anonymous letters. Formal complaints ('plaintes') are much more common.[7] A private individual who feels he is the victim of a criminal offence has the choice of reporting the offence to the police, or direct to the procureur. While the reasons underlying the decision of an individual to report to the procureur rather than the police are often obscure, the commonest reasons are that the complainer distrusts the police or is not satisfied with their ability or competence to handle the affair, or the complaint concerns a member of the police force, or in the hope that the procureur will institute criminal proceedings thus allowing the complainer to enter subsequent appearance as 'partie civile' (i.e. as an alternative to a civil action).[8] There is no set form for a 'plainte', and while the majority take the form of letters, some are made by telephone calls. The content of the letters varies considerably, sometimes being accompanied by witness statements, medical reports and any other relevant documentary evi-

[6] CPP Art. 40.

[7] In 1970, apart from offences dealt with in the tribunal de police, the procureur in Paris received 477,870 reports of criminal offences, of which 40,780 (i.e. approximately 10%) took the form of 'plaintes'. The corresponding figures for 1971 were 516,593 reports and 47,000 'plaintes'.

[8] See para 27, and Appendix 3, especially 'plaintes' number 1 and 2.

dence. This is especially the case where the complainer has sought legal advice before writing to the procureur. Other letters are brief, lacking in specification and sometimes so vague that it is virtually impossible to ascertain why the complainer has written to the procureur.[9]

On receipt of the 'plainte' the procureur, once he is satisfied that he has jurisdiction, that any potential proceedings are not time-barred, and that the matter has not already formed the subject of criminal proceedings, will normally send the 'plainte' to the police, instructing them to make inquiries and report back to him.[10] In due course the procureur will receive a report ('procedure') from the police in the usual form and will then decide whether or not to prosecute. If he decides to institute proceedings, he will normally notify the complainer, thus giving him an opportunity to enter appearance as 'partie civile'. Should he decide to take no proceedings ('classer sans suite'), the procureur will normally instruct the police to notify the complainer of his decision. He may explain his reasons to the complainer (such as that he has merely decided to exercise his discretion not to prosecute, or that the offence is a civil matter and not criminal) or he may give no reason. The police are also instructed to notify the complainer of what further rights are available to him, namely instituting proceedings himself by citing the accused to court or informing a juge d'instruction. The complainer is told that he might be entitled to legal aid and is warned against the consequences of raising a vexatious action.[11] The police will obey these instructions submitting a final report to that effect, this report being signed by the complainer. As noted above, if the complainer institutes proceedings, the procureur will take over the conduct of the prosecution.

The Police

40 Since in the first instance the majority of criminal offences is reported by the public to the police, who in turn report to the procureur de la République, it follows that the police are the commonest source of the procureur's information. In Paris and other large cities, the procureur insists that all offences made known to the police are in turn reported to him, regardless of whether there is enough evidence to identify the accused, and as a result the procureur can follow the progress of the police inquiries if he so desires. Other procureurs, especially in provincial areas leave the police with more discretion, and, apart from serious offences, only insist that offences are reported when there is sufficient evidence to identify an accused—although strictly speaking only the procureur may decide that no further proceedings should be taken.

A report sent by the police to the procureur is known as a 'procédure'. It commences with a summary ('rapport'), usually by a commissaire, containing the name and personal details of the accused, the nature of the charge,[12] and a summary of the facts of the case. The 'rapport' is followed by 'procès verbaux'. A 'procès

[9] Typical examples of 'plaintes' are given in Appendix 3.

[10] If he has no jurisdiction, the procureur will normally send the 'plainte' to the appropriate procureur. In sending the 'plainte' to the police (or another procureur), the procureur will usually attach a formal printed note known as a 'Soit Transmis', examples of which are given in Appendix 3.

[11] The instructions given by the procureur to the police are contained on a form called 'Avis de classement', of which an example is given in Appendix 3.

[12] 'Il exist contre l'interessé des indices graves et concordants de nature à motiver des inculpations de . . .'—here follows the nomen juris of the offence and its statutory reference.

verbal' is a formal document, usually by an 'officier' of the police judiciaire recording the steps he has taken or the evidence he has obtained. It must be written shortly after the events it records and be transmitted to the procureur with the minimum of delay; it must be dated and bear the name, address and signature of the author.[13] The police report submitted to the procureur usually contains 'procès verbaux' recording the following—interviews of the witnesses by an 'officier' of the police judiciaire, wherein the officer gives the personal particulars of the witness, the time and place of the interview, the witness's statement verbatim, any questions put to the witness and his answers thereto, and bearing the signatures of both the witness and the 'officier'; the seizing of productions by the 'officier'; the initial interview of the accused by an 'officier' of the police judiciaire, informing the accused that he is being detained in custody[14] as from a particular time and the reasons in brief for such detention,[15] the 'procès verbal' bearing the accused's signature as well as that of the 'officier'; the subsequent questionning of the accused by the police commencing with questions about his personal background, then continuing with questions about the offence, at the end of which the accused is asked to subscribe his signature;[16] any confrontation between different witnesses, or a witness and the accused, for the purpose of clarifying the evidence or resolving any conflict, will be embodied in a 'procès verbal' giving full details of the confrontation and quoting verbatim what the parties said; any other action taken by the 'officier', such as, 'I notified the procureur who instructed that . . .'; informing the accused at the end of the police inquiry what is going to happen to him next—being liberated, or brought before a court etc.; and finally that the police inquiries are finished and the entire police report was transmitted to the procureur on a particular date.

PRE-TRIAL INQUIRIES

Before considering court procedure, it is necessary to examine pre-trial inquiries which play a predominant rôle in French criminal procedure. There are three types of pre-trial inquiry—'l'enquête flagrante', 'l'enquête preliminaire' (both of which are conducted by the police and the procureur de la République) and 'l'information judiciaire' (which is conducted by a juge d'instruction).

'L'Enquête Flagrante'[17]

41 The type of inquiry known as 'l'enquête flagrante' is competent when the offence is classified as a 'crime' or 'délit' and has either been detected while actually being committed, or which has recently been committed. As a general rule, the procureur will not treat an offence as 'flagrant' unless it is reported to the authorities immediately on discovery. There are no rules as to the time which may elapse between commission and discovery—for example if a householder returned from four weeks' holiday to find that his house had been broken into a few days after his de-

---

[13] 'Procès verbaux' are a survival of the times when illiteracy was common, so that a witness required to give his evidence verbally to the authorities who recorded the same immediately on receipt.

[14] See para 45 'garde à vue'.

[15] e.g.—'Pour les besoins de l'enquête'.

[16] It is not uncommon for an accused, in answer to questions concerning the offence, to refuse to answer—'Je n'ai rien à répondre à cette question'; nor is it unusual for an accused to refuse to sign the 'procès verbal'.

[17] CPP Arts. 53–74.

parture, and reported the matter as soon as he returned, the offence would be treated as 'flagrant'. If the police are in doubt as to whether an offence is 'flagrant' the procureur will rule on the matter, deciding each case on its merits. The main feature of 'l'enquête flagrante' is the wide power given to 'officiers' of the police judiciaire and the procureur de la République to investigate the offence as one of urgency. As soon as the police learn of the offence they must notify the procureur who is permanently 'on call' for this purpose. At this point the procuruer has a choice of two courses of action. He may request the immediate intervention of a juge d'instruction who then takes charge of the inquiry. The procureur loses his wide powers of investigation and the police come under the direct control of the juge d'instruction, losing their right of independent action. In the provincial areas of France the procureur will normally adopt this course, dealing only with matters of extreme urgency which cannot await the arrival of the juge d'instruction. There is, however no rule governing the timing of the request by the procureur for the intervention by a juge d'instruction, it being left to the procureur's sole discretion. This provides him with an alternative course. In Paris and in most large towns, the procureur as a general rule, will delay his request for a period of fifteen or even twenty one days, provided progress is being made in the inquiry. During this period, the procureur is in personal control of the inquiry, the police acting subject to his directions. If the accused is arrested within this period the procureur will request the juge d'instruction to take over the inquiry if the offence is a 'crime' or requires further investigation. If no accused is arrested within this period, the procureur will then decide what further action should be taken. He may at the end of the period request the intervention of a juge d'instruction, or being more fully aware of the nature of the case and provided it is not a 'crime', he may decide it is not of sufficient importance to warrant investigation by a juge d'instruction and will instruct the police to continue their inquiries with the important difference that such subsequent inquiries will be classed as 'preliminaire' and not 'flagrant'. The role of the procureur in 'l'enquête flagrante' thus depends on the timing of his request for intervention by a juge d'instruction.[18]

Powers of the Procureur

42 When the procureur is in charge of the investigation (either because he has not requested intervention by a juge d'instruction or is awaiting his arrival) he may visit the locus of the crime and give detailed instructions to the police judiciaire concerning the obtaining and preserving of evidence. Unofficially he might even suggest which police officer should be made responsible for certain duties, but this depends on his personal relationship with the police. He may give written observations and questions for the police to answer, such writings being known as 'Notes Dossier' and being retained with the 'dossier'. He may order an 'expertise'— i.e. use of experts—to examine aspects of the evidence. This will include ballistic, handwriting and analytical experts, but the commonest is naturally the medical expert.[19]

[18] It is sometimes suggested that one of the reasons why the procureur delays the intervention of the juge d'instruction is that the latter is frequently encumbered with too much work. By retaining control of the inquiry, the procureur can be more selective as to which cases he wishes the juge d'instruction to investigate. Since, however, all 'crimes' must be investigated by a juge d'instruction, this reasoning could only apply to 'délits'.

[19] As to the choice of experts available, see para 63. The form used by the procureur when ordering a post mortem examination is contained in Appendix 4.

Post Mortem examinations

43 Post mortem examinations will usually be preceded by an X-ray of the whole body. Only one doctor will be employed if the cause of death seems straightforward, regardless of the degree of foul play, hence for example, if it is obvious that death occurred by shooting, stabbing, strangulation etc. On the other hand, if the cause of death seems dubious or complex, the procureur will employ two doctors.[20] Even if the accused has been arrested prior to the post mortem, he may not be represented by a lawyer or a doctor at the post mortem itself. The procureur will however order that any relevant parts of the body should be retained for evidential purposes. As a general rule, the defence do not contest expert evidence, since the procureur will employ sufficient experts to give a result beyond all reasonable doubt. In one celebrated case, where a female died as a result of stab wounds in the back, the first expert suggested that the wounds could have been self inflicted. The procureur asked for the opinion of a second expert who disagreed with the first. Eventually the procureur instructed a total of seven experts to give their opinions, who while not all agreeing in full, eventually gave as their consensus that the wounds might possibly have been self inflicted. As a result it was decided that the accused should not be sent for trial on a charge of murder owing to lack of evidence.

Search and Seizure

44 The powers of search and seizure are also important. The procureur may order an 'officier' of the police judiciaire to seize any weapons or tools apparently used in the commission of the offence and show them to any person who appears to be responsible for the offence (if present at the locus) for identification purposes.[21] If it seems that evidence might be obtained by examining documents or other objects in the possession of any person who appears to be responsible for the offence, the procureur may order the 'officier' to search that person or his domicile[22]—for example if the police find someone in possession of explosives, they may search his house and any evidence they find may be used, even if it relates to entirely different offences. There is a similar power to search the house of any person who appears to be in possession of documents or other evidence. Such searches must be carried out in the presence of the householder or his nominated representative, failing which in the presence of two witnesses chosen by the police. It should be noted, that all that is required is the householder's presence (if possible) and not his consent. Such consent is only required if the search takes place between 9 p.m. and 6 a.m.[23]

Arrest and Detention—'Garde à Vue'

45 Another important feature of 'l'enquête flagrante' is the power given to the police to arrest and detain. The police may prohibit any person from leaving the

[20] See Appendix 4 for examples of how the procureur will deal with different types of sudden deaths reported to him.

[21] The 'officier' may do this on his own initiative if the procureur has not yet intervened to take charge of the inquiry.

[22] 'Domicile' includes any places where the person resides. The 'officier' may make such a search on his own initiative if the procureur has not yet intervened to take charge of the inquiry.

[23] There are some minor exceptions to this rule concerning timing—notably offences concerned with prostitution. With regard to the general power of search, there are certain restrictions if the premises concerned are occupied by a person such as a lawyer or doctor who is bound by rules of professional secrecy.

scene of the crime until their initial inquiries there are terminated.[24] If the police think that any person may be able to provide information concerning the offence, they may request that person to attend a police station and if he refuses, the procureur can authorise the police to use force to compel his attendance. In addition to these powers, the police may, without the procureur's authority, take into custody any person whose identity they wish to verify, or any person against whom there is substantial incriminating evidence ('indices graves et concordants'). If the person refuses to be taken into custody or resists, the police may use force. This custody is called 'garde à vue'. A person detained under 'garde à vue' may be questioned by the police and is not entitled to legal advice or representation during his detention.[25]

There are various rules concerning the operation of 'garde à vue' which must be strictly observed. Only an 'officier' of the police judiciaire may order such detention. The length of time during which a person may be detained is limited to twenty four hours, unless there is substantial incriminating evidence against the person so detained, in which case the procureur may authorise a further extension by twenty four hours (making a total of forty eight hours[26]) if so requested by the police. Without such written authorisation, the period is strictly limited to twenty four hours. The police may not extend the period improperly by releasing the person shortly before the expiry of the twenty four hour period, then re-arresting him immediately, as the total of all the periods of detention must not exceed twenty four hours—unless the person was released, and after further evidence having come to light, he was re-arrested on a later date. If several offences are being investigated simultaneously all involving the same person, he may still only be detained for one period of 'garde à vue'. The period commences when the person is first taken into custody, so he can not 'willingly' attend a police station for several hours and only technically and formally be detained 'garde à vue' at the end of that period.

The procureur may order that any person detained 'garde à vue' be medically examined, and in any case where the 'garde à vue' has been extended beyond twenty four hours, the person detained may make a similar request. The purpose of such an examination is not to obtain evidence (the procureur having the power to order an expert examination at any time, without the accused's consent), but rather to ensure that the person is medically fit to be detained, or as a safeguard against police brutality.[27] A Ministry of Justice circular of 1961 specifically states 'A person detained by "garde à vue" must be treated properly, both mentally and physically and must have an opportunity for proper rest between examinations and questionnings.'

The police must keep a record of each 'garde à vue' giving its time of commencement and total duration, the duration of any examinations and what took place

[24] In cases of extreme urgency, such as if the witness is dying, an 'officier' of the police judiciaire may put the witness on oath before taking his statement.

[25] It should be remembered that 'l'enquête flagrante' and therefore the power to detain 'garde à vue', only applies to offences classed as 'crimes' or 'délits'.

[26] In certain cases involving drugs, a law passed in 1970, allowed the 'garde à vue' to be extended up to ninety-six hours. In an address to the Congress of Police Commissaires on 15th March 1972, the Minister of the Interior stated that since this extension was proving efficacious, it would be worthwhile studying if such an extension could not be made in other cases concerning known criminals acting together in gangs. In 1970, in Paris, out of 41,247 persons detained 'garde à vue', an extension to forty-eight hours was authorised by the procureur in 3,000 instances.

[27] In Paris, the procureur usually orders a few such examinations each year; about 5% of the persons detained make such a request.

thereat, and the reasons why the person was detained (usually given as 'necessary for the inquiry', or 'substantial incriminating evidence'). In addition to such individual records, the police must maintain a composite register giving details of all 'garde à vue' detentions. The register must state the name and personal particulars of the detainee, the offence being investigated, the exact time of the commencement and termination of the detention, and the exact timings of any examinations of the detainee.[28] Both the record and the register must be signed by the person detained, and if he refuses to sign, this fact must be noted. The procureur examines the register closely each year to ensure that the provisions concerning 'garde à vue' have been strictly observed.

If any person is improperly detained (for example if the 'garde à vue' extended beyond twenty four hours without the procureur's authority, or if the offence being investigated was merely a 'contravention') the 'officier' responsible is liable to be disciplined. The procureur will notify the 'officier's' superior of any such instances coming to his notice. In addition, since illegal detention is a criminal offence, the 'officier' concerned is liable to be prosecuted, but the procureur, except in flagrant breaches, will not normally institute such proceedings unless he receives a formal complaint from the person illegally detained (who may as an alternative course, institute such proceedings himself).

The power of the police to detain a suspect by 'garde à vue', allows the police to question him in the absence of legal representation. This power disappears if a juge d'instruction is in charge of the inquiry, since the police may then only arrest a suspect on his instructions and only he has the right to examine him. The effect of the questions and the answers thereto may well be more restricted if the accused's lawyer is present, as is the accused's right when appearing before a juge d'instruction.[29] Some critics suggest that this provides the procureur with another reason for delaying the intervention of the juge d'instruction but such criticism would appear to be without foundation bearing in mind the frequent refusal of accused persons to answer the police while giving full explanations to the juge d'instruction, the reserve placed by the courts on confessions made to the police, and the general attitude of the 'magistrats' of the 'Ministère public'. Furthermore, unless substantial incriminating evidence already existed against a suspect, it would be pointless for the police to arrest him in the hope of gaining a confession, since failure to do so would only result in the accused's release at the end of the period of detention.

Termination of 'Garde à Vue'

46 Detention by means of 'garde à vue' will be terminated when the purpose for the detention has been accomplished, or the maximum period has expired, whichever is the earlier. The procureur may instruct that the detainee be released at any time. The fact that a suspect has been released from 'garde à vue' does not necessarily mean that he will not be prosecuted as he may be cited to attend court at a later date. In the case of an inquiry conducted as an 'enquête flagrante', the police may bring a suspect before the procureur at the termination of 'garde à vue'. The suspect may then be further detained in custody beyond the limits of 'garde à vue', but only for the length of time necessary to bring him before the procureur—a

---

[28] It was noted that in Paris, the average time for the examination of the accused was 15–30 minutes. A possible explanation may be that this was the time taken to dictate any statement made by the accused, exclusive of any prior 'conversations', etc.

[29] Except for his first formal appearance.

period known as 'delai de transfer'—and he must be brought before the procureur as quickly as possible, regardless of the day of the week or public holidays.[30]

Power of the Procureur to Question the Accused: Termination of L'Enquête Flagrante

47 When the accused appears before him, the procureur has the right (which he usually exercises) to question the accused if the procureur so desires. During such questioning the accused may not be legally represented. The present attitude of most procureurs is that the purpose of this examination is to ensure that there is a reasonable case to answer and that proceedings are not taken against an innocent person. The accused has an opportunity to put forward any explanation, which, if accepted by the procureur, may lead the procureur to drop the proceedings and liberate the accused immediately,[31] The examination is not intended as a means of extracting a confession or obtaining further evidence against the accused. The procureur will normally commence by confirming the accused's personal particulars, then ask him a few questions about the main facts of the case. If the accused denies the charge against him, the procureur will not normally cross-examine him in length, leaving that function to the trial judge or a juge d'instruction, depending on the disposal of the case.[32] If the accused makes a statement, or answers any questions, the procureur will dictate this in narrative form to a clerk or typist and the accused will sign the statement, as will the procureur. This is done in the form of a 'procès verbal'. The procureur will then decide how to dispose of the case and will tell the accused of his decision. The choices of action available to the procureur are (a) take no further proceedings and liberate the accused, (b) liberate the accused to be cited to court later, (c) if the offence is classed as a 'délit' and no further inquiries are necessary, place the accused before the court the same day or the following day. This last mentioned procedure is known as 'flagrant délit' (not to be confused with 'enquête flagrante'). The procureur will issue a warrant called a 'mandat depôt' authorising the detention in custody of the accused until his court appearance. In addition to telling the accused that this will be done, the procureur will tell the accused that he now has a right to legal advice and that when he appears in court, he has the option to ask for an adjournment to allow him to prepare his defence. The accused will sign a note that he has been given this advice by the procureur.[33] (d) the procureur may order that the accused be taken immediately before a juge d'instruction, while at the same time, the procureur will request the juge d'instruction to investigate the offence. This course will always be followed if the offence is a 'crime'; it will also be adopted if the offence is a 'délit' but further inquiries are necessary which the procureur estimates could best be made by a juge d'instruction, or if the offence is a 'délit', requiring further minor inquiries, but where it is desirable that the accused be detained in custody (e.g.

---

[30] In Paris, in view of the number of such cases, the suspect will be detained overnight in a place of detention known as the 'Depôt'—such detention being treated as a 'delai de transfer'. The suspect will appear before the procureur on the following morning. In Paris the department of the procureur's office dealing with such cases is called the 'Petit Parquet'.

[31] See example I in Appendix 5.

[32] For examples of this examination, see Appendix 5.

[33] For court proceedings dealing with 'flagrant délit', see para 80. The examination by the procureur takes place in private. The only persons present being the police escorting the accused, the accused, the procureur and his clerk. The public is not admitted.

because he has no fixed place of abode). The procureur will only place an accused before the court by means of 'flagrant délit' procedure if no further inquiries are necessary, and apart from such procedure, the procureur has no powers to order that an accused be detained in further custody,[34] although a juge d'instruction may order such detention.[35]

If the suspect is brought before the procureur for examination, that terminates 'l'enquête flagrante' by one of the means above described. Should the suspect not be arrested and brought before the procureur, 'l'enquête flagrante' may be terminated by the procureur deciding that no further proceedings should be taken, or ordering that the police should continue their inquiries by means of 'l'enquête preliminaire'. If the offence is a 'crime', or serious offence, or if it is obvious that further inquiries are necessary, the procureur will terminate 'l'enquête flagrante' by requesting a juge d'instruction to take over the investigation.[36]

'L'Enquête Preliminaire'[37]

48 This type of inquiry is used where the offence is not 'flagrant' (thus not permitting the use of 'l'enquête flagrante') and as an alternative to investigation by a juge d'instruction (although such an investigation may follow on an 'enquête preliminaire'). It is used in all 'contraventions', and in all cases where the offence was not reported as soon as it came to light, obvious examples of which are frauds. It is also the method usually employed to investigate road traffic offences.[38] In minor road accidents, if they are reported to the police and investigated by them, the police will retain the report only forwarding it to the procureur for action if he receives a formal 'plainte' from one of the parties. This is especially true if the damage only involves the vehicles and not personal injury. It therefore follows that there are no criminal proceedings taken in many road accidents. If however the accident is serious the procureur will normally consider proceedings, the preliminary inquiries having been made by the police, with or without instructions from the procureur.

Powers of the procureur

49 In 'l'enquête preliminaire', the powers given to the procureur and the police are considerably more restricted than in 'l'enquête flagrante'. The procureur, in general, has the same power to order examination by experts (on the fiction that such an examination can not be delayed), but the police do not have this right (which they have in 'l'enquête flagrante' prior to the intervention of the procureur). The powers to search premises and seize evidence is much more limited, the consent of the occupier in writing being essential. This written consent usually takes the following form—'Knowing that I can object to the visit to my house, I give you my express consent to go there, make a search, and take as productions anything you judge to be of use to the present inquiries.' If the occupier refuses to give this consent,

---

[34] See Appendix 5, example 11.

[35] Very occasionally an accused person who is not in custody will come direct to the procureur rather than the police to 'give himself up', usually the case being a 'crime passionnel'. The procureur will question the accused, then dispose of the case in one of the ways above described. Since the accused is not in custody at the time of the questionning, he may be legally represented thereat.

[36] See para 54 for further detail of this matter.

[37] See CPP Arts. 75–78.

[38] Except for minor offences dealt with by 'on the spot' fines—see para 86.

the police are powerless and can only report the matter to the procureur who may then request the intervention of a juge d'instruction, who can order that the search take place.

Arrest and Detention

50 The power to arrest and detain under 'garde à vue' is also much more limited than under 'l'enquête flagrante'. Since the police are not present at the scene of the offence at the time of its discovery, they can not detain anyone there. They may only use detention 'garde à vue' if such detention is 'necessary for the inquiry' and may not use force to effect such detention. The person detained must have been found in a public place, unless the police have the occupier's consent to enter a building— in other words if the suspect is in his house, he can refuse the police entry, and if he is in the street, he may refuse to accompany the police. The police may only request a suspect or witness to attend the police station and that person has the right to refuse. If a suspect agrees to come to the police station and is detained 'garde à vue', the police can not bring him before the procureur at the end of the period of 'garde à vue'. Their only remedy, if they wish the accused to be detained in custody, is to make a request to the procureur to ask a juge d'instruction to take over the inquiry in the hope that the juge d'instruction will order that the accused be detained, all this being accomplished before the end of the period of 'garde à vue'.

The 'enquête preliminaire' will come to an end when the procureur orders no further proceedings, cites the accused to court, or requests a juge d'instruction to take over the inquiry.

Discretion of the Prosecutor to order 'No further proceedings'

51 In all cases classed as 'crimes' the procureur must request an investigation by a juge d'instruction, and in cases classed as 'délits' he has a discretionary right to request such an investigation. If the juge d'instruction has not made an investigation and if there are no legal bars to taking proceedings,[39] the procureur has a discretion as to whether or not to institute criminal proceedings. The following factors may have a bearing on how he exercises that discretion. If the victim of the offence institutes the proceedings, the procureur has no discretion, except to comment at the trial, giving his views as to the desirability of the prosecution and its conduct by the 'partie civile'. In cases where the victim does not institute proceedings, in certain instances, the procureur may only prosecute if he has the concurrence of the victim of the offence. Cases falling into this class usually involve matrimonial disputes. In certain other circumstances, the procureur, while not required to do so by law, will not normally institute proceedings unless he receives a formal complaint from the victim, although such a practice depends on the attitude of the individual procureur. The cases covered by this practice usually include minor road traffic accidents, the issuing of cheques without sufficient funds to cover them where the amount was less than 100 francs or the victim was subsequently re-imbursed,[40]

---

[39] See para 76.

[40] The practice concerning 'bounced cheques' is particular to Paris, but illustrates the point. Approximately 160,000 such cases were marked 'no proceedings' in Paris in 1970. Under a law coming into effect in 1972, anyone issuing a cheque which is not met by the bank will be given an immunity from prosecution if he makes payment to the victim within 10 days and pays a sum equal to 10% of the amount involved to the Ministry of Finance. Failure to observe this provision will result in prosecution, regardless of the amount involved.

and cases of relatively minor importance. The procureur, waiting to see if any complaint is made to him by the victim, will mark such cases 'classer en etat' and if such a complaint is received he will then decide whether or not to prosecute. If no such complaint is received, the case is treated in the same way as if it had been marked 'No proceedings'. While to this very limited extent the action of the procureur depends on the attitude of the victim, he is in no way bound by the victim's wishes unless the latter himself institutes criminal proceedings.

In some cases involving pornographic literature, the procureur is required to obtain the views of a commission before instituting proceedings. The commission consists of former 'magistrats', a professor of law, and representatives from the Ministry of Education and associations designed to protect the rights of authors, public morality and family life. The commission whose deliberations are not open to the public must be consulted if the literature has no illustrations, the author and editor are not identified and a copy has not been lodged with the 'depôt legal' (which receives copies of all printed matter for record purposes). All of these conditions must be present, otherwise whether or not the commission is consulted is left to the discretion of the procureur. The role of the commission is purely advisory and while giving its views on the nature of the literature and the desirability of a prosecution, it is not meant to exclude expert evidence at the trial,[41] nor are its views binding on the procureur. In certain other types of offence, such as breach of price control regulations and merchant marine offences, the procureur must notify the appropriate government department of his intention to prosecute, but this does not affect his decision as to whether or not to prosecute.

All the above cases only fractionally impinge on the wide discretion given to the procureur to decide whether or not to institute criminal proceedings.[42] Even where there is no legal bar to proceedings, where the accused has been identified and there is sufficient evidence to justify proceedings (which is often a question of law or interpretation of the evidence), the procureur still has the discretion to refuse to prosecute ('classer sans suite'), and is not required to state the reasons for his decision. The most common reasons underlying such a decision are that the offence is of a trivial nature ('ne trouble pas suffisamment l'ordre public') or that the taking of criminal proceedings would be out of all proportion to the offence itself—such as a case involving a respectable middle aged woman committing a minor shoplifting offence, or a road accident where the only person injured was the driver or his wife. The decision to mark a case 'classer sans suite' is not final and may be reviewed if further evidence comes to light, nor does it count as a judicial decision, and hence can not be founded on for a plea of 'res judicata'. The extent to which the discretion to take no proceedings is exercised, can be illustrated by the following statistics for Paris for 1970.

Total number of cases made known to the procureur (exclusive of 3,473,792 'contraventions')	477,870
Less cases where the author of the offence was not identified	134,400
	343,470
Total number of prosecutions instituted	66,324
Cases marked 'classer sans suite'	277,146

[41] In a recent case, it was held in a cour d'appel that experts called to give an opinion on the literature could not be heard in evidence on the grounds that the court was concerned with obscenity not artistic merit.
[42] CPP Art. 40.

—in other words approximately 80% of the cases made known to the procureur in Paris were marked 'classer sans suite'. It must be borne in mind that of the 277,146 cases marked 'no proceedings', 160,000 represented cheque bouncing cases, and if proceedings had been taken in these 160,000 cases, the percentage of cases marked 'no proceedings' would be nearer 30%. Furthermore, the procureur in Paris insists that all cases be referred to him for a decision, whereas in other parts of France, the procureur may give the police more discretion as to what cases they refer to him. Even so the national average percentage for the whole of France of cases marked 'classer sans suite' in 1969 was 25.9%

It must be remembered that the procureur has no discretion to order 'no further proceedings' if proceedings are ordered by a juge d'instruction or the Chambre d'accusation, when the procureur must institute proceedings regardless of his views of the case.

'L'Information Judiciaire'[43]

52 Unlike 'l'enquête flagrante' and 'l'enquête preliminaire' which are made by the procureur de la République, the type of pre-trial enquiry known as 'l'information judiciaire' is undertaken by a 'magistrat' specially designated for this purpose and called a juge d'instruction. The juge d'instruction is independent and in particular is not subject to control by the court,[44] the procureur or the police.

Appointments as juges d'instruction are usually made from among the judges of the tribunal correctionnel, but there is nothing to prevent a procureur or a newly appointed 'magistrat' becoming one. A juge d'instruction is appointed on the formal advice of the Conseil Supérieur de la Magistrature[45] and usually holds office for three years. At the end of that period the appointment will normally be renewed unless the person concerned has been found unsuitable or requests a change, in which case he will be given a different magisterial post. There is at least one juge d'instruction attached to each tribunal correctionnel. In small courts where there is not sufficient work to justify a full time appointment, the juge d'instruction will also be required to sit on the bench, judging civil and criminal cases. In busy courts there may be more than one juge d'instruction—Paris has 68, each handling between 200 and 300 cases per annum. In 1971 there were 381 juges d'instruction in France. If there is more than one juge d'instruction attached to a court, the president of the court is responsible for allocating cases to the different juges d'instruction, but unofficially the procureur may often make suggestions concerning such allocation.[46] Once a juge d'instruction has begun his investigation he may only be removed therefrom if the procureur requests the president of the court to remove him, stating that it is necessary for the proper administration of justice (the accused and the 'partie civile' can not make such a request). The president must answer such a request within eight days, either rejecting it or appointing another juge d'instruction. If a juge d'instruction is unable to complete his inquiries because of personal illness or other urgent reason, another juge d'instruction can be appointed to complete the inquiry.

[43] This procedure is sometimes called 'L'instruction criminelle'.

[44] Although his decisions are subject to appeal.

[45] See para 20 supra.

[46] In Paris the juges d'instruction tend to specialise in different types of cases which correspond to the specialisation of the 'magistrats' in the procureur's office and the police.

Method of instigating inquiries by a juge d'instruction

53 A juge d'instruction can not initiate an inquiry unless requested to do so by the procureur de la République or by a 'partie civile'. The procureur requests the juge d'instruction to intervene by means of a written request known as a 'réquisitoire introductif'. There is no set form for a 'réquisitoire introductif', but it must be dated, which is of importance when considering the question of prescription. It normally states that there is evidence that a criminal offence has been committed contrary to a specific provision of the Code pénal, and may also state that there is particular evidence that the offence was committed by a named accused. It is not, however essential that the accused be named, in which case the investigation will be requested 'contre x'. If the procureur has requested the intervention of the juge as soon as the offence was discovered, it is almost certain that the investigation will be 'contre x'.[47] Since the juge's duties are to investigate the case and not the individual, if the procureur has specified an accused by name, this is not binding on the juge who may suggest an alternative or additional accused; if the procureur has not specified an accused, the juge in the course of his inquiries may do so; before any person specified by the juge as the accused may be formally designated as such (and thus benefit from the rights given to accused persons), the juge must notify the procureur and receive from him a further request that the person so specified should be formally designated as the accused. This further request by the procureur is called a 'réquisitoire aux fins d'inculpation'. Although the 'réquisitoire introductif' of the procureur will give the 'nomen juris' of the offence, the juge is not strictly bound thereby—for example he may decide to treat an offence designated as fraud as a case of theft; he may also investigate any factors which act as an aggravation, mitigation and complete or partial defence to the charge. In the course of his investigation, if he discovers further facts giving rise to fresh charges he may not investigate such charges except on the request of the procureur (who has a complete discretion to decide whether nor not such charges should be proceeded with); should the juge investigate such new charges without the request of the procureur, his investigation quoad these charges will be declared null and void. In his 'réquisitoire introductif' the procureur may request the juge to take specific action such as detaining the accused in custody, or having him mentally examined. The juge is not bound by such requests and will decide on them as he sees fit.[48]

The investigation on the request of the procureur will only concern the criminal and not the civil aspect of the case; if, however the victim enters appearance as 'partie civile' or if the victim instigates the proceedings by himself requesting the intervention of a juge d'instruction (no such request having been previously made by the procureur), the juge will also investigate the civil aspects of the case. Should such appearance be entered, the juge will notify the procureur.

If the intervention of the juge has not been requested by the procureur, the victim of the offence may request such intervention as 'partie civile', by making a formal complaint to the juge and requesting him to investigate it—'plainte avec constitution de partie civile'. This will compel the juge to make an investigation regardless of the wishes or prior knowledge of the procureur, but the juge must notify the procureur of such an occurrence, so that the latter may consider his position. The

---

[47] Re the timing of the request by the procureur, see para 41.

[48] Subject always to an appeal by the procureur against his decision to the chambre d'accusation.

RÉQUISITOIRE INTRODUCTIF

Le Procureur de la République près le Tribunal de grande instance de Paris.

Vu les pièces jointes _____
_____

Attendu qu'il en résulte contre _____
_____
_____
_____
_____
_____
_____

Des présomptions graves d_____
_____
_____
_____

Vu les articles _____
_____
_____

Requiert qu'il plaise à M. le Juge d'instruction informer par toutes voies de droit et décerner _____
_____

Fait au Parquet, le _____
LE PROCUREUR DE LA RÉPUBLIQUE,

45

procureur may then concur in the action of the 'partie civile' and himself request the juge to investigate by means of a 'réquisitoire introductif', or if there is some legal bar to proceedings, he may request the juge not to make an investigation ('réquisitoire refus d'informer'). As a general rule, however, the procurer will have little or no knowledge of the alleged offence and will therefore not be in a position to make either of these requests. Instead he will request the juge to take all legal steps to investigate the case quoad any person who appears to be responsible, such a request being known as a 'réquisitoire aux fins d'informer'. Should the investigation reveal that a criminal offence has been committed and there is sufficient evidence to warrant proceedings against a particular accused, the procureur will then issue a réquisitoire aux fins d'inculpation'. There is one important difference if inquiries are instigated by the 'partie civile', in that if he names a specific accused, the juge may only investigate the case quoad the named person unless he receives a request from the procureur to the contrary.

If a juge d'instruction is requested to investigate a case either by the procureur or the 'partie civile', he must make such an investigation, unless he issues an 'ordonnance de non informer'. He may only issue this and thereby refuse to make an investigation if he is satisfied, before he commences his investigation that criminal proceedings are incompetent (for example if there is a legal bar to proceedings, or the alleged offence does not constitute a breach of the criminal law).[49] A request to issue an 'ordonnance de non informer' may be made by the procureur, and such an 'ordonnance' may be appealed to the chambre d'accusation either by the procureur or the 'partie civile'. Like all decisions by a juge d'instruction, the 'ordonnance' must be accompanied by the juge's reasons therefor based on law.

Type of Offence which may be Investigated[50]

54 All offences classed as 'crimes' must be investigated by a juge d'instruction. While there is nothing to prevent offences classed as 'contraventions' being investigated, such an occurrence would be so rare as to be almost theoretical—unless an offence had been wrongly classified and the investigation by the juge allowed it to be properly classified as a 'contravention'. Whether or not a 'délit' is investigated rests entirely on the discretion of the procureur (except for a few minor exceptions where statute requires such an investigation). The way in which each procureur exercises this discretion may vary, but the commonest considerations which lead him to request the investigation of a 'délit' by a juge d'instruction are: because further inquiries are necessary and the police have neither the ability nor the legal competence to make such inquiries; because it is desirable that the accused be detained in custody awaiting trial while further inquiries are made; or because the accused's whereabouts are unknown and it is necessary to obtain a warrant for his arrest.

With regard to the need for further inquiries, this covers a very wide field. The procureur will not place an accused before the court unless he is satisfied that all the relevant evidence has been obtained in a manner suitable for its presentation at the trial. Since the wide powers of investigation available to the procureur and the police are restricted to 'l'enquête flagrante' (which may only be used in a specific class of

[49] If he makes such a decision after the commencement of the inquiry, he will terminate the inquiry by means of an 'ordonnance de non lieu'—see para 67.

[50] Offences committed by persons aged less than 18 years are investigated by a juge d'instruction, the offence being dealt with in the appropriate juvenile court.

cases) and since the powers of inquiry are greatly restricted under 'l'enquête preliminaire', the procureur will frequently request that the investigation be made by a juge d'instruction. Such instances include cases where an accused has not been identified but are of sufficient gravity to warrant further inquiry. Also included are cases where there are several accused or several charges and it is desirable that all should be conjoined;[51] cases where the evidence obtained by the police contains contradictions of a serious nature, or requires clarification, verification or is incomplete;[52] cases of a complex or important nature or which, because of the persons involved, the evidence or the type of offence require careful handling; cases where the procureur thinks that more detailed inquiries should be made about the accused's background[53] which may sometimes entail a medical or mental examination;[54] or cases where it is felt desirable that the accused should be examined prior to the trial, and the police have been unable to conduct such an examination because of their restricted powers (i.e. under 'l'enquête preliminaire').

With regard to cases where it is desirable that the accused be detained in custody while further inquiries are made, a juge d'instruction is the only person who may order this (unless the court so orders and adjourns the case part-heard). In view of the restricted time limits applicable to 'garde à vue', the procureur has often no option but to place the inquiry in the hands of a juge d'instruction[55] who may order such detention. The juge is however free to decide on the question of detention as he sees fit, not being bound by the views of the procureur.[56]

A further minor factor which may occasionally have a minimal bearing on the procureur's decision to involve the juge d'instruction, is the personal attitude of the procureur. In many of the larger cities, juges d'instruction are overburdened with work, and the procureur may consider this factor in marginal cases. On the other hand, there a few critics who complain that some procureurs unnecessarily send cases to a juge when the nature of the further inquiries is such that they could be made by the police or dispensed with. Such criticism is rare and not in accordance with the general opinion.

The vast proportion of cases investigated by the juge d'instruction fall into the category of 'délits' in the first instance, even allowing for the fact that some 'crimes' will ultimately be treated as 'délits' by virtue of 'correctionnalisation'. In 1970, the total number of prosecutions for 'crimes and délits' instituted by the procureur of

[51] See Appendix 5, example 9.

[52] See Appendix 5, example 10.

[53] See Appendix 5, example 8.

[54] If the procureur has reason to believe that an accused is mentally ill and if the accused has been arrested, the procureur may order a doctor to examine the accused prior to his court appearance. Bearing in mind the restricted length of time in which the accused is in custody, there is often no opportunity to arrange such an examination, which if it occurs, must because of the time factor, be brief. If no such examination takes place, or if the doctor says the accused is mentally ill, or at least requires further examination, the procureur will refer the inquiry to a juge d'instruction, who alone has the power to order that the accused be detained in custody in order to be mentally examined. Since such examinations are usually very thorough, and especially in Paris where there is often considerable delay in obtaining the results thereof, this can often lead to the type of case where a middle aged woman, with no previous convictions, charged with stealing several bottles of whisky from a shop, was detained in prison for 6 weeks merely in order to have her mentally examined—see also Appendix 7, case 6.

[55] See Appendix 5, example 11.

[56] See Para 59 for a more detailed discussion on this point.

Paris was 66,324. Of that number, the procureur requested an investigation by a juge d'instruction in 11,939 cases. The total number of cases prosecuted as 'crimes' in the cour d'assises in Paris in 1971 was 78, and while this can not be accurately related to the above figures (since an investigation in Paris by a juge d'instruction averages over twelve months and therefore only the majority of the 1971 trials would be reported in 1970), it gives a fair indication of the ratio of 'crimes' to 'délits'.

Secrecy
55 One of the features of the investigation by a juge d'instruction is the private nature of the proceedings. While the accused, the procureur and the 'partie civile' are at all times kept fully informed of the progress and content of the inquiry, the investigation is otherwise regarded as secret. The public is not admitted and should the juge himself, or his clerk, or the procureur or any person lawfully entitled to obtain information concerning the inquiry, divulge such information, he would be liable to prosecution.[57] The rule of secrecy is designed to protect the accused's reputation should no trial proceedings be ordered at the end of the inquiry or alternatively to ensure he receives a fair trial by preventing any potential jurors from receiving prior knowledge of the case. Unfortunately this purpose is usually frustrated since the prohibition of divulging information does not apply to the accused and his lawyer, the 'partie civile' and his lawyer, nor any of the witnesses. Since such persons may divulge information to the press, who may also make their own inquiries, and since the press is only restricted from publishing comment on the case, but may freely print the facts,[58] some cases may be given pre-trial publicity, which can be very extensive in certain instances. While this may result in the press giving a distorted view of the case owing to their ignorance of some of the facts, it often means that the secrecy of the inquiry is more derisory than real. This constitutes one of the major problems in France today as a case can virtually be judged by the press in advance of the actual trial.[59]

The 'Dossier'
56 All the steps taken by the juge d'instruction in his investigation, including statements made by the accused and the witnesses must be recorded in a 'dossier', which is kept in duplicate. This 'dossier' is usually divided into four parts: (a) 'Pièces de fond'—which includes the original police report and statements made to them, the 'réquisitoire introductif' by the procureur (the note by the president of the tribunal appointing the juge d'instruction to investigate—if applicable), the examination by the accused and any statements made by him, the witness statements, the results of any confrontations,[60] experts' reports—in other words a full record of all the evidence as obtained firstly by the police and thereafter by the juge d'instruction.

[57] The penalty being a term of imprisonment for not less than 1 month and not more than 6 months and a fine not less than 500 francs and not more than 3,000 francs—CP Art. 378.

[58] See para 35.

[59] In 'l'affaire Leroy' in 1972 a 'notaire' was charged with the murder of a 16 year old girl. The case attracted a great deal of publicity, the newspapers printing all available information and reporters interviewing the witnesses as soon as they left the office of the juge d'instruction. As a result, when the juge decided to reconstruct the accused's movements on the night of the crime, which required visiting various public places, the crowds who attended to see the reconstruction were so vast, that special police had to be drafted to control them.

[60] See para 62.

(b) a record detailing the history of the accused's detention in custody awaiting trial, including the original warrant by the juge d'instruction committing the accused to prison, requests by the accused to be liberated, details of any appeals in connection with such detention—this section of the dossier being entitled 'Détention préventive'; (c) a section entitled 'Renseignements et Personnalité' giving a full life history of the accused including any previous convictions and the results of any medical or mental examination;[61] (d) a final section entitled 'Pièces de Forme' containing miscellaneous correspondence and other papers not essential to give an appreciation of the case.

The procureur and the legal representatives of the accused and the 'partie civile' (but not the accused or 'partie civile' in person)[62] have a right of access to this 'dossier' to study its contents at all times, regardless of the stage of the proceedings. Furthermore, the procureur has the right to demand that the 'dossier' be sent to him at any time, on condition he returns it to the juge within 24 hours (although there is no sanction to apply if the procureur fails to observe this condition). Therefore although the investigation by the juge is secret, and made outwith the presence of the parties to the case, the parties are at all times kept fully informed of the nature, content and progress of the inquiry.

Duties and Powers of the Juge d'Instruction

57   The function of the juge d'instruction is to take responsibility for the collection, examination and investigation of all the evidence relating to a particular case and thereafter to decide whether or not the case should be remitted for trial, and if so, in which court the trial should proceed. In deciding whether or not a case should be sent for trial, he is only required to ascertain if a criminal offence has been committed and if there is sufficient evidence, which if believed by the court, would constitute a reasonable case for the accused to answer. He is not required to decide on issues of credibility, nor to interpret the evidence, this being left to the trial court. His personal views as to the guilt or innocence of the accused are of no relevance. All his decisions,[63] including the final one must be motivated in law, which thus excludes his opinions on credibility and his personal views. Appeals against his decisions may be taken to the chambre d'accusation.[64] The investigation by a juge d'instruction is inquisitorial; he has the responsibility of ascertaining the facts, rather than leaving it to the parties to present their cases to him, although the parties may suggest lines of inquiry or witnesses to be examined. In order to perform these duties, the juge d'instruction is given extensive powers which include the right to issue warrants of arrest, to detain the accused in custody, to examine the accused and the witnesses, to order experts to examine the accused or the evidence, to order a search for and seizure of evidence and to direct the police.

Warrants to Arrest

58   If the accused has not already been arrested (by provision of the police powers of 'garde à vue'), the juge d'instruction has the power to issue a warrant for his arrest of which there are three types—the 'mandat de comparution', the 'mandat

---

[61] For full details see para 66.

[62] Which makes it essential for the accused to be legally represented.

[63] Known as 'ordonnances'.

[64] See para 72.

d'amener' and the 'mandat d'arrêt'. The 'mandat de comparution' is not so much a warrant as a request by the juge to the accused to appear before him. It will not normally be used in serious cases, or if the juge thinks the accused is liable to ignore it. If the accused fails to appear, the juge will then issue a 'mandat d'amener', having first invited the procureur to give his views on the issue of such a warrant. A 'mandat d'emener' may only be issued if the offence is at least a 'délit' punishable by imprisonment. The warrant authorises the police to arrest the accused, using force if necessary, but such an arrest may not be effected in a private house between the hours of 8 p.m. and 6 a.m. As soon as the accused is arrested, he must be brought before the juge d'instruction, or if that is impossible, at least within twenty-four hours of his arrest, being detained in a police station in the interim. If the juge d'instruction does not examine the accused within twenty-four hours of his arrest, the procureur may request the president of the court (or a judge nominated by him) to conduct such an examination. Should such an examination not be made within twenty-four hours of the request, or if no such request is made (and the juge has not examined the accused), the accused must be liberated from custody. In the event of an accused being arrested more than 200 kilometers away from the juge's office, the accused will be brought before the nearest procureur to his scene of arrest. The procureur will verify the accused's identity then tell him he has the right to make or refuse to make a declaration. If the accused makes a declaration, the procureur will note it, and then ask the accused if he wishes to be transferred before the juge d'instruction who issued the warrant, or prefers to remain in custody where he is until that juge's decision is known. When the accused agrees to be transferred, this is done immediately, but if he elects to stay in custody where he is, the procureur will send all the available information, including any declaration made by the accused, to the juge who issued the warrant. The juge on receipt of this information may then order that the accused be brought before him, or may order his release (if for example he thinks that the wrong person has been arrested or the accused's explanation clearly proves his innocence). A 'mandat d'arrêt' is basically the same as a 'mandat d'amener', but is used where the accused has fled or gone abroad. The main difference is that the accused must be brought before the juge within forty-eight hours of his arrest (and not twenty-four hours as with the 'mandat d'amener').

Detention in Custody

59   When the accused appears before him by virtue of his arrest on such a warrant, or having been brought before him on the orders of the procureur at the end of an 'enquête flagrante' (or before the end of the 'garde à vue' in 'l'enquête préliminaire'), the juge d'instruction after examining the accused, must decide whether the accused is to be detained in custody, released on conditional liberty, or released completely until the date of the trial. The law dictates the factors which a juge should consider when making his decision, but the law is loosely worded, and leaves so much discretion to the juge that it has virtually no effect and in practice is often ignored. The law, which came into effect on 1st January 1971[65] states that with regard to pre-trial detention in custody ('détention provisoire'), such detention may only be ordered if it is necessary for the inquiries or as a measure of security, and the penalty for the offence exceeds two year's imprisonment. Furthermore, conditional liberty must be inappropriate as an alternative. To illustrate what may be considered as

[65] CPP Arts. 137–148.

'necessary for the inquiries' or 'as a measure of security', various examples are given such as where detaining the accused is the only way to preserve the evidence or to prevent the accused interfering with the witnesses or forming a scheme to produce false evidence to defeat the ends of justice, or where detention is necessary in the interests of public order, or to protect the accused, or to prevent the offence being continued, or further offences being committed, or to keep the accused at the disposal of the legal authorities. A final example is where an accused has been placed on conditional liberty but has failed to observe the conditions. The juge must give his reasons for the detention. Such reasons are frequently given as—'detention is necessary in view of the gravity of the charge and the necessities of the inquiry'. No further detail is given in amplification as to why detention is necessary for the inquiry, but in October 1971 the Cour de Cessation overturned a decision of a chambre d'accusation confirming a decision of a juge d'instruction detaining an accused in custody where the only reason given for such detention was—'necessity of the inquiries'. The Cour de Cassation held that this phrase alone was not sufficient to justify detention and that full details must be given. While the decision of the Cour de Cassation only applied to the case before it, an indication may be taken as to how it would decide similar such appeals.

With regard to conditional liberty ('contrôle judiciare') the juge may only consider such a course if it is necessary for the inquiries or as a measure of security. The juge may allow the accused to remain at liberty but may impose certain conditions such as that the accused must not leave a certain area, must not change his address, must not visit specific places, must present himself at regular intervals to persons specified by the juge, must visit any person as ordered by the juge, must conduct his business or employment as directed by the juge, must surrender his identity papers or passport, must refrain from driving motor vehicles and surrender his driving licence, must refrain from meeting or communicating with individuals specified by the juge, must submit himself for medical examination if ordered by the juge, and must lodge caution to ensure his subsequent appearances, the amount being determined by the juge bearing in mind the accused's resources. All or any of these conditions may be imposed, the above list not being exhaustive but merely illustrative of the type of condition the juge may consider. The juge can add or modify the conditions at any time, or remove all the conditions, leaving the accused in complete freedom. The juge may do so on his own initiative or on the request of the procureur or of the accused (in which case the procureur must be notified of the accused's request). The juge must answer such a request within five days, failing which the request may be submitted to the chambre d'accusation. If the latter fails to deal with the request within fifteen days, the conditions fall. Should the accused fail to obtemper one of the conditions deliberately, the juge has a discretion to issue a warrant for his arrest and detain the accused in custody. Unfortunately one of the difficulties concerning the operation of conditional liberty is the lack of manpower and resources to ensure that the conditions are complied with, and in practice, the juge may have to decide between the alternatives of custody or complete freedom.

As a result the juge will frequently decide that the accused should be detained in custody, which is almost automatic where the offence is classed as a 'crime'. Similarly most juges would almost automatically detain persons accused of certain 'délits' such as assaulting a police officer, or drunk driving involving injury to a third party. Despite the decision of the Cour de Cassation in October 1971 and several ministerial circulars, the discretion left to the juge d'instruction is such that the law of 1st January 1971 would appear to have little effect.[66] It must of course be remembered that the juge may frequently have to make such a decision at the outset of his inquiries when he knows little or nothing about the case, and he may well decide to detain the accused until the evidence has been properly examined. In France, the liberty of the individual tends to be subordinated to the right of the state to investigate criminal offences. It is also worthy of note that the number of cases not committed for trial at the end of the juge's investigations is very small,[67] and the majority of trials result in a verdict of guilty.

When the juge is deciding initially whether or not to detain the accused, the procureur, the accused and the 'partie civile' may express their views. The procureur may state his views in the 'réquisitoire introductif' or in a separate 'réquisitoire', and will usually give his views very briefly, such as 'gravity of the offence', 'necessary for the inquiries', 'accused liable to flee if liberated', etc. In about 80% of the cases, the juge will initially follow the views of the procureur, who may also appeal against the juge's decision to the chambre d'accusation (in which case the procureur's views will be elaborated on in greater detail both in writing and orally by the procureur général). If the juge decides to detain the accused he issues a 'mandat depôt' which transfers the accused to prison and detains him there until liberated in due course of law.[68]

The period for which the accused may be detained awaiting trial may not exceed four months, but the juge, on cause shown, may extend this period by a further four months as often as he wishes (the procureur and the accused having the right to comment on such extensions). In Paris, the average length of pre-trial detention is eighteen months to two years, whereas in country districts where there is less pressure of business, the average is much lower and only 2.4% of all pre-trial detentions in France exceed eight months. In one provincial district where there were two juges d'instruction, the average time was four to six weeks. All time spent in custody is counted towards any prison sentence ultimately imposed for the offence, the sentence being automatically backdated to the date of the accused's arrest.

The juge may release the accused from custody at any time, setting him at liberty with or without conditions provided he first notifies the procureur, and the accused agrees to attend all future hearings. The procureur or the accused may also at any time request that the accused be liberated. This request is known as a 'demande de mise en liberté'. The procureur will take this course if he estimates that the evidence elicited by the juge is not sufficient to warrant further inquiries or proceedings.[69] This may be contrary to the juge's view of the case, in which instance he is likely to refuse the request. On the other hand if the juge in the course of his inquiries finds

[66] In 1971 the total number of persons detained in prison was 33,000, of whom 12,700 were detained awaiting trial. The corresponding figures for 1972 are 37,000 and 15,000.

[67] The proportion for the whole of France for 1968 was 2.63%.

[68] The juge also has the sole authority of deciding which visitors the accused may see while in prison.

[69] In the case of Leroy (see footnote 59), the juge was quoted as saying 'I have no actual evidence against Leroy at present, only presumptions'. The case against Leroy virtually rested on his inability to account for his movements about the time when the murder could have been committed. Leroy was a well known lawyer, a local dignitary and had no previous convictions. The juge detained him in custody. The procureur requested Leroy's release, and when the juge refused this, the procureur appealed to the chambre d'accusation against the juge's refusal.

that the case against the accused is very weak, and that while the inquiries are not finished, it is likely that the case will not proceed to trial, the juge may consult the procureur, who, if he agrees with the juge, will request that the accused be liberated. (The alternative course would be for the juge to liberate the accused without the prior concurrence of the procureur and thus involve a possible appeal by the procureur if he disagrees with the juge.)

If the accused makes a request to be liberated, the juge must notify the procureur and the 'partie civile' of the request immediately. The juge must decide on the request within five days, his decision being accompanied by reasons. As noted above these reasons may be brief—such as 'necessities of the inquiry', but if he thinks it advisable, he may specify in more detail why the detention should be continued. If the juge fails to make a decision within five days, the accused may apply direct to the chambre d'accusation, who must give a decision within fifteen days, failing which the accused is automatically liberated (unless the delay is due to the chambre d'accusation requesting further information before making its decision). Should the juge refuse the accused's request, the accused at that stage may appeal against the refusal to the chambre d'accusation—similarly if the juge grants the request, the procureur has the right of appeal to the chamber d'accusation. There is no limit to the number or timing of the requests which the accused can make to be liberated, nor is there any such limit to the appeals he may make to the chambre d'accusation. If there are no new circumstances arising since the previous request, a further request may seem pointless, but nevertheless many accused continue to make repeated requests and appeals using such procedures for the improper motive of delaying the inquiry as long as possible. Such a delay has two potential benefits for an accused. Firstly there is always the chance that an essential witness may disappear, or become forgetful. Secondly if the accused knows he is ultimately bound to be convicted, and that his sentence will be backdated to his date of arrest, he will be anxious to undergo as much of his sentence as possible as an untried prisoner, since such prisoners are much less restricted than those detained after conviction. The rights of untried prisoners include lighter prison discipline, the right to buy their own food, and more frequent visitors, etc.

At the conclusion of the investigation by the juge d'instruction, the question of the accused's detention may again be considered by the court to which the accused is remitted for trial. If the accused requests such a court to liberate him prior to the trial, the procureur and the 'partie civile' have the right to be notified of the request and to address the court thereon.

If any person, having been detained on the orders of a juge d'instruction, is subsequently acquitted at his trial, or is released and not committed for trial, that person may be entitled to financial compensation if it is shown that his detention has caused him to suffer what is clearly an abnormal and particularly serious prejudice. Such claims are considered by a commission consisting of judges of the Cour de Cassation. The procureur général has a right of audience before the commission. Any compensation awarded will be paid from public funds unless the detention was the direct result of a third party having made a malicious accusation or committing perjury, in which case a civil action may also be competent.

Right to Examine the Accused

60 The juge d'instruction has the right to examine the accused. Such an examination will take place in the juge's office and will lack some of the formality of a court

appearance.[70] On the accused's first appearance he is not legally represented. The juge will satisfy himself as to the accused's identity and inform him of the nature of the offence. He will also tell the accused that he has the right to make or refuse to make a statement, and if the accused elects so to do, the juge will merely note it. The juge will not question the accused about his statement except to clarify any ambiguities therein, although he may ask the accused if he recognises the accuracy of any prior statements made by the accused to the police. The juge will then advise the accused that he is entitled to legal representation (making a note of the giving of the advice and any reply thereto). It is particularly important that the accused should have a lawyer who is entitled to examine the dossier at any time and in particular twenty-four hours in advance of any subsequent examination of the accused. At the conclusion of the first examination, the juge decides whether or not the accused should be detained in custody, this decision being made before the accused is legally represented.

The juge may subsequently examine the accused on as many future occasions as seem necessary to the juge, there being no limit to the number or duration. At such subsequent examinations in addition to the juge, his clerk and the accused, the following persons have the right to be present—the accused's police escort, the accused's lawyer, the 'partie civile' and his lawyer, and the procureur de la Republique.[71] At such subsequent examinations the juge will question the accused in great depth, in the same way as an accused would be examined and cross-examined in a British trial. There is no restriction to the nature, content, form or number of the questions that may be put, but the accused always has the right to refuse to answer and can never be compelled to speak.[72] The juge will put contradictory evidence to the accused, and may read witnesses' statements to him. If the juge wishes, he may confront the accused with witnesses, or arrange a reconstruction of the offence. While each individual juge has his own style, many feel that the informality of the proceedings—as opposed to the trial itself—is more conducive to the accused speaking freely. In that way an innocent person has nothing to lose and has a better chance to establish his innocence since the juge will investigate any defence evidence with the same resources, thoroughness and impartial approach which he brings to bear on the prosecution evidence. At these examinations the accused's lawyer is free to suggest questions for him to put to the accused, the lawyer for the 'partie civile' and the procureur having a similar right. Whether or not such questions are put depends on the juge who alone may ask questions. The juge will dictate the accused's answers in the form of a statement, either at the end of the examination, or in the course thereof if it is lengthy. The statement is typed by the juge's clerk as it is dictated. Sometimes important questions and answers will be noted verbatim. At the end of the examination, the juge will read the statement over to the accused who may correct any inaccuracies. Thereafter it is signed by the accused and the juge.

[70] The juge does not wear a gown, and as in any office the proceedings may be frequently interrupted by telephone calls, messages, etc. It should be noted that at no time does the accused answer questions under oath.

[71] In practice the procureur seldom attends, as he leaves the juge with the responsibility of the investigation. He may however decide to attend in cases of exceptional importance or cases which have serious political implications. In some provincial areas where the procureurs ignore this practice and frequently attend such examinations, the practical effect is to turn this part of the pre-trial inquiry into a 'rehearsal' for the trial itself.

[72] The same rule applies to the accused's spouse. At the trial, the court is free to draw what inferences it pleases from the accused's silence.

In some very complex or important cases, the juge will hold a final examination of the accused, recapitulating the main points of the case and the accused's answers thereto.

Examination of Witnesses

61 The juge d'instruction has the power to cite any witnesses whose evidence may be relevant. In the first instance he will learn of the witnesses from the police report, but in the course of his inquiries he may learn of more. The parties to the case may suggest witnesses and while the juge is not bound to cite them, he will usually do so. The juge may ask a witness to attend his office by sending him a letter (in which case the witness's appearance is treated as being voluntary), or the juge may have him formally cited, in which case failure to attend without reasonable excuse will result in a fine. Witnesses who are ill may be examined at their homes or in hospital. All witnesses must give evidence under oath—'to tell the truth and nothing but the truth'.[73] Witnesses must answer all questions put to them (unless bound by rules of professional secrecy) and failure to answer a question may result in the witness being fined.

The initial questions by the juge establish the witness's identity and any relationship (being blood, business or social) with the accused or the 'partie civile'. The witness is then asked to give his evidence in brief narrative form, which the juge dictates, as it is given, to his clerk. The juge will then question the witness and if the questions and answers are important, they will be noted verbatim. In some instances where the evidence is purely formal, the juge will merely verify the statement made by the witness to the police, in which case his statement to the juge will read—'I confirm the statement I made to the police (and further add . . .)'.

The witness will read the typed statement (or the juge will read it to him) and after rectifying any inaccuracies, the witness and the juge will both sign the statement. No one may be present when the witness is giving his statement,[74] but as the statement is embodied in the dossier, all the parties to the case may study it shortly after it is given.

Confrontations; Reconstructions of the Crime

62 If conflicting evidence is given by different witnesses, the juge may confront these witnesses with each other in his presence. Similarly if the evidence given by the accused contradicts that given by a witness, the juge may confront the accused and the witness with each other. Should such a confrontation involve the accused then the accused's lawyer, the 'partie civile' and his lawyer, and the procureur may be present, although in practice the procureur never attends (the confrontation being treated as an examination of the accused). The juge will normally ask one of the parties to give his evidence in the presence of the other party, then vice versa. He will then ask each to comment on the evidence of the other, and will compare both sets of evidence closely. He will cross examine both parties forcefully on any points of difference. The purpose of the confrontation is to ascertain if one party is lying, forgetful or mistaken and to find out why the discrepancy in the evidence occurs. The confrontation does not necessarily result in resolving all the conflicts and need

---

[73] An exception is the 'partie civile', any person with an interest in the outcome of the case, certain persons with criminal records, etc., i.e. the same persons who may not take the oath at the trial—see para 83.

[74] Except if a confrontation is arranged.

not continue till this is done. The aim is to find the truth, not to remove all conflict from the case.[75]

The judge d'instruction must retain full control of the situation otherwise proceedings could degenerate into an undignified argument. By putting conflicting parties face to face with each other it is often easier to find the truth, especially if one of them is lying or forgetful, as the parties may be examined together and point by point.[76] It is felt that this is much more effective than the British method, whereby the contradictory evidence of one party is only put to the other party when he is cross examined perhaps hours or even days later in the course of the trial; moreover the second party may merely deny such contradictory evidence and the first party may not be recalled.

Similar to confrontations are reconstructions. The judge may request the accused or a witness to re-enact parts of his evidence, if need be at the locus itself. In such a way inaccuracies or discrepancies in the evidence may be resolved.

Use of Experts

63 The judge d'instruction may instruct experts to examine any aspect of the case or the accused in person. He may do so on his own initiative or on the request of one of the parties. If he refuses a request by a party for expert examination, or the employment of further experts, his refusal must be motivated and may be appealed to the chambre d'accusation. There is no limit to the type of expert that may be employed, but the usual ones concern such matters as ballistics, analysis, handwriting or medical matters. In complex fraud cases, accountants may be employed as experts. Experts are normally chosen from a national list, but on cause shown experts not on the list may be employed. Normally only one expert will be used unless the evidence is fundamental to the issue when two or more will be used. The expert will be given an express remit which may include a time limit for completing his task. Once appointed, an expert must perform his duties to the best of his ability, failure to do so being a criminal offence. An expert will have access to the evidence and to the 'dossier'. He may also question witnesses, but can not compel them to answer. He may ask the juge to put particular questions to the accused, or with the accused's consent, the expert may examine him direct. (Whether or not the accused's lawyer is present at such examinations is left to the discretion of the accused.) In exceptional cases the expert may make a physical examination of the accused (for example if looking for signs of injury) on the instructions of the juge, whether or not the accused consents.

The expert will then send a report of his findings to the juge who will include it in the 'dossier'. Once the parties have studied the report they may request that further experts be employed to confirm or contradict the opinion of the original expert. The juge has a discretion whether or not to agree to such requests, his decision being appealable to the chambre d'accusation. The purpose of allowing the use of several experts is to explore all the implications of expert evidence and resolve any technical issues before the trial.

Search and Seizure

64 The juge d'instruction has the power to search premises for evidence and to

---

[75] A confrontation would not be arranged for the purposes of identifying the accused. If his identity were in question an identification parade would be held.

[76] For an example of a confrontation see Appendix 6.

seize any evidence so found. Such searches may not take place inside premises between the hours of 9 p.m. and 6 a.m. but otherwise there is no restriction. The juge may also delegate this power to the 'police judiciaire'.

Direction of the Police

65 As soon as a juge d'instruction takes over the inquiry, the police lose all powers of independent action in that inquiry and may only act subject to the control and direction of the juge. In certain instances the juge (if he has been requested by the procureur to intervene) will attend the scene of the crime immediately after its discovery and will thus take charge of the inquiry right from the outset. This results in the police investigation being made subject to the juge who will decide what discretion, if any, should be left to the police.

In addition to directing the police, the juge may delegate some of his powers to them by a document called a 'commission rogatoire'.[77] In theory this course should only be adopted where it is impossible for the juge to act in person, but in practice, the juge will always find it 'impossible', and no objection is ever taken. There are restrictions on the use of a 'commission rogatoire'. It can only be given to a named individual who must be an 'officier' of the 'police judiciaire' and must specify the offence to be investigated. A typical 'commission rogatoire' will be worded as follows—'Proceed to hear all necessary witnesses under oath; undertake in accordance with the law all confrontations, visits, searches, seizure of evidence and all necessary steps to identify the person or persons and their accomplices responsible for the offence above specified'. On the other hand the powers delegated may be more limited and more specifically expressed.

A juge can not delegate his power to issue warrants of arrest, nor may he delegate his power to examine the accused. If in the course of questionning a witness the police come to the belief that because of substantial incriminating evidence, the witness should be treated as a suspect, they must cease to question him (as failure to do so could infringe on the rights of the defence). Such a situation is less frequent in Paris and the larger towns since the procureur will delay the intervention of the juge until the accused has been identified,[78] thus giving the police the right to question the suspect regardless of the strength of the evidence against him. The prohibition on questioning a suspect binding the police while acting under a 'commission rogatoire' can be partly evaded in so far as the questioning must cease only when the person becomes a suspect in the mind of the investigating officer (who may be anxious to avoid coming to hasty conclusions)—nor does such a prohibition prevent the police from noting any statement spontaneously made by the suspect. It may also happen that the police might tell a suspect that they no longer have the power to question him and he is entitled to be brought before a juge d'instruction, unless the suspect himself waives this right by agreeing to be voluntarily questioned. Such a practice is however strictly against the spirit of the law and it is understood that it is seldom resorted too.

Background Inquiries—'Dossier du Personnalité'

66 In accordance with the doctrine that the court should judge the accused, and

---

[77] Similarly if the juge wishes inquiries made outwith his jurisdiction, he may delegate his powers to the appropriate juge d'instruction who may in turn authorise the police to act by means of a 'commission rogatoire'.

[78] See para 41.

not merely confine its attention to the evidence concerning the offence, it is necessary for the court to have detailed information concerning the accused.[79] In order to provide such information the juge will make a detailed examination of the accused's life history and embody the same in the section of the 'dossier' entitled 'Renseignements et Personnalité, colloquially called the 'Dossier du Personnalité'. Such investigations will cover the accused's family background from birth, and includes his education, work record, military service, and previous convictions. It will contain opinions on his character given by his parents, teachers, employers and anyone else—sometimes including a witness to the offence—who may be in a position to do so. Such information is given in extremely full detail and where possible every aspect of the accused's life up to the moment of the offence will be checked and verified. All possible information will be given whether it is favourable or unfavourable to the accused. If a medical examination or the accused's health record contains anything of note, this will also be included. In most cases the accused is examined by a psychiatrist on the orders of the juge d'instruction, and this report likewise forms part of the 'dossier'.[80] In practice if the offence is a 'crime' the background inquiries will be much more extensive than if the offence is a 'délit', but the aim is to give a full balanced picture of the character and personality of the accused. While a juge d'instruction is not compelled to make such inquiries,[81] in practice he will always do so.

Since the 'dossier' is given to the president of the court, all this information is available at the trial, and in the cour d'assises, where the jury has no access to the 'dossier', it will be elicited by verbal evidence, usually in the form of questions to the accused. The numerous witnesses giving evidence to the juge d'instruction on this aspect of the case are not usually cited to give evidence at the trial.[82]

Termination of Inquiries by the Juge d'Instruction

67 The juge d'instruction may terminate his inquiries whenever he deems it appropriate to do so, there being no time limit. At the end of his inquiries the juge will send the completed 'dossier' to the procureur so that the latter may express his views. In theory these views should be given within three days of receipt of the 'dossier', but in practice this time limit is ignored, the 'dossier' being given to the procureur unofficially and only officially sent to him when he has had time to study it and is in a position to decide on his position. The juge must notify the accused and the 'partie civile' that he has sent the 'dossier' to the procureur, to allow them an opportunity to study a copy of the 'dossier' in its completed form and make their comments thereon known to the juge.

On receipt of the 'dossier', the procureur may suggest that the juge should make further inquiries,[83] or he may suggest that the juge should order no further proceedings (because of lack of evidence, lack of criminal responsibility or legal bars to

[79] See paras 31 and 57.

[80] For details of the type of information, and the way in which it is used by the court, see Appendix 8.

[81] Crim. Avril 1960 D. 1960 p. 654.

[82] Where there has been no investigation by a juge d'instruction, the only evidence of the accused's background will be a few facts contained in the police report and any information supplied to the court by the accused himself.

[83] If the juge refuses this request the procureur has the right to appeal to the chambre d'accusation.

RÉQUISITOIRE DÉFINITIF
DE NON-LIEU

Le Procureur de la République près le Tribunal de grande instance
d

Vu les pièces de l'information suivie contre

inculpé.. d

Attendu que l'information a établi les points suivants :

T, S. V. P.

Attendu, en conséquence, qu'il ne résulte pas de l'information charges suffisantes contre l—— susnommé—— d'avoir commis le délit ci-dessus visé,

Vu les articles 175 et 177 du Code de Procédure pénale,

Requiert qu'il plaise à M. le Juge d'instruction déclarer qu'il n'y a pas lieu à suivre en l'état et ordonner le dépôt de la procédure au greffe pour y être reprise en cas de survenance de charges nouvelles.

Ordonner la mise en liberté d—— inculpé—— s'—— n—— détenu—— pour autre cause.

Statuer sur la restitution des objets saisis,

Statuer ce que de droit sur la condamnation de la partie civile aux dépens.

Fait au parquet, le ————————————————

LE PROCUREUR DE LA RÉPUBLIQUE,

COUR D'APPEL
DE PARIS

TRIBUNAL
DE GRANDE INSTANCE
de PARIS

PARQUET
DU
PROCUREUR DE LA RÉPUBLIQUE

N° du Parquet : _____

N° de l'Instruction : _____

RÉQUISITOIRE DÉFINITIF
DE RENVOI DEVANT LE TRIBUNAL CORRECTIONNEL

Le Procureur de la République près le Tribunal de grande instance de Paris

Vu les pièces de l'information suivie contre _____

inculpé___ de

Attendu que l'information a établi les faits suivants :

T. S. V. P.

61

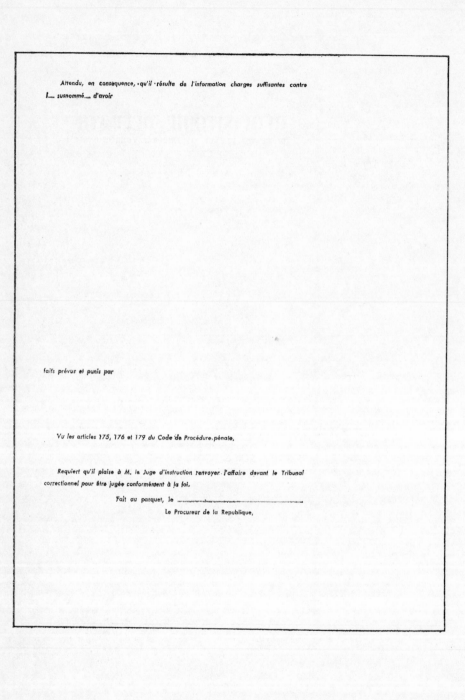

Attendu, en conséquence, qu'il résulte de l'information charges suffisantes contre l..... susnommé..... d'avoir

faits prévus et punis par

Vu les articles 175, 176 et 179 du Code de Procédure pénale,

Requiert qu'il plaise à M. le Juge d'instruction renvoyer l'affaire devant le Tribunal correctionnel pour être jugée conformément à la loi.

Fait au parquet, le ....

Le Procureur de la Republique,

proceedings). The commonest course, however, is to issue a request known as a 'réquisitoire définitif', asking the juge to remit the case to the appropriate court for trial. The 'réquisitoire définitif' gives a full summary of the facts of the case and the character of the accused, considering the evidence both for and against the accused. It may be fairly brief, or it may consist of ten, twenty or even more pages in a complex case.

After considering the views of the procureur and the other parties to the case, the juge will decide what future action to take. He is not bound by the attitude of the parties, and in particular he does not require to accept the view of the procureur. The basic question for him to answer is—is there sufficient evidence, which if believed, could constitute a case for the accused to answer? He has three courses of action viz.—order no further proceedings, or remit the case to the appropriate court, or (if the offence is a 'crime') arrange for the case to be placed before the chambre d'accusation, so that the latter may remit the case to the cour d'assises.

If he decides that no further proceedings should be taken, he will issue an 'ordonnance de non-lieu', at the same time releasing the accused from custody and restoring any items seized as evidence to the rightful owners. He has the option in certain circumstances to make an award of expenses against the 'partie civile'. If his decision is based on law, the proceedings are completely terminated unless the decision is overturned on an appeal to the chambre d'accusation, or unless further evidence comes to light affecting the legal position—for example if the juge ordered no further proceedings because the offence was a 'délit' for which the time for taking proceedings was barred by prescription. Should evidence later come to light aggravating the offence and allowing it to be classed as a 'crime', the question of proceedings could be reconsidered. On the other hand if his decision is based purely on lack of evidence, or some factual matter, if fresh evidence subsequently comes to light, the case may be re-considered, provided such a request is made by the procureur.

Should the juge decide that further proceedings be taken, he will remit the case to the appropriate court for trial (unless the offence is a 'crime'). This is done by an 'ordonnance de renvoi' ordering that the case be tried in the court competent to deal with the offence—usually the tribunal correctionnel[84]—and that the 'dossier' be transmitted to the prosecutor. The procureur must prosecute the case in the tribunal correctionnel if so ordered by the juge, regardless of his personal views about the prosecution.

Should the juge decide that further proceedings should be taken and the offence is classified as a 'crime', he will order that the dossier be sent to the procureur général, who must arrange for the case to be brought before the chambre d'accusation which alone has the power to remit cases to the cour d'assises for trial.[85]

Appeals Against Orders by a Juge d'Instruction

68 The prosecution may appeal against any decision made by the juge d'instruction, except his decision to transmit the dossier to the procureur général at the end of the inquiry. Such appeals will be marked by the procureur de la République, but

---

[84] Although if the offence is a 'contravention', the juge will remit the case to the tribunal de police. Similarly if the appropriate court is the 'tribunal des enfants' or a military court, the case will be remitted there.

[85] See para 72.

when the appeal is heard in the chambre d'accusation, the prosecution will be represented by the procureur général who is not bound by the views of the procureur de la République.

The accused's right of appeal is much more restricted, being limited mainly to decisions by the juge concerning pre-trial custody, refusal to employ an expert (or additional experts) and allowing the entering of appearance by a 'partie civile'. He may also object to the competency of the juge to make an inquiry, and if the juge repels this objection, the accused may appeal. While he may not appeal against a decision remitting the case for trial, this is sometimes done by raising the matter as an issue of competency, the accused claiming on appeal that the juge was not competent to investigate the offence, thus rendering the remit for trial void.

The 'partie civile' may appeal against a juge's decision not to investigate the case, or an order that no further proceedings should be taken, or in general any decision by the juge which is adverse to the civil claim (including the refusal by a juge to employ an expert or additional experts).

Appeals must be made within set time limits varying from forty-eight hours to ten days and are heard by the chambre d'accusation. If the appeal is upheld, the chambre itself will order what action should follow—e.g. employ an expert, release the accused, etc.—but it can not order the juge d'instruction himself to perform the act, unless the decision of the juge on which the appeal was based was ultra vires.

In theory, if a juge d'instruction commits an ultra vires act, there are disciplinary, civil and penal sanctions, but in practice these would never be applied, the only sanction being to declare the act null. If the appeal concerns a point of law, the decision of the chambre d'accusation may itself be appealed to the Cour de Cassation which will consider each case on its merits and in deciding whether or not an irregularity should render the proceedings null, will be mainly concerned with whether or not the irregularity diminished the rights of any party to the case. If the Cour de Cassation holds that an irregularity is substantial it may declare that all the proceedings are null, or that all proceedings following on the irregular act are null. This means that the proceedings (or the appropriate part of them) must be begun again.

While any party may appeal on a plea of nullity, if the juge d'instruction himself discovers he has done something irregular—for example forgetting to notify the accused's lawyer of an examination arranged for the accused, he may remit the case to the chambre d'accusation for a ruling. The procureur may also lodge such an appeal at any time, but the accused and the 'partie civile' are restricted to raising such a plea at the diet of trial.

Summary of the Rights of the Parties before a Juge d'Instruction
(a) The procureur
69 While the juge d'instruction is an independent 'magistrat', the procureur de la République has extensive powers. The juge must wait until he receives a request from the procureur (or 'partie civile') before starting his investigations. The procureur has a discretion to decide whether or not a 'délit' should be investigated, and even in the case of 'crimes' which must be so investigated, the timing of the request for intervention by a juge d'instruction rests with the procureur. Unofficially, the procureur may select which juge (if there are more than one) should make the inquiry. If the 'partie civile' institutes the proceedings, the procureur must be informed and has the right to state his views. The procureur has the right to decide whether or not

a particular suspect should be treated as the accused, and may request that certain steps be taken with regard to that person (such as matters dealing with custody, mental examination, etc.). If further changes come to light, these may only be investigated if the procureur so requests. In the course of the inquiries the procureur may request that experts be employed, and may be present when the accused is being examined by the juge. The procureur has a right of access to the dossier and may demand it be sent to him at any time. If the procureur is not satisfied with the way in which the juge is conducting the inquiry, he may request that the juge be replaced. At the conclusion of the inquiry, the procureur must be given an opportunity to state his views as to what further proceedings should be taken. Should the juge not accede to any request by the procureur, the latter has the right of appeal.

In addition to these powers, there is an undefinable bond between the juge and the procureur in that both are 'magistrats', and thus members of the same profession —as opposed to the lawyers who act for the accused and the 'partie civile'. As 'magistrats' they have the same aim of making an impartial inquiry, which is usually started by the procureur and then taken over by the juge. The procureur is usually slightly higher in the magisterial hierarchy than the juge[86] although this does not give him the power to give orders to the juge. As a result of such factors, there is usually a very close liaison between the juge and the procureur. They will have frequent informal discussions concerning the conduct of the inquiries and any problems that have arisen. While the juge is never bound to accept any requests or suggestions from the procureur, he will usually bear them in mind if for no other reason than to ignore the procureur's views is to run the risk of him taking numerous appeals. In practice therefore, it may frequently happen that the independence of the juge is more illusory than real, although the degree to which a procureur may influence the juge will depend on their respective personalities and attitudes.

As to the need for the office of juge d'instruction, the general view of most procureurs and juges is that such an office is essential in order that the prosecution of an offence should be kept entirely separate from its investigation. Apart from the fact that most procureurs approach their duties with an impartial mind, this argument fails to consider that the vast majority of criminal offences are not investigated by the juge, but by the procureur, and that even when a juge does investigate, the inquiry has usually been commenced by the procureur. During the recent war in Algeria, while it was still a French province, it is understood that the prosecutors there performed most of the duties of the juge. The main difficulty in the procureur taking over such duties lies in relation to the juge's role in deciding on pre-trial custody (which could obviously not be left to the decision of the prosecutor) and in his powers to examine the accused. Most accused persons would naturally exhibit a certain antagonism to the procureur, while regarding the juge as impartial. If the procureur were given the duty of examining the accused, it is probable that the accused would refuse to speak, or at least not speak so freely, and the character of the pre-trial proceedings would be completely different, thus affecting the trial which is based on these inquiries. On the other hand, if the right to examine the accused were given to a 'magistrat' other than the procureur, while leaving the latter with the responsibility of investigating the remainder of the case, the examination of the accused could not be thorough unless the 'magistrat' examining him were fully conversant with all aspects of the case and the investigation.

[86] and until recently commonly inserted notes in the personal dossier of the juge giving his views as to how the juge performed his duties.

(b) *The accused*

70 The rights of the accused may be briefly summarised. He can not be compelled to answer any questions, and if he does so, he is not required to take the oath. He is entitled to be legally represented at all stages (except the first formal examination) and his lawyer has the right of access to the 'dossier' at all times. He has a limited right of appeal.

(c) *The 'partie civile'*

71 He has the right to institute the inquiry by the juge d'instruction, but thereafter he loses control of the conduct of the inquiry. He may insist on his lawyer being present before answering any questions and his lawyer has a right of access to the 'dossier'. He has limited rights of appeal, basically in so far as any decision affects the civil case.

THE CHAMBRE D'ACCUSATION[87]

The main functions of the chambre d'accusation are to remit cases to the cour d'assises, and to act as an appeal court against decisions by the juge d'instruction.[88] All proceedings are in private—i.e. the public is not admitted. As the chambre d'accusation is a section of the cour d'appel, the prosecution is represented by the procureur général or his depute ('avocat général').

Remit to the Cour d'Assises

72 When the juge d'instruction orders that the 'dossier' be sent to the procureur général at the end of the pre-trial inquiry, the procureur général must commence proceedings in the chambre d'accusation within forty-eight hours of receiving the 'dossier'. He has no power of discretion in this matter. The procureur général will then lodge with the court his written submissions giving his views as to what further action should be taken in regard to the case, and in this respect he has complete freedom, being in no way bound by the attitude of the juge d'instruction. At the same time the accused and the 'partie civile' may also lodge written submissions. The chambre d'accusation will then appoint one of the judges to act as 'rapporteur' which requires him to investigate the case by studying the 'dossier' and all prior proceedings in the case. He then prepares a written summary to which is attached the written submissions of the parties. A date for the hearing will then be fixed, all parties being given advance notice so that they may study the 'dossier' and the written submissions of the other parties. At the hearing, proceedings commence with the 'rapporteur' (being one of the three judges at the hearing) giving his summary. The parties may supplement their written submissions with verbal argument and may comment on the submissions of the other parties. The court must base its decision on these submissions and the facts contained in the 'dossier', but it has the power to examine the accused if it thinks such a course is necessary. The court must conduct all proceedings with the minimum of delay. At the end of the hearing, the court may decide that further inquiries are necessary and can order that such inquiries be made by one of its own judges, or by the juge d'instruction. When such further inquiries have been made, the court will make its final decision. The final decision may be that no further proceedings should be taken ('arrêt de non-lieu') which terminates the case in the same way as an 'ordonnance de non lieu' by a juge

---

[87] For the composition of the chambre d'accusation, see para 13.

[88] See para 53 et seq., especially para 68.

d'instruction.[89] Alternatively the court may decide that the case should be remitted for trial ('arrêt de renvoi'). If it decides the offence is a contravention, the case will be remitted to the tribunal de police; if it decides the offence is a 'délit', the offence will be remitted to the tribunal correctionnel—such courses being unusual since the case will only be brought before the chambre d'accusation if the juge d'instruction considers it is a 'crime'. If the case is a 'crime' and is remitted to the cour d'assises, this is known as a 'mise en accusation' and the accused is formally known as 'accusé'. The remit to the cour d'assises gives that court jurisdiction to try the offence, and also cures any prior defect or irregularity in the proceedings, which means such matters may not be raised at the trial.

The remit itself gives a summary of the facts of the case and of the accused's background.[90] A warrant is issued ordering the arrest and detention in custody of the accused until the date of the trial. If already in custody, the warrant has the effect of continuing the same; if, however, the accused is not already in custody, the accused must give himself into custody on the day before the first hearing of the case,[91] failing which he will be arrested.

Other Functions of the Chambre d'Accusation

73   In addition to the above functions, the chambre d'accusation has certain other powers, the most important of which is to advise on cases of extradition. A request by a foreign government to extradite someone from France will be received by the French Ministry of Justice. Depending on the urgency of the matter, the request may be made by means of a telegram, or in full legal form. A warrant will be issued for the suspect's arrest and he will normally be brought before the procureur de la République who will verify his identity. Thereafter the suspect will be brought before the chambre d'accusation which for this purpose sits in public. The suspect, who may be legally represented, will be asked if he consents to extradition, and if he does so, this will be arranged. If he objects to extradition, the court will then decide on the matter, unless it requires further information, when the case will be adjourned, usually for fifteen days, and usually remanding the suspect in custody. Whether or not the court recommends extradition will depend on the terms of the treaty between France and the other country. As a general rule, the offence must also be recognised by French criminal law and not be of a political nature. The court will never recommend that a French national be extradited from France. The proceedings before the court will follow the same basic form as described above. The court can not order that extradition take place, but only judge on its competency. If it decides that extradition is incompetent, this binds the government, but if it holds that extradition is legally competent, the final decision as to whether or not extradition takes place will rest with the government and not with the court.

Further functions of the chambre d'accusation include disciplinary proceedings against an 'officier' of the 'police judiciaire' (whom it may punish for improper conduct of his duties), resolving any questions of competence or jurisdiction involving a juge d'instruction, and an inherent power to extract facts from a 'dossier' brought before it for another purpose and instruct that since no prosecution has already been based on these facts, but that they constitute a criminal offence, proceedings should now be instituted.

[89] See para 67.
[90] The remit is read aloud at the start of the trial in the cour d'assises.
[91] —i.e. his examination by the president prior to the trial proceedings—see para 88.

Since all decisions of the chambre d'accusation may be appealed to the Cour de Cassation on a point of law, the legal reasons for the decision must also be specified.

Criticism of the Chambre d'Accusation

74 One of the criticisms of the chambre d'accusation relates to its function in remitting cases to the cour d'assises. Since it invariably agrees with the recommendations of the juge d'instruction, it is often suggested that its role in this respect is limited to examining the contents of the 'dossier' and the regularity of the prior proceedings. There is also the psychological factor in that many jurors, unaware that the chambre d'accusation does not decide on the issues of the case, may believe that the accused has already been found guilty by a court of law.

Powers of the President of the Chambre d'Accusation

75 It is perhaps appropriate at this point to mention some duties which are given to the president of the chambre d'accusation in person, which concern the liberty of the individual. The president must satisfy himself that the juge d'instruction and the police (acting under 'commissions rogatoires') performed their duties efficiently, and in particular without unjustifiable delays. He receives a three-monthly return of all persons detained in custody on the orders of a juge d'instruction and will examine the progress of the inquiry involving such persons. He will visit the prison where such persons are detained at least once every three months, and more often if he deems it necessary, and on such visits, persons detained may request to see him. If he considers that an accused person is being improperly detained he may refer the matter to the chambre d'accusation which will then decide whether such detention should continue.

7. Proceedings in Court: Trials[1]

Since an accused person can not 'plead guilty' in a French criminal court, all court appearances take the form of trials.[2] As there is no occasion prior to the trial when the accused may be brought before the court to state his attitude to the charge against him, the trial diet is the only time when the court may consider any objection by the accused to the competency or relevancy of the proceedings or any other plea in bar of trial.

Objections to the Proceedings

76 An objection may be taken on the grounds that the court is not competent to try the offence in that it has no jurisdiction so to do. The power of the court is bounded by territorial limits, and while for the cour d'assises, the limit is France, for the tribunal correctionnel either the offence must have been committed within the geographic area over which the court has jurisdiction, or one of the accused must normally be domiciled in that area, or one of the accused must have been arrested there. The court is further limited to dealing with a specific type of offence, for example, the tribunal de police may not deal with a 'délit'. Objection may also be taken if the proceedings were not commenced within the time limits determined by statute—namely ten years for 'crimes', three years for 'délits' and one year for 'contraventions'. A criminal court may not decide on a question of legal status (legitimacy, marriage, nationality, etc.) if this is involved in a criminal charge, and must await until the appropriate civil court has decided such issues.

An objection may be taken to the relevancy of the proceedings if the law giving rise to the offence has been revoked, or an amnesty has been pronounced. Criminal proceedings may not be instituted against an accused who is insane, whether such insanity occurred at the time of the offence, or at the time of the trial. Another plea which would successfully bar criminal proceedings is 'res judicata'. If a criminal court has already decided on the same matter—i.e. the same accused, offence, etc.— subsequent criminal proceedings may not be based thereon. Thus an accused acquitted of murder, can not be re-tried for the same offence under the 'nomen juris' of culpable homicide. As a general rule only the verdict of a criminal court will act as 'res judicata'. The decision by the procureur not to prosecute is regarded as an administrative decision and not the verdict of a court. The decision of a juge d'instruction might in some cases act as 'res judicata'.[3]

[1] For Scotland—see para 199 et seq.
[2] See para 32.
[3] See para 67.

TRIAL PROCEDURES—TRIBUNAL CORRECTIONNEL[4]

As trial procedures in the tribunal de police are basically the same as in the tribunal correctionnel, it is perhaps appropriate to consider the tribunal correctionnel first, since it deals with a more serious type of criminal offences.

There are four methods by which a case may be brought before the tribunal correctionnel—direct citation, voluntary appearance, remit by the juge d'instruction (or chambre d'accusation) and 'flagrant délit' procedure.

Direct Citation

(a) *Direct citation*

77 This is the commonest method for instituting proceedings[5] and is used when the accused is not in custody. Once the procureur has obtained all the information he requires about the offence, he will obtain personal details about the accused (such as his full name, date and place of birth, parents' names, marital status, children, nationality, military service, employment, domicile, education, reputation and any other relevant facts) by writing in the first instance to the police in the accused's home town. At the same time, the procureur will obtain a record of any previous convictions relating to the accused.[6] The procureur will then complete a form known as a 'ordre de citation' or 'cédule' giving the accused's name and address, the name and address of any 'partie civile' (if known), the names and address of any witnesses whom the procureur wishes to be cited, and the charge against the accused. The 'ordre de citation' will then be sent to an officer of the court known as a 'huissier' (or 'huissier-audiencier') asking him to cite the accused and witnesses for a specified date. If the 'partie civile' is instituting the proceedings, he does so in the same way.

The 'huissier' will then serve a citation on the accused personally, the citation giving the time, date and place of the trial, and a copy of the charge as contained in the 'ordre de citation' drafted by the procureur. If the accused is not at home, but the 'huissier' is satisfied that the address is correct, the 'huissier' may serve the citation on another inmate of the house. Should this not be possible, the 'huissier' will leave the citation at the office of the local mayor and at the same time send a registered letter to the accused telling him what has been done. It is then the responsibility of the accused to collect the citation and it is presumed he has received the citation until the contrary is proved. The 'huissier' will complete an execution of service specifying how service was effected. One of the difficulties of the last method of service is that if the post office is unable to deliver the registered letter, they will retain it for fifteen days, leaving a note for the accused to this effect. If the accused is unable or unwilling to collect the letter, or does not receive the note from the post office, he will thus have no knowledge of the citation. Furthermore the 'huissier' will not know that the letter has not been received until fifteen days have elapsed. Since the minimum notice that must be given to an accused about his trial is five days (longer if he stays outwith the department), the case may call in court prior to the 'huissier' being informed that the letter was not delivered, and since it is presumed that the accused has been properly cited, when the accused fails to appear, he may be

---

[4] These notes should be read in conjunction with Appendix 7.

[5] In 1970 in Paris, out of 66,324 cases in which proceedings were taken 44,574 were dealt with by means of direct citation.

[6] Any previous convictions must be carefully examined to see if they act as an aggravation to the offence, possibly thus changing its classification from a 'contravention' to a 'délit', or a 'délit' into a 'crime'.

judged in his absence.[7] In such circumstances, the first knowledge the accused will have of the proceedings will be when the penalty is enforced. He will however be entitled to appeal and have the case re-heard by means of a process known as 'l'opposition'.[8]

If the 'huissier', in attempting to effect service finds that the accused does not reside at the specified address, he will report to the procureur who may instruct the police to trace the accused. Should the police be unable to do so, the procureur must either drop the case, or place the matter before a juge d'instruction who alone has the power to issue a warrant for the accused's arrest.

(b) *Voluntary appearance*

78 In theory, the accused may present himself voluntarily before the court and thus dispense with the need for a formal citation. In some provincial areas of France, the procureur may send a registered letter to the accused instructing him to come to court, using this method as an alternative to a formal citation, which will only be used if the accused fails to appear. In practice however, most procureurs will prefer to cite the accused direct in the first instance, and the only use to which voluntary appearance is put is where the accused presents himself in answer to a citation in which some legal flaw is found.

(c) *Remit by the juge d'instruction or chambre d'accusation*

79 If the case is remitted for trial by the juge d'instruction, the procureur after lodging the 'dossier' with the clerk of court, will either cite the accused to attend for trial (if liberated), or arrange he be brought to the court (if in custody). While a remit from the chambre d'accusation is more uncommon, it would occur where such proceedings had been ordered on an appeal from a juge d'instruction; or if the chambre decided that the offence was a 'délit' and not a 'crime'; or if the offences concerned various charges some of which were 'crimes' and some were 'délits' and the accused's whereabouts were unknown. In such circumstances the cour d'assises may try the accused in his absence by a procedure known as 'contumace',[9] which can only be used for 'crimes'. While the cour d'assises may try a 'délit' along with a 'crime', it may not do so in the absence of the accused, and the chambre d'accusation in such a case might decide to remit the 'délit' to the tribunal correctionnel which may judge a 'délit' in the absence of the accused.

(d) *'Flagrant délit' procedure*[10]

80 If at the end of 'l'enquête flagrante' where the accused is in custody and the procureur decides that no further inquiries are required, the procureur may bring the accused before the court for trial forthwith. One disadvantage of this method is that the procureur does not have time to obtain further details concerning the accused's background and must rely on what is contained in the police report. At the same time as he decides on such procedure, the procureur will order the 'police judiciaire' to instruct any witnesses to attend the trial, which means that such witnesses may only receive a few hours' notice.[11] In many cases, however, the procureur

---

[7] Although the court may decide to continue the case and order that the accused be cited again.

[8] See para 107.

[9] For 'contumace'—see para 95.

[10] See para 99.

[11] See Appendix 5, example 5.

will decide that no witnesses are necessary. If an essential witness does not appear, the court must either adjourn the case, or the procureur before the start of the trial will require to place the investigation before a juge d'instruction. The accused has the right to ask for an adjournment of three days to prepare his defence. The court must inform the accused of this right and his reply must be noted. The court may adjourn the case on its own initiative to obtain further information, in which case it has the discretion to liberate the accused or detain him in custody.

One of the difficulties about 'flagrant délit' procedure is that the accused must be brought before the court on the day on which the procureur makes his decision, or at the latest, on the following day, which means that if necessary, a special court may require to be convened on a Sunday or public holiday. Nevertheless, 'flagrant délit' procedure is commonly used especially in the busier areas.[12]

Personal Appearance by the Accused

81   If an accused person has been detained in custody prior to the trial, he will obviously be present at the trial proceedings. Should he not be in custody, an accused may request the court to deal with the case in his absence, usually by writing a letter to the president of the court. The letter may contain any mitigating factors, or the accused may be represented by a lawyer who will give such factors. Such a course is only competent if the maximum penalty for the offence is less than a fine plus two year's imprisonment.[13] The court may still insist on the personal appearance of the accused and on receipt of a letter from him, may adjourn the case, ordering him to appear in person.

If the accused has been properly cited, and either fails to attend or write a letter, he will be judged in his absence—i.e. by default—but may later have the right to have the case reheard.[14]

Should an accused person fail to behave during trial proceedings and continually interrupt them, the president has a discretion to remove him from the court, the trial then proceeding in his absence. At the end of the proceedings, the clerk of court will read him an account thereof.

If there are several accused, the president may request one or all of them to leave the court while a witness is being examined, and then question each accused separately concerning the witness's evidence. In such a case, the president must subsequently inform the accused what has taken place in his absence.[15]

Examination of the Accused

82   After the president has ordered the trial to begin and the accused has answered to his name, the president will normally commence the proceedings by examining the accused. The examination may often commence with the president explaining to the accused the nature of the trial proceedings, and the rights available to him, unless the accused is legally represented. He will then question the accused about

---

[12] In Paris in 1970, out of the total number of cases prosecuted, which was 66,324 (not counting cases in the tribunal de police), the number dealt with by means of 'flagrant délit' procedure was 7,361.

[13] In exceptional cases the court may allow this to be done when the penalty is greater, but this is very rare. The court may also visit the sick bed of an accused too ill to attend court.

[14] See 'l'opposition'—para 107.

[15] CPP Art. 339. While this rule is specifically given for the cour d'assises, it is understood it also applies to other criminal courts.

his identity and background history, including any previous convictions. The president is in possession of the 'dossier' (if the case has been investigated by a juge d'instruction) or the police report (if there has been no investigation by a juge d'instruction). The amount of personal detail elicited depends on the case and the attitude of the president.

The president will then read aloud the details of the charge and question the accused about it. He may read aloud excerpts from the witnesses' statements (to the police or juge d'instruction) and will consider all the facts of the case, both against the accused and in his favour. If the accused disagrees with a statement made by a witness, or gives evidence contrary to it, the president will frequently question him vigorously—in the same manner as cross-examination at a British trial. He will certainly do so if he thinks the accused is lying or withholding evidence. He may ask the accused to demonstrate his evidence by referring to any sketch plans or other real evidence that is produced. While the president must be impartial, eliciting all evidence in the accused's favour to the same degree as any evidence against him, and must not indicate his opinions as to the guilt or innocence of the accused, the president's role is that of an investigating judge, and not as an arbiter between the parties to the case. At the conclusion of the examination, the procureur may question the accused; the lawyer for the 'partie civile' and the accused's lawyer may suggest questions for the president to put to the accused (whether or not this is done will depend on the discretion of the president). If the president agrees, he may rephrase the question, or may merely tell the accused to answer it. Provided the examination by the president has been thorough, the number of such questions will be relatively few, and frequently none are suggested.

Throughout the examination, the accused, who does not take the oath, may refuse to answer any question put to him, but the court is then free to comment on his silence and draw any conclusions it wishes therefrom.[16] If the accused is in custody he will remain with his police escort in special compartment—similar to the 'dock' in a British court, but if he is at liberty, he will answer questions while standing at the bar of the court, sitting nearby when not being examined.

The other two judges also have the right to question the accused, but this is seldom if ever done.

Examination of the Witnesses

83 After he has examined the accused, the president will examine any witnesses who have been cited, in any order he thinks appropriate. The prosecution, 'partie civile' and defence may all cite witnesses to the trial[17] by requesting the 'huissier' to do so. Failure to comply with a citation is a criminal offence punishable by a fine and an award of any expenses incurred as a result of the witness's non-attendance; the witness is also liable to be arrested and brought to court. If necessary the court may attend a witness's sick bed to hear his evidence. A witness attending court is entitled to any expenses incurred and is immune from civil or criminal proceedings on any matter arising from his evidence in court. All persons may be compelled to attend court and give evidence (except the accused and his spouse), but the following

---

[16] The court may also consider any statement made by the accused to the police or a juge d'instruction.

[17] If an accused can not afford to pay witnesses expenses, the president may order this to be done at public expense. In appeal courts, the only witnesses heard are those cited by the court itself.

persons may not give evidence on oath—children aged less than sixteen years, persons with criminal records (excluding minor road traffic offences, etc.), any person related to the accused, anyone with a direct personal interest in the outcome of the case (including the 'partie civile') and any persons suffering from a loss of civil rights (which is a penalty for certain criminal offences).

Since the court may base its decision on facts contained in the 'dossier' or police report, the procureur will frequently refrain from citing any witnesses. He is most likely to take this action if there has been an investigation by a juge d'instruction, on the grounds that it is pointless to put the witness to further inconvenience and that the juge has already investigated the case fully. Even it if is clear from the 'dossier' that the accused disagrees with such evidence, the procureur may still decide not to cite the witnesses.[18] If however, there has been no such pre-trial investigation, and especially where 'flagrant délit' procedure is being used, the procureur will usually cite any witnesses whose evidence he estimates will not be accepted by the accused since such evidence has not been fully examined before the trial.[19] Although whether, all or any of the witnesses for the prosecution are cited to court depends on the decision of the procureur (and the attitude of individual procureurs may vary), the court has an over-riding right to adjourn the case and decide to hear the witnesses in person if it is not satisfied with the contents of the 'dossier' or the police report. A complainer whose evidence does not seem to be in dispute will usually be notified of the trial by the procureur (thus giving him an opportunity to enter appearance as 'partie civile') but will not normally be cited as a witness. If the court insists on proceeding in the absence of a witness whose presence is claimed by one of the parties to be essential, that party has the right to appeal at the conclusion of the trial.

When a witness is present in court, the president will normally hear him. The president will ask him his identity and whether or not he has any relationship to any of the parties to the case. He will then administer the following oath—'Do you swear to tell all the truth and nothing but the truth?' to which the witness answers—'I swear'. The president will then tell the witness to give his evidence in narrative form. In principle, the president will only interrupt to clarify any ambiguities, leaving any questions to the end of the narration. The president will examine the witness on any further points he wants brought out, and will question him about any contradictory evidence (including that of the accused) often reading such statements to him verbatim. The president may also confront witnesses giving conflicting evidence and may question them jointly. If a witness's evidence contradicts that of the accused, the president may interrupt the witness to question the accused further. The president may also question the witness about any prior statement he has made to the police, the juge d'instruction or any other person. In theory, a witness should give his evidence without the aid of notes, but this rule is not strictly adhered to. At the conclusion of the president's examination the procureur may question the witness and the parties to the case may suggest further questions to put to the witness (in exactly the same way and with the same effect as at the end of the examination of the accused).

Before giving evidence, witnesses are kept out of court and thus separate from witnesses who have already given evidence and who remain in court. A brief record

[18] See Appendix 7, cases 1 and 2.

[19] When using 'flagrant délit' procedure, the procureur will cite the witnesses by means of the police. This is also the method he will use in all cases where the witness is a police officer.

of the witness's evidence is made by the clerk of court. The president will normally start with the witnesses cited by the prosecution, police witnesses usually being heard first. Whether the witnesses for the 'partie civile' are heard before any witnesses for the defence, depends on the president. Expert witnesses are often heard last and take a different oath—'Do you swear to give an account of your inquiries and findings on your honour and conscience?' The defence may adduce evidence at any stage of the proceedings, whether or not such evidence was disclosed during the pre-trial inquiries, although if such evidence is to be accepted as credible, a reason should be given if necessary why such evidence was not made known during the pre-trial inquiries.

Since perjury is a criminal offence, a witness who has given evidence under oath and is suspected of lying, will usually be invited to remain in court and given a chance to retract his evidence. If he does so, he may not be prosecuted for perjury. All cases of perjury must be reported to the procureur who will decide what action should be taken. Although witnesses give evidence on oath before a juge d'instruction, no perjury proceedings may be based on a statement made to a juge d'instruction.[20]

In general, it should be noted that with regard to the placing of evidence before the court, there is a marked absence of procedural rules, the court being given as much freedom as possible to obtain all the facts about the case. This is in accordance with the inquisitorial nature of the proceedings.

Closing Addresses

84 At the conclusion of the evidence, the 'partie civile' has the right to make a closing address, in which he will review the evidence and comment thereon. He will usually ask the court to convict the accused and it is not uncommon for him to use very forceful terms in making this demand. He will then concentrate on any civil issues, often addressing the court at great length and sometimes stressing the suffering and inconvenience he has sustained as the victim of the offence.

The procureur will address the court after the 'partie civile', and while he may also review and comment on the evidence, his remarks are often very brief. He will usually give his views as to an appropriate sentence (which, of course, the court is free to ignore).

The defence will then address the court, either asking for an acquittal, or urging points that should be considered in mitigation. The accused may have a separate lawyer to deal with the criminal and civil aspects of the case (in which case both may address the court), but if not, the closing address will deal with both these matters.

The 'partie civile' and the procureur have the right to address the court further in reply to the defence, in which case the defence may make a final speech, as the defence must always have the right to the last word.

Verdict and Sentence

85 After listening to the closing addresses the court may adjourn the trial to obtain further evidence, or adjourn to consider its verdict, or may proceed to give its verdict immediately.

If the court decides it requires further information (perhaps as a result of what was said in a closing address, or to verify some fact given in mitigation, or to clarify the

[20] CPP Art. 361, note 1.

evidence), the court will adjourn the hearing to a later date. The court may then request the procureur to make further inquiries, giving him (or the other parties) the right to cite further witnesses to the adjourned diet. As an alternative, but more unusual course, the court will appoint one of the three judges to make further inquiries, in which case, the judge has the powers of a juge d'instruction, and may order an examination by experts, issue instructions to the police by means of 'commissions rogatoires', etc.

Should the court adjourn merely to consider its verdict, this may be for a period of several minutes or several days—fourteen days being not uncommon. In deciding on its verdict, the court must consider whether or not it is competent to judge the offence.[21] All verdicts must be motivated—i.e. must specify the legal reasons on which they are based. The verdicts available to the court are: not guilty, guilty, guilty by default (non appearance of the accused) or absolution.

If the verdict is guilty, the court may specify any factors which aggravate or mitigate the offence. The court may also find the accused guilty of an offence other than the one specified in the charge (for example it may find the accused guilty of theft although he is charged with fraud). The sentence must be pronounced at the same time as the verdict; the court may not find an accused guilty then adjourn to consider sentence. The sentence must be within the limits specified by law, but the reasons for deciding on a particular sentence need not be given.

If the verdict is not guilty, the court may award the accused damages against the 'partie civile' if the latter was responsible for instituting the proceedings and the court decides he acted vexatiously. Expenses and damages may not be awarded against the procureur.

A verdict of 'absolution' is very exceptional and only available in a restricted number of cases, mainly where one of the accused ceased to participate in the offence at the outset and thereafter attempted to prevent his co-accused continuing in their actings. A verdict of absolution has the same effect as an acquittal.[22]

At the same time as deciding on verdict and sentence, the court will settle any civil issues. If the accused is acquitted, the court can not make an award of damages against him in favour of the 'partie civile'. Should he be convicted, such an award may be made, the court not being bound by the specification and amounts of the civil claim.

In certain instances, the procureur is required to give notification of a conviction to a particular body or person, for example if the accused is a doctor, lawyer, school teacher, policeman, member of the armed forces, etc., the procureur must notify the appropriate governing or disciplinary body.

TRIAL PROCEDURES—TRIBUNAL DE POLICE

The tribunal de police has competence to judge offences classed as 'contraventions' which are divided into five classes.

---

[21] While the tribunal correctionnel has competence to judge a 'contravention', it may not judge a 'crime'. If it holds that the offence should be classed as a 'crime', the court will remit the case to the procureur to allow him to commence proceedings in the cour d'assises. The proceedings in the tribunal correctionnel will not act as 'res judicata' since no verdict has been given.

[22] Except in the cour d'assises where an accused given such a verdict may still lose the civil claim and have an award of damages made against him.

86 Some minor 'contraventions', such as parking offences may be disposed of without the need for court proceedings. Prior to 1972, the accused paid a fixed penalty known as 'l'amende forfaitaire' to the policeman detecting the offence. If the accused was unable or unwilling to pay the fine on the spot, he could purchase a stamp to the value of the penalty and send the same to the appropriate authorities within certain time limits. If the accused failed to pay the penalty, he was either cited to court, or dealt with by a shortened form of proceedings known as 'procedure simplifiée'. The latter proceedings were competent where there was no civil claim, the maximum fine was less than 400 francs, there were no previous convictions to aggravate the offence, no other offences were committed at the same time, inquiries had not been commenced by a juge d'instruction, and statute did not prohibit the use of such proceedings—all of which conditions had to apply. The police lodged the complaint with the procureur who placed it before the judge in the tribunal de police within ten days. The judge determined the fine (known as 'l'amende de composition') within five days. The clerk of court notified the accused of the fine within fifteen days, the accused having a further fifteen days to pay the fine. If the accused paid the fine, he could not later lodge an appeal and the offence counted as a conviction for record purposes. If the accused failed to pay the fine, he was cited to attend court, and the case was dealt with in the usual way.

In a report to the Conseil de legislation pénale, Professor Vitu stated—'In 1968 in Paris and the Parisien region less than 50% of the offenders took advantage of the 'amende forfaitaire' procedure when such procedure was used. In the same year, out of 1,602,000 cases where an 'amende de composition' was imposed, in only 950,450 instances (i.e. 55.65%) was the fine paid. As a result, normal court proceedings were instituted in 597,528 cases of which more than 75% were parking offences. The court was required to deal with an average of 3,000 cases per day.'

A law passed on 3 January 1972 made the following changes—The 'amende de composition' was replaced by a system known as the 'ordonnance pénale'. By this procedure the court may convict the accused without the necessity of a trial or any form of hearing. The accused has, however, a right of appeal by means of 'l'opposition'.[23]

Article 524 of the French Code Penal states in paragraph (1)—'All cases falling within the jurisdiction of the tribunal de police may be dealt with by means of an 'ordonnance pénale', even where the accused has a previous conviction for an analogous offence'. (There are some minor exceptions to this rule). Therefore although the 'ordonnance pénale' may be used for offences which attract only a monetary penalty, Article 524(1) extends its use to cover offences which carry a penalty of imprisonment as an alternative to a fine, or which entitle the court to impose disqualification from driving. However, if the judge decides that imprisonment is the only appropriate penalty, he will return the case to the procureur de la République who will then re-commence proceedings in the normal way (i.e. by direct citation).

The use of l'ordonnance pénale is not compulsory and the procureur has a discretion to proceed in the normal way[24] or by the 'ordonnance pénale'.

Where he decides to proceed by means of an 'ordonnance pénale' he will lodge

[23] See para 107.

[24] See para 77 et seq.

the police report with the judge, together with written submissions giving his views on the appropriate penalty.

The judge is not bound by such written submissions. Furthermore should the judge decide that the case should be examined more fully by means of a trial, or that a penalty other than a monetary one should be imposed, the judge will return the case to the procureur so that it can proceed to trial in the usual way. Where the procureur has taken proceedings by way of an 'ordonnance pénale' and the judge decides that the case may be disposed of by such procedure, the judge has a complete discretion as to the amount of the fine (provided it is within the minimum and the maximum limits proscribed by law).

The judge will base his decision on the facts submitted by the procureur in the form of a police report. This report may contain a minimal amount of information about the accused's personal circumstances. The judge's decision does not require to be accompanied by the reasons therefor (which is the normal rule). It is not necessary to serve a notice of the court's decision on the accused personally, but such a notice is sent to the accused by registered post, and the accused is required to acknowledge receipt thereof. Since the procureur may appeal (by means of 'l'opposition') against sentence within ten days of the determination of a case, the notice of the court's decision is not posted to the accused until a period of ten days has elapsed.

After the decision has been notified to the accused by registered letter and he has acknowledged receipt, the accused has a period of thirty days from the date of notification within which to lodge an appeal.

(The 'ordonnance pénale' procedure differs from a trial in absence of the accused in that the latter proceedings take the form of a trial in open court after the accused has been cited and has failed to appear. Further, the accused does not have the same automatic right of appeal which he is given by 'ordonnance pénale'). Once the penalty has been intimated to the accused, he has the following choices of action:

Firstly—He may pay the fine and not exercise his right of appeal. If he follows this course, the 'ordonnance pénale' has the same effect as a decision given at the end of a normal trial. The case is thus disposed of without the necessity of personal appearance by the accused.

Secondly—The accused may fail both to pay the fine and to appeal. In these circumstances, the accused, by failing to appeal will be taken as acquiescing to the court's decision and steps will be taken to enforce payment of the fine, unless it can be shown that the accused in person did not receive intimation of the court's decision—(for example, if the registered letter was accepted by the accused's wife or other member of his household). Should no personal intimation have been received the accused has the right to appeal within a period of ten days of the court's decision coming to his personal knowledge, no matter how he learned of it. With regard to enforcing the penalty, it should be noted that this is not done by the court, but by an official employed by the Ministry of Finance. If the accused is unable to pay the fine immediately, he must arrange with this official whether time is to be allowed for payment, or whether payment by instalments is acceptable. It is only where the accused fails to pay, that the procureur will order the police to arrest the accused and take him to prison where he will serve an alternative period of imprisonment.[25]

[25] See para 100.

Thirdly—The accused may exercise his right to appeal, in which case the matter is remitted to the court for trial and the decision given by the 'ordonnance pénale' is set aside. The accused will be cited to attend for trial but, if he fails to do so, the trial will proceed in his absence, in which case the court has no option but to re-impose the finding and sentence pronounced by means of the 'ordonnance pénale'. The accused may not lodge any subsequent appeal (except on a point of law) by means of a 'pourvois en cassation.[26]

The effect of l'ordonnance pénale' on the rights of the 'partie civile' is as follows: Should he institute criminal proceedings prior to the court deciding the criminal case by means of an 'ordonnance pénale', then the latter procedure is incompetent. On the other hand, where a decision has been made by an 'ordonnance pénale' and the procureur has lodged an appeal, the 'partie civile' may still lodge a civil claim after the original decision but before the court has decided on the appeal (i.e. before the re-trial), in which case the court may also give a decision on the civil issues. Finally where a 'partie civile' only lodges his claim after the case has been decided by an 'ordonnance pénale' and no appeal has been taken by the procureur, the 1972 Act states that the tribunal de police is competent to decide the civil case even although the criminal case has been concluded. However, when a civil claim is lodged after the criminal case has been decided by an 'ordonnance pénale', the tribunal de police or any court before which the claim is pursued, is not bound by the decision of the criminal court. (Prior to 1972, a conviction in a criminal court was sufficient to establish fault on the part of the accused in any subsequent civil action).

Parking Offences

The 1972 Act also introduced changes relating to parking offences. Any person who is charged with committing a parking offence but who refuses to pay the fixed monetary penalty within a period of fifteen days following the commission of the offence, or within fifteen days of the offence being notified to the owner of the vehicle, may send notice of his refusal to pay to the body responsible for dealing with the offence (e.g. to the local authority, if the offence contravenes local authority parking regulations). They in turn will intimate the case to the procureur de la République who may order no further proceedings, or take proceedings by way of an 'ordonnance pénale' or may take proceedings in the usual form (i.e. by trial).

Should the accused neither pay the penalty nor notify his refusal to pay, a fixed penalty will be imposed and such a penalty will be recoverable by the Treasury. This is the principal innovation effected by the 1972 Act, since under the former procedure where an accused failed to pay the penalty, it was necessary to prosecute him by means of an 'amende de composition' and, if that failed, then by proceeding to trial in the usual way.

Under the procedure contained in the 1972 Act, it is necessary to have the written concurrence of the procureur de la République before the penalty can be recovered by the Treasury. The accused may appeal to the procureur within ten days of being notified of the latter's concurrence to the enforcement of the penalty. If such an appeal is lodged, the procureur may order no further proceedings, or proceed by means of an 'ordonnance pénale' or proceed to trial

[26] See para 106.

79

in the usual way. In order to discourage frivolous appeals, the Act provides that, where the accused is convicted following an appeal, the penalty imposed by the court may not be less than the original penalty.

The 1972 Act defines which persons may be deemed to be guilty in relation to parking offences. Paragraph 21(1) states that the person in whose name the vehicle is registered shall be liable for the payment of any monetary penalty for parking offences in which the vehicle was involved. When the vehicle belongs to a firm or a company the liability will fall on such persons who are otherwise legally responsible for the acts of the firm or company. It must be noted that this provision applies only to parking offences (for other offences the responsibility lies with the driver of the vehicle). The purpose of the above provisions is to eliminate any conflict or dispute as to responsibility which could otherwise have the effect of complicating or delaying the proceedings.

The responsibility is not, however, absolute. The owner of a vehicle is entitled to prove that at the material time, the vehicle was on hire to a third party and, if such proof is accepted, then the third party will be held to be responsible for the offence. A further exception is allowed where the owner of a vehicle has delegated certain functions to one of his employees, and, if such functions include the care or control of a motor vehicle, then the employee to whom such duties are entrusted might be held to be legally responsible for the vehicle. The owner of a vehicle may also escape responsibility for the penalty if he furnishes information as to the identity of the person who committed the offence. Finally, the owner will not be found liable to pay the penalty if he can prove that the offence was committed due to circumstances beyond his control, such as that the vehicle had broken down, or had been stolen.

Trials in the Tribunal de Police

87 All accused appear before the court by means of direct citation (although 'voluntary appearance' may be used to cure any defect in the citation). While a remit from the juge d'instruction or chambre d'accusation is competent it is exceedingly uncommon. No accused will be brought to the court in custody since the police power of arrest ('garde à vue') does not apply to 'contraventions'. While in theory, the trial proceedings are identical to the tribunal correctionnel, in practice it depends on how the 'contravention' is classified. Should it fall into the first four classes, the accused is presumed to be guilty unless he establishes his innocence. These offences include most minor road traffic infractions such as exceeding the speed limit, ignoring traffic lights, etc. The accused will step forward when his name is called in court, the president will ask if he admits the offence, and if he does, he will be fined—the entire proceedings lasting less than ten seconds. If he has an explanation to make, the president will listen to the same and either ignore it, accept it or adjourn the case for a fuller hearing at a later date.[27] While the prosecution in court is repre-

---

[27] In Paris, extensive use is made of modern techniques for dealing with such road traffic offences. The police have cars equipped with an apparatus for photographing moving vehicle offences, the photograph showing the time and if need be the speed of the vehicle. The owner of the offending car will be presumed to be the driver until the former proves to the contrary. If the owner is a company, it must disclose the particulars of the driver. Paris deals with approximately 3½ million such cases per annum. While the prosecution process has effectively been reduced to a system which is in the hands of the police, the procureur has overall control, and it is he who deals with any legal point or other difficulty arising from a case.

sented by a 'police commissaire',[28] the procureur has the overall responsibility and will intervene if required. Should some difficult legal point arise, the court will almost certainly adjourn the proceedings to allow the procureur an opportunity to take over the conduct of the proceedings.

If the 'contravention' falls within the fifth class (which covers such offences as assaults, road accidents causing injury, etc.) the prosecution is conducted by the procureur in person. This class of 'contraventions' were formerly 'délits', but were reduced by statute to 'contraventions' because of the pressure of business in the tribunal correctionnel and the relatively minor nature of the offences compared with the other cases taken in that court. They are however dealt with in exactly the same way as 'délits' in so far as the pre-trial inquiries or court proceedings are concerned. The trial will follow the exact pattern of trials in the tribunal correctionnel, and since such offences include road accidents, there is often a 'partie civile'.[29] The civil issues may often play a larger role in the trial than the criminal, and since lengthy and detailed written submissions are often made concerning the civil claim, the court will frequently adjourn for fourteen days to consider its verdict, sentence and finding on the civil claim. There are two points of interest in such cases. Firstly it is quite common in a road accident case involving two accused and several civil claimants representing injured parties, for the entire trial proceedings (covering the criminal and civil aspects) to be concluded within one hour. Secondly, since because of the rules of prescription the institution of criminal proceedings can not be delayed, the trial will frequently take place before any injured party has fully recovered or before the full extent of the civil liability can be known. In such cases the court may make an interim award of damages, then continue the case (if need be several times) quoad the civil aspect of the case, until the full extent of the civil liability is known.

TRIAL PROCEDURES—COUR D'ASSISES

88 When the chambre d'accusation decide that a case is to be tried in the cour d'assises, the 'dossier' is sent to the clerk of that court, and a copy of the remit is served on the accused. The remit gives a summary of the facts of the case and of the accused's background. The accused is interviewed by the president of the cour d'assises prior to the trial. If he is at liberty, he must give himself into custody on the day before this first examination, but if he is in custody, he will be transferred to the prison nearest the court, if not already there. The president will have the accused brought to his chambers in order to examine him. While the public is not admitted, the accused's legal adviser may be present, as may the procureur général (who in practice never attends). The 'partie civile' and his lawyer may not be present. The purpose of the examination is to allow the president to verify the accused's identity, that he has received a copy of the remit from the chambre d'accusation and to ensure he is legally represented. If the accused does not have a lawyer, the president will arrange for one to be appointed. In very exceptional cases, the accused may request that he be represented by a parent or friend, which is competent. At this examination the facts of the case will not be discussed, although there is nothing to prevent an accused protesting his innocence. A record of the examination is made, being signed by the clerk of court, the president and the accused.

[28] See para 21.

[29] As in the tribunal correctionnel, a motor insurance company can enter appearance as 'partie civile', hence the accused may be defended by two lawyers, one representing the criminal interests and the other concerned with defending the civil claim.

At any time before the start of the trial, the president has a discretion to order further inquiries if he thinks such a course is necessary. He may make such inquiries personally, or delegate this task to one of the other judges or to a juge d'instruction. The president may also order a separation or joinder of trials, provided that in the case of joinder, the other trial or accused must have been put down for the same session. On his own initiative, or on the motion of the procureur général, the president may adjourn the trial to a later session.

The prosecution must notify the defence of any witnesses it seeks to call at least twenty-four hours before the start of the trial; the defence have a similar obligation to notify both the prosecution and the 'partie civile'; the 'partie civile' must notify the defence, but need not notify the prosecutor, nor need the prosecutor notify him. Failure to give the above notification would allow the party not notified to object to the witness at the trial, but the president has a discretionary right to allow the witness to be heard. Each accused is sent a copy of each witness's statement and each expert report before the start of the trial, and the accused's lawyer has right of access to the 'dossier'. A list of potential jurors must be sent to the accused at least forty-eight hours before the trial, although minor amendments may be made to the list at a later time. The trial may not take place within five days of the first examination of the accused by the president unless the defence waive this right.

Trial[30]

89 The trial commences with the president asking the accused his full name, date and place of birth, address and occupation. As the accused is in custody he will be in the dock with his police escort. The clerk of court then reads out the names of all potential jurors to ensure all are present. All the names are then put into an urn, and the president draws nine names therefrom. As each juror's name is called, he takes his place on the bench, four sitting on one side of the three judges and five on the other. The prosecution is allowed four peremptory challenges to jurors, and the defence five, regardless of how many accused there are.[31] No reason is given for the challenge. If the trial promises to be extremely long, the president has a discretion to order that one or two extra jurors be ballotted. These supplementary jurors will sit beside the original jurors being then able to replace any of the original jurors who falls ill, etc., during the course of the trial. After the jury has been selected the president reads out their names and administers the oath—'Do you swear and promise before God and man to examine with the most scrupulous attention the charges brought against (the accused); not to betray either the interests of the accused person or those of society which accuses him; not to communicate with any person until after you have reached your verdict; to be guided neither by hate, malice, fear nor affection; to come to your decision after hearing the charges and defences according to your conscience and personal conviction with the impartiality and resolution of an honest, free man; and to maintain the secrecy of your deliberations even after the termination of your duties'. Each juror in turn replies 'I so swear'.

[30] See Appendix 1—'The French Jury System' and Appendix 8—'Excerpts from Trials in the cour d'assises.

[31] If there are more than five accused, they will draw lots as to who may exercise the challenge —Mazurier, C. de Cass. 15 December 1959. As a general rule, the prosecution will not challenge a juror, accepting the jury as it is ballotted. However, some prosecutors may challenge a juror at the latter's request if the juror has some urgent personal business to attend to on the day of the trial.

During the course of the trial a juror may ask the president to put specific questions to the accused or witnesses, and if authorised by the president, may put such questions in person—such an occurrence being very rare. The part of the oath requiring the jurors 'not to communicate with anyone' means that the jurors must not discuss the facts of the case with anyone else prior to reaching their verdict. The jurors must pay close attention to the proceedings—for example a juror falling asleep could render the proceedings null and void. A juror must not display any prejudice to any party to the case, nor indicate in any way that he has prejudged the case. A juror breaking one of these rules could invalidate the entire trial, in which case the president would probably stop the proceedings and order that they be recommenced at the next session.

90 The 'huissier' (who is responsible for citing the witnesses) will then read out the names of the witnesses, each answering to his name. If any witness is absent, and if all the parties agree to proceed in his absence, the president may allow the trial to continue, failing which he will adjourn the trial to the next session. If any of the parties has brought a witness to court who has not been cited, he will intimate the presence of this witness, at the same time explaining why the witness was not properly cited and intimated to the other parties, who at this stage may object to the witness. Normally the president will not give a ruling until later. All witnesses will then be taken from the court to the witness room.

91 The clerk of court then reads the remit from the chambre d'accusation in full.
  The president will then commence by examining the accused, followed by the witnesses—the procedure being the same as in the tribunal correctionnel. The oath administered to the witnesses is slightly different, the witnesses swearing 'to speak without hatred or fear, and to tell the whole truth and nothing but the truth'. As a general rule no record is kept of the evidence in the cour d'assises since no appeal is competent, but the president may order the clerk of court to note the evidence of a witness making contradictory statements. The principle difference between the cour d'assises and the tribunal correctionnel is that since the jury do not have access to the 'dossier' all the evidence should be placed before the court orally. In other words any witness whose evidence is to be given to the jury for consideration, must be cited to court and examined. With regard to the accused's background, such evidence is elicited during the examination of the accused. The president of the cour d'assises also has a discretionary power to 'take all steps which he believes to be useful in order to discover the truth', which is not given to presidents of inferior courts.[32] This power includes the right to summon and obtain evidence from witnesses not cited by the parties, call for further productions to be lodged, order any document (including anonymous letters) to be read aloud, order an examination by experts and give the jury anything which may assist them in their deliberations (for example sketch plans, written statements by witnesses, etc.). Such a power, however, does not allow the president to break the rules of procedure (for example he may not place evidence before the court if it has been improperly obtained). The president may not use this power to adjourn the trial to a later date, except on cause shown and with the consent of all the parties.

[32] Although the president of an inferior court may adjourn the trial to obtain further information—see para 85.

92 At the conclusion of the evidence, the president will frequently adjourn the court for thirty minutes after which the parties to the case will address the court. The procedure is exactly the same as in the tribunal correctionnel except that since the parties are addressing a lay jury the address will tend to be longer and more reasoned. After the lawyer for the defence has finished his address, the president normally asks the accused in person if he has anything further to say.

93 The president then addresses the jury. He will determine the issues for the jury to decide, reducing the same to questions for the jury to answer. In theory the questions should always be read aloud to the court, but the parties may dispense with such reading, and in practice, while it depends on the attitude of the individual president, the questions are seldom read aloud in many courts. The questions must be formed in such a way as to be capable of being answered by a simple affirmative or negative. The basic questions are—'Is the accused guilty of . . . (specifying the offence in detail)?'; 'Was the offence accompanied by . . . (specifying aggravating circumstances)?'; 'Were there any mitigating circumstances in the accused's favour?' The president then tells the jury—'The law does not require judges to account for the means by which they are convinced, nor does it prescribe rules by which they must assess the sufficiency of evidence; the law only requires that they ask themselves in silence, in reflection and with a sincere conscience what impression the evidence brought against the accused and his defence thereto has made upon them. The law only asks them one question which encompasses their entire duties— 'Are you thoroughly convinced?' This formula is also prominently displayed in the retiring room.

94 The jury, the president and the other two judges then retire to the same room to consider verdict and sentence. No one may enter or leave the jury room until this is given. In their deliberations, they may not consider any evidence that has not been given orally at the trial. The court (i.e. judges and jury) must answer each of the president's questions. This is done by writing 'Yes' or 'No' on a slip of paper which is folded and put into an urn. This ensures secrecy of the votes. The president then counts the votes. Any blank paper or one that is indistinct, or does not answer by a simple 'Yes' or 'No' will be counted as a vote in favour of the accused. After the voting, the ballot papers are burnt. Every answer unfavourable to the accused must have at least eight votes to be binding—thus requiring at least the majority of the lay jurors. The verdicts can be guilty, not guilty or 'absolution'—as in the tribunal correctionnel.[33] If the verdict is guilty, the court then proceeds to vote on sentence, which must be within the minimum and maximum limits specified by the law. Each person writes down what he thinks is an appropriate sentence and the voting is dealt with in the same way as when voting on the verdict—except a simple majority (i.e. seven votes) is sufficient to determine sentence. If on the first ballot, there is no majority, the most severe proposed sentence is struck off, and the matter again voted on—this procedure being followed until a majority is obtained.

The answers to all the questions and the sentence are noted, the note being signed by the president and the foreman of the jury. The court then reconvenes and reads the questions and answers, including the sentence, to the accused. If the accused is convicted, the president will inform him briefly of the steps he may take if he wishes to appeal.

[33] See para 85.

Should there be a civil claim, the court will adjourn briefly, then reconvene without the jury. The parties to the case may then address the court further in relation to the civil claim. While the procureur général also has such a right, he seldom exercises it. The court may have appointed one of the judges to investigate the civil claim, in which case he will give his report at this stage. The court normally then adjourns to consider the civil claim, then reconvenes to give its decision. The court can still award damages against the accused if he is acquitted or given a verdict of 'absolution'.

The clerk of court must write a minute with the verdict, sentence and statutory provisions contravened. Within three days of the verdict, he must write a further minute, recording the proceedings (but not the evidence). Both minutes are signed by the president.

It should be noted that no appeal is competent from the cour d'assises, except to the Cour de Cassation on a point of law.

'Contumace'—Trial in Absence

95 'Contumace' is a procedure whereby the cour d'assises may try an accused in his absence if he fails to appear for trial. The trial is held without a jury, and the court only considers the dossier, not hearing evidence from the witnesses. If the accused is convicted and is arrested before the time for enforcing the penalty has prescribed, he must be re-tried in the normal way. The main effect is that all the accused's possessions are sequestrated and any civil claim is settled. A subsequent re-trial will however lift the sequestration and reconsider the civil issues. 'Contumace' is not frequently used, especially since persons accused of 'crimes' are invariably detained in custody awaiting trial. If an accused has been liberated and fails to appear for trial, the court would normally proceed by 'contumace', rather than adjourn the trial, the court having no power to issue a warrant for the accused's arrest.

Procureur Général

96 It will be seen from an examination of the chambre d'accusation and the cour d'assises, that the role of the procureur général is to represent the prosecution, his duties in the cour d'assises being identical to those of the procureur de la République in the tribunal correctionnel. He is superior in rank to the procureur de la République, but does not have the same function in investigating cases before the trial. In the chambre d'accusation, as in the cour d'appel itself he represents the prosecution in appeals taken against the juge d'instruction or tribunal correctionnel. He has no responsibility for initiating these appeals, but is not bound by the views of the procureur de la République. In the cour d'assises, he prosecutes cases remitted for trial by the chambre d'accusation, and while he has a right of audience when the remit is being considered, once the remit has been ordered, he must prosecute regardless of his personal opinion, which, of course, he may express at the trial.

8. Penalties

97   The penalties applicable to each offence are determined within the limits fixed by the Code pénal. The way in which they are enforced is described in the Code de procedure pénale. The treatment of the offender and the application of penalties is a separate subject outwith the scope of this present book. The following remarks merely give some of the details, in particular concentrating on the role of the public prosecutor who is largely responsible for enforcing the penalty imposed by the court.

The Death Penalty
98   The death penalty may be imposed for particide, premeditated murder, continual illtreatment of children with intent to kill, wrongful detention accompanied by physical torture, wilful fire raising of an occupied house, perjury in the trial of an offence carrying the death penalty, kidnapping a child less than 15 years of age when the child dies, and certain types of robbery and theft.

In practice juries in such trials often find some mitigating circumstances which prevent the death penalty being imposed. Furthermore the President de la République may grant a reprieve by exercising his discretion. The following figures give the number of times the death penalty was imposed in recent years, the figures in brackets showing the number of times in which it was actually executed: 1965—16(1); 1966—17(1); 1967—6(1); 1968—4(0); 1969—13(1). In practice therefore the number of times when the death penalty is actually carried out is very infrequent. The method of execution is by guillotine. Women are never executed.

Imprisonment
99   Imprisonment may be imposed for life (which does not necessarily mean 'natural life') for certain offences and may or may not be ordered to be in solitary confinement. Imprisonment is always backdated to include any time in custody awaiting trial. Once a sentence of imprisonment is executed, the way in which the sentence is served is controlled by a 'magistrat' called the 'juge de l'application des peines'. Normally a prisoner will start by being given work to do in his cell; he may then pass through various stages, including working outside the prison for government contractors, etc. Eventually he may be placed on semi-liberty whereby he is allowed to work outside the prison and is only detained outwith working hours and at weekends and public holidays; and ultimately be released on conditional liberty. There are various rules concerning such progress, and the procureur of the court pronouncing the sentence must be consulted before the prisoner is released on conditional liberty.

When the court imposes a sentence of imprisonment, it may not be executed until

86

the time limits for lodging an appeal have expired,[1] unless the court specifically orders that the sentence be executed forthwith (in which case the sentence must exceed one year's imprisonment). The prosecutor is responsible for enforcing the sentence, hence this duty lies on the procureur général if the sentence is imposed by the cour d'assises or confirmed or imposed by the cour d'appel. When the sentence is imposed by the tribunal correctionnel or the tribunal de police, the procureur de la République will enforce the sentence. The prosecutor has no discretion to decide whether or not the sentence should be enforced.

In the cour d'assises, the sentence may be enforced within three days of its imposition, this being the time limit allowed to an accused (who is present when the sentence is pronounced) to lodge an appeal with the Cour de Cassation. In the tribunal correctionnel, if the accused was present in court when the sentence was pronounced, the sentence may be enforced after the expiry of ten days (this being the time limit for lodging an appeal with the cour d'appel). Should the sentence be pronounced in the accused's absence, the 'huissier' will serve a notice on the accused informing him of the court's sentence.[2] The same rules apply to service of this notice as apply to service of a citation on the accused to attend for trial.[3] The sentence becomes enforceable within ten days of personal service, or if this has not been effected, within ten days of the accused signing the receipt for the delivery of the registered letter telling him the notice has been left at the local mayor's office (ten days being the time limit for appealing against a judgement by default by means of the appeal procedure known as 'l'opposition'). If service of the notice is not effected, then the procureur may instruct the police to trace the accused. Should the accused not be traced within five years and if the penalty has not been extinguished by prescription, the penalty may be enforced on the accused without notification, if he is found. All penalties prescribe if not enforced within a certain time limit namely, penalties for 'crimes'—twenty years; penalties for 'délits'—five years; penalties for 'contraventions'—two years. When the penalty of imprisonment becomes enforceable, and the accused is in custody, the sentence begins to run, commencing from the date when the accused was taken into pre-trial custody. If the accused is not already in custody, the procureur will send an extract of the court's verdict and sentence to the police, with instructions to arrest the accused and take him to prison. Should the accused live outwith the district of the procureur, he will send the extract to the procureur who has jurisdiction, requesting him to enforce the penalty.[4]

Fines
100 If the penalty is a fine, the procureur is not responsible for collecting it, this duty being given to an official called a 'percepteur' who is employed by the Ministry

---

[1] It need not wait until the expiry of the two month time limit given to the procureur général to lodge an appeal against a judgement of the tribunal correctionnel.

[2] Unless the court orders that the penalty is to be enforced forthwith, in which case a warrant to arrest the accused will be issued.

[3] See para 77.

[4] In Paris when the accused is arrested, he is brought before the procureur who examines him to ensure that the person arrested by the police is the person to whom the extract applies. It should also be noted that while the penalty may become enforceable within ten days, in Paris because of pressure of work it is not uncommon to have a period of up to nine months before the penalty is enforced.

of Finance. After the accused has been notified of the fine (and the time for appealing has expired), the accused may make arrangements with the 'percepteur' for the time limits and methods by which the fine is to be paid. If the accused fails to pay the fine, the 'percepteur' will request the procureur to order the accused's arrest. The procureur will then instruct the police to arrest the accused and take him to prison where he will be detained for a specified period, the periods being determined by the Code de procedure pénale.[5] The accused can only avoid going to prison if he pays the fine on the spot, or if the 'percepteur' agrees to a further arrangement for payment thereof. Exceptions to these rules are made for age and for indigence. If the accused is aged between 60 and 70 years and fails to pay the fine, the alternative period of imprisonment is halved; if he is aged over 70 years no alternative of imprisonment may be enforced. In certain circumstances if the accused can prove he is without means, the alternative period of imprisonment may be halved.[6] It should be noted that if the accused is also ordered to pay damages or make restitution to the victim of the offence, this takes priority over payment of the fine. Should the accused die before paying the fine, it will be regarded as a civil debt against his estate. The court has no control over how a fine is paid.

If any expenses are awarded against an accused, these are dealt with in the same way as fines.[7] If the accused is ordered to pay damages to the victim ('partie civile') then the latter has the responsibility for enforcing payment thereof. An accused can not be sent to prison for non-payment of damages.

Loss of Civil Rights, etc.

101 In addition to the above penalties, for certain offences, the Code pénal allows the court to deprive an accused of certain civil rights, such as the right to vote, to exercise a particular profession or to dispose of his property (the latter being in the case of life imprisonment). The court may also order confiscation of goods used in the commission of or gained as the result of a criminal offence. Other offences allow the court to banish the accused from France or a certain area thereof (the latter provision being frequently employed in Paris). The court can sometimes order that details of the offence and the conviction be prominently displayed in certain areas—for example in the accused's home town.

While all the above penalties are prescribed by the Code pénal, there are two measures which allow the court to ignore these penalties at its discretion. These measures are suspended sentences and probation.

Suspended Sentences

102 When pronouncing sentence, the court can state that it will be suspended, provided the accused has not been previously convicted of a 'crime' or a 'délit'. The court may impose conditions on the accused during the period of suspension. If the accused is not convicted of a 'crime' or 'délit' and sentenced to more than two months' imprisonment during the period of five years after which the suspended sentence was pronounced, the sentence subject to the suspension will not be en-

---

[5] CPP Art. 750.

[6] If the accused is already serving a sentence of imprisonment, the alternative period for non payment of a fine will only commence when the first term has expired.

[7] If proceedings were instituted by a 'partie civile' and the accused is convicted, the court has a discretion to award expenses against an accused. Such a course is fairly uncommon.

forced. A suspended sentence does not affect any award of damages or expenses against the accused, who is still required to pay them. If the accused commits a further offence during the period that the sentence is suspended, then the suspended sentence will be treated as a previous conviction.

The court may also state that part of the sentence is to be served and the remainder is to be suspended. In 1969, when the provisions relating to suspended sentences were more restricted (having been modified by a law of 17th July 1970), 63,727 persons were given suspended sentences as opposed to 86,948 persons who were sent to prison—i.e. approximately 42% of all prison sentences were suspended.

Probation

103 The court can not place an accused on probation if he has a previous conviction for more than twelve months' imprisonment, or if he has two previous convictions each for more than two months' imprisonment. Probation must be for at least three years, and not more than five years. The 'juge de l'application des peines' is responsible for supervising the probation, and may impose the conditions he thinks are necessary. Failure to obey the conditions of probation may entail the accused being arrested and placed in prison until being brought before the court. His arrest is made on the instructions of the procureur de la République acting on the request of the 'juge de l'application des peines'.

Amnesties: Pardons

104 From time to time a law may be passed giving an amnesty in relation to certain types of offence. This will have the effect of preventing the penalty being enforced, or if the matter has not yet come to trial, it will act as a plea in bar of trial.

The President de la République has a discretionary power to grant a pardon, absolving the accused from serving all or part of his sentence. The accused may apply for a pardon at any time, such requests being frequent. While the number granted depends on the personal attitude of the President de la République, at present about 10% of the requests for pardon are granted.

9. Appeals[1]

There are four methods of appealing against the judgement of a French criminal court—an appeal to the cour d'appel, an appeal to the Cour de Cassation ('pourvois en cassation') being the two common methods of appeal proper. There is also a method of appeal available when the accused was judged in his absence ('l'opposition') and an extremely rare type of appeal to the Cour de Cassation known as 'pourvois en revision'. The means of appeal available depend on the circumstances of the case, but all have the effect of suspending execution of sentence until the appeal is decided.[2]

'L'Appel'—Appeal to the Cour d'Appel

105   The cour d'appel has jurisdiction to hear appeals against any judgement given in the tribunal correctionnel, and any judgement of the tribunal de police (if the sentence exceeds five days' imprisonment or a fine of sixty francs). It can not consider an appeal against a judgement of the cour d'assises.

An appeal may be considered before the termination of the trial in the inferior court if the appeal concerns a refusal to liberate the accused from custody (i.e. after the case has been remitted for trial by the juge d'instruction) or any decision by the inferior court concerning a preliminary plea, which if upheld would have the effect of terminating proceedings before the trial proper had started. (Such as pleas concerning jurisdiction, amnesty, prescription, insanity, etc.). Appeals concerning pre-trial custody must be considered within twenty-four hours of the appeal being lodged, otherwise the time limit for deciding an appeal is one month.

At the end of the trial in the inferior court, an appeal may be lodged against verdict or sentence. While the cour d'appel would normally consider both these matters, it is always open to the party lodging the appeal to indicate which particular aspect of the case he is appealing against, in which case the cour d'appel will normally concentrate its deliberations on that aspect.

An appeal may not be taken to the cour d'appel if an appeal by way of 'l'opposition' is competent, until the proceedings by 'l'opposition' have been decided.

An appeal may be lodged by the accused, the 'partie civile', the procureur de la République or the procureur général, and if one party lodges an appeal, this entitles the others to lodge a counter-appeal. If the accused lodges an appeal and there is no counter appeal, the cour d'appel may not increase his sentence. In practice therefore

---

[1] For Scotland see para 231 et seq.

[2] Unless in the exceptional case where the court orders that the sentence be executed as soon as it is pronounced.

the procureur de la République will always lodge a counter appeal, so that the cour d'appel has the power to increase or decrease sentence as it sees fit. If there are several accused, of whom only one lodges an appeal, the procureur will probably lodge notice of appeal concerning all accused. Should he only lodge a counter appeal against the one accused who had appealed, then that accused could claim in the cour d'appel that he only played a minor part in the offence and that his co-accused were the main culprits. If the cour d'appel accepted this, they would be powerless to do anything quoad the other accused, unless the counter appeal by the procureur included them also. In the proceedings before the cour d'appel, the procureur général will explain this as the reason for the appeals lodged by the prosecution.

Apart from any right to lodge a counter appeal, the procureur may appeal on his own initiative, even if such an appeal concerns sentence only (which is known as an 'appel à minima'). Furthermore in certain exceptional instances where the procureur thinks that the sentence imposed is unjust, he may even appeal in the interests of the accused—for example, if an accused having been judged in absence, lodges an appeal by way of 'l'opposition' giving new facts indicating his innocence, then fails to appear at the 'l'opposition' hearing, the original verdict must stand. In such circumstances if the procureur accepted that the accused was innocent, he might lodge an appeal which would result in the accused being acquitted. The procureur might also appeal if he thought the sentence was improper or illegal, since it would be his duty otherwise to enforce such a sentence.

If only the procureur or the accused appeals, the court may not increase any award of damages made to the 'partie civile', but should the 'partie civile' appeal, the award may be increased up to the limit originally asked by him plus any further loss incurred due to the delay in enforcing payment of the award. Should the 'partie civile' be the only party to appeal, the cour d'appel may only consider the civil aspect of the case, but may not decrease the award made by the inferior court. If the 'partie civile' appeals against an acquittal verdict, the procureur will also normally lodge a similar appeal (since failure to do so would merely entitle the cour d'appel to award damages if it upheld the appeal, but not to convict the accused), but if the original proceedings were instituted by the 'partie civile' the procureur will not normally lodge such an appeal.

All notices of appeal must be lodged with the clerk of court within ten days of the judgement being given. If the accused is in prison, he may lodge his appeal with the prison governor who will forward the same to the clerk of court. The procureur général has a general power to lodge an appeal within two months of the date of the judgement. There are minor exceptions to the ten-day rule—such as where the accused was not present in court at the time of the judgement.

The appeal is heard by the cour d'appel (or more accurately by the chambre des appels correctionnels de la cour d'appel) which will normally appoint one of its judges to investigate the case and make a report thereon. The report merely concerns the facts of the case, and does not give the judge's opinions. At the appeal hearing, the court will consider the report. The court may also re-examine the accused (which is quite frequently done) and has a discretion to re-hear the witnesses. It will also examine the notes of the evidence taken by the clerk of the original court, but can not consider fresh evidence.[3] The appeal hearing virtually involves a re-trial of the

[3] See 'pourvois en revision'—para 108.

case, the procedure being the same as in the tribunal correctionnel, unless the parties have stated that the appeal refers to one aspect of the case only.

At the conclusion of the hearing the court may uphold the original verdict, or modify it (by reducing the charge or the sentence—it can not increase the gravity of the charge) or reject the appeal. If it acquits the accused it may award him damages (but this is most unusual). If it decides that there was a procedural irregularity in the original proceedings, the appeal itself will act as a fresh trial, giving a verdict and sentence at the end thereof. Should it hold that the offence was a 'crime' and therefore that the trial in the tribunal correctionnel was incompetent, the cour d'appel will set aside the original verdict and report the case formally to the prosecutor who then has a discretion to commence proceedings leading to a fresh trial in the cour d'assises. When the cour d'appel finds that the tribunal de police dealt with an offence classed as a 'délit' the cour d'appel will try the case itself. Finally, it may be open to the cour d'appel to find that the appeal itself is time barred or incompetent in some other way.

Cour de Cassation—'Pourvois en Cassation'

106 An appeal may be taken to the Cour de Cassation on a point of law provided no other appeal procedure is competent. Thus for example, an appeal may not be taken against the ruling of a juge d'instruction since such appeals may be taken to the chambre d'accusation, but an appeal is competent against a decision of the chambre d'accusation. Similarly, an appeal may not be taken from the tribunal correctionnel, since such appeals may competently be taken in the cour d'appel, but an appeal may be taken from that latter court. Appeals may be taken direct from the tribunal de police if the sentence is less than five days imprisonment or a fine of sixty francs, since in such cases no appeal may be taken to the cour d'appel. Appeals may also be taken direct from the cour d'assises.

The appeal must concern a point of law—i.e. procedure. Thus the court may not consider if the evidence was sufficient to justify the verdict but may consider any matter concerning the constitution of the original court (e.g. if the prosecutor was not present at all stages); questions of competency (e.g. the tribunal de police dealing with a 'délit'); any ultra vires act of the court; any judgement not properly motivated in law; any sentence not in conformity with the law; an improper decision that a particular course of conduct constitutes a criminal offence, and violation of procedural rules or breach of the Code de procédure pénale.

Any party may lodge an appeal provided he has been prejudiced by the decision or actings of the inferior court. Notice of appeal must be lodged within five days of the judgement being given in the inferior court, unless a valid reason is given for a later lodging. The notice of appeal is lodged with the clerk of court and the other parties must be notified. Caution for expenses must be given and the full grounds of the appeal (as opposed to the formal notice) must be lodged within ten days. If the sentence of the original court was more than six months imprisonment, and the appeal is taken by the accused, he must give himself into custody unless the original court allows otherwise.

The appeal is heard by the Chambre Criminelle de la Cour de Cassation which will first hear a factual report by one of its judges and then hear the parties to the case. The general procedure is as in the cour d'appel. The court is not restricted to considering the aspect of the case that is appealed but may consider any aspect of procedure, but it may not consider the civil aspects of the case unless the 'partie civile' appeals, and likewise may only consider the civil aspects if the 'partie civile' alone appeals.

The court has the following powers—to refuse the appeal because the appellant failed to appear at the hearing or abandoned his appeal, or because the appeal itself was incompetent, or on the merits of the appeal itself. The court can also find that an irregularity had occurred, but that the irregularity was so trivial or technical that the original judgement should stand. If however the irregularity was grave and caused prejudice to the appellant, the court may annul the earlier judgement. In theory the court may annul only part of the earlier judgement, but in practice it usually annuls the whole judgement.

The Cour de Cassation will then remit the case for re-trial to another court[4] (e.g. if the case came from the tribunal correctionnel it will be remitted to a tribunal correctionnel composed of different judges from the original court, or if the Cour de Cassation decided that the offence was a 'crime', it would remit the case so that it could be tried in the cour d'assises).

The court to which a case is remitted is not bound by the decision of the Cour de Cassation (e.g. the trial court might decide it was incompetent to deal with the offence). If the court does not follow the ruling of the Cour de Cassation, a second appeal may be taken on the same grounds to the Cour de Cassation. At the second hearing in the Cour de Cassation, the court will sit with a full bench of thirty-five judges (Chambres réunies), the court not being bound by its own previous decision. The final decision of the Cour de Cassation must be followed in the court to which the case is again remitted for trial.

In addition to the above type of appeal, the procureur général has the right to appeal to the Cour de Cassation merely with a view to obtaining a decision to clarify the law. In such a case, the decision of the court can not affect any of the parties to the case. The Minister of Justice can also instruct that such an appeal be taken at any stage in the proceedings and if this is done the decision of the court can not be applied if adverse to any of the parties to the case.

L'Opposition

107 The procedure known as 'l'opposition' is not so much an appeal, but merely a means to have the case re-tried. It applies to the tribunal de police and tribunal correctionnel where the accused has been judged in his absence. Such an accused may request the court to re-hear the case in his presence. It is only competent when the absence of the accused was due to the fact that he was not properly cited, or had no knowledge of his citation.[5] 'L'opposition' proceedings must be commenced within ten days of the accused receiving notification of the court's judgement.[6] To commence such proceedings all that is required is that the accused should notify the procureur that he wishes to appeal by means of 'l'opposition'. (If the accused is only concerned with the civil aspect of the case, he will notify the 'partie civile'.)

The effect is that the original verdict is reduced, and proceedings re-commence

---

[4] Unless the Cour de Cassation holds that the course of conduct did not constitute a criminal offence, or legal proceedings were barred or incompetent. If the appeal only concerned the civil aspects of the case, only such aspects will be reconsidered at the re-trial.

[5] See para 77—where the 'huissier' leaves the citation with the local mayor and sends a letter to the accused, the accused might not receive the letter or the citation, but will be presumed to have been properly cited until he proves to the contrary.

[6] See para 99—the period is extended to one month if the accused lives outwith France.

as if the first trial had never taken place. The accused is cited to attend the new diet of trial, but if he fails to attend, the new diet of trial, the court at the second trial can merely re-affirm the original judgement, whether or not any new facts have arisen in the interim. Only one appeal by means of 'l'opposition' is competent, so that if the accused fails to appear at the new diet of trial, he can not request further 'l'opposition', regardless of his reasons for failing to attend.

Pourvois en Revision

108 A 'pourvois en revision' is a means of appeal whereby the Cour de Cassation may reduce a verdict of guilty because of new evidence coming to light after the trial. The evidence must not have been available at the time of the trial and must be such as to raise a serious doubt as to the accused's guilt. It does not apply if the case is a 'contravention', nor is it a remedy available to a prosecutor seeking to overturn a verdict of acquittal. Obvious examples of when this type of appeal is competent are—in a case of murder where it is later proved that the victim is alive; if another person is subsequently convicted for the same offence, thus making it impossible for the accused to be guilty; if a witness at the trial is later convicted of perjury in regard to his evidence, provided knowledge of the perjury was not available at the original trial.

The accused, or the prosecutor will apply to the Minister of Justice who will set up a commission consisting of three directors (i.e. heads of departments) of the Ministry of Justice and three 'magistrats' from the Cour de Cassation to examine the new facts. Depending on the advice of the commission, the Minister of Justice may recommend that the case be brought before the Cour de Cassation by means of a 'pourvois en revision'. The court may then base its decision on the evidence available or may instruct further inquiries (having the power to issue 'commissions rogatoires' to the police, etc.).

If the court grants the appeal it has a choice of action. Either, it may reduce the earlier judgement and remit the case for re-trial (in which case if the accused is again convicted his sentence can not exceed that imposed at the first trial). Alternatively, the court may reduce the earlier judgement and terminate the proceedings, without ordering a re-trial. The court will adopt the latter course if the accused was clearly innocent (as in the 'Dreyfus' case) or if no criminal offence was committed (for example if the 'victim' of a murder is alive) or if a re-trial is impossible.

If the second course is adopted, the accused is liberated, any fine or damages paid by him will be reimbursed, the court's decision is widely published in an attempt to restore his reputation, and he may be paid compensation from public funds.

Scotland

1. Historical and Political Background

The Legislature

109 The historical and political background to Scots criminal law and procedure has remained relatively stable since the beginning of the 18th century. Prior to 1603, Scotland was an independent kingdom and the Union of the English and Scottish Crowns in that year had little effect on the government of Scotland except to remove her king to London, with the result that more of the government was left in the hands of persons appointed by the king, one of the most important being the Lord Advocate. Scotland retained its own parliament until 1707 when the parliament of England and Scotland were united to form the parliament of Great Britain. While this new body was the sole source of legislation, Scotland continued to maintain its separate legal system completely independent of that practised in England and in the realms of criminal law, widely different from the English system.

The British constitution is of course unwritten, and consists of the Queen in parliament. There are two Houses of Parliament—the House of Commons and the House of Lords. Members are elected by the country to the House of Commons and the leader of the majority party (the Prime Minister) forms his government which is formally appointed by the Queen. The House of Lords is comprised of hereditary lords and those appointed for life only. A legislative measure, which is called a 'bill' must be approved by both Houses of Parliament then receive the Royal assent. The House of Lords basically only has the power to use delaying tactics, and as the Royal assent is a formality, to all intents and purposes, the laws are passed by the House of Commons. Once a bill has received the Royal assent, it is known as an Act of Parliament. Many Acts of Parliament contain provisions concerning delegated legislation, which is the power given to a particular Minister to make rules and regulations which become operative without the formal legislative machinery and consent of Parliament. The amount of delegated legislation is enormous, much of it being concerned with the criminal law.

The Secretary of State for Scotland; the Lord Advocate

110 While Scotland is directly governed in this way, there are two government ministers with particular responsibility for Scottish affairs, one being the Secretary of State for Scotland and the other the Lord Advocate. By tradition the former is always a member of the House of Commons and has responsibility for a wide range of administration including health, education, housing, roads, etc. One of his duties includes the administration of the courts, and in particular the sheriff court, but in this sphere, he works in the closest consultation with the Lord Advocate. The actual body responsible for this administration and organisation is known as the

97

Scottish Courts Administration.[1] The Lord Advocate on the other hand is appointed from among the senior advocates at the Scottish bar. He is not only the public prosecutor, but is also the chief law officer or legal adviser of the government in Scotland. He is a member of the British government and while in the past he was by tradition a member of the House of Commons, in recent years Lord Advocates have sometimes been appointed who were not members of that House.[2] As the Lord Advocate may be subject to criticism (of the way in which he conducts his duties) only in parliament, there being no other effective check on his powers, it was formerly considered advantageous that he be a member of parliament and thus in a position to answer in person any attack made on him there. In practice however, no serious attack has been made in parliament against a Lord Advocate since 1823, and this factor need no longer be considered as important. Should any matter concerning legal administration be raised in parliament, it can be answered by the Secretary of State for Scotland. In addition to his duties as public prosecutor, the Lord Advocate has many responsibilities of an administrative nature which include the drafting of legislation applicable to Scotland, the appointment and control of the procurator fiscals (the prosecutors in the sheriff court) and the 'de facto' appointment of judges.[3]

Local Government

111 In addition to the central government, Scotland has a system of local government which will be reorganised in May 1975. Prior to that date, Scotland was divided into counties governed as regards local issues by an elected county council. In addition, the larger towns and cities had their own elected councils. In 1975, all these bodies will cease to exist, and instead, Scotland will be divided into regions, which in turn will be divided into districts. Each region and each district will have its own elected councils. All councils have the power to make local regulations, usually known as bye-laws, and in many cases, breach thereof is a criminal offence. Local government to a large extent is subject to the control of the central government which provides much of the required finance.

The Scottish Legal System

112 With regard to the position of criminal law in the general legal system, Scots law can be divided into different bodies many of which have their own special courts—viz: civil law and the civil courts; agricultural law and the Scottish Land Court; heraldry and the court of the Lord Lyon; and various other courts and administrative tribunals dealing with elections, building regulations, liquor licences, income tax and many other such matters. With regard to criminal offences committed by children and young persons, some are not dealt with by the courts, but are considered by administrative bodies known as juvenile panels; others appeal before special juvenile courts.

---

[1] Which was created in 1971, the first director being the Rt. Hon. Baron Wilson of Langside, Q.C., a former Lord Advocate and sheriff.

[2] In one instance a Lord Advocate was created a life peer, thus making him a member of the House of Lords.

[3] For fuller details re the Lord Advocate, see paras 132–133.

2. Sources of Criminal Law

Scots criminal law has not been codified hence it relies mostly on numerous statutory provisions and on common law.

Legislation

113 Statute law consists of the Acts passed by the Scottish Parliament prior to 1707,[1] Acts passed by the parliament of Great Britain prior to 1800, and Acts passed by the United Kingdom parliament since 1800. All legislation passed by the United Kingdom parliament in theory also applies to Scotland, but in practice an Act will usually state whether or not it applies specifically to Scotland. In some instances only part of the Act will have a Scottish application. The same rules apply to delegated legislation. Again in theory an Act of parliament becomes operative when it receives the Royal Assent, but in many instances the Act itself states that it will not come into force until a later date, or when made effective by delegated legislation (which for this purpose usually takes the form of a Statutory Instrument). A Statutory Instrument issued by a government minister may often specify that certain parts of the same Act should come into force at different dates. Acts of parliament may be repealed or amended by subsequent Acts and there is no comprehensive collection of the amended Acts.[2] Hence before an Act can be given effect by the legal practitioner or the courts, it must be examined to see if it applies to Scotland, if it has been made operative and if it has been repealed or amended.

There are numerous rules for interpreting the language of Acts of Parliament, the two most important being that an Act can not be interpreted to have retroactive effect, nor against the interests of an accused person. The courts play an important role in interpreting the law (such decisions being binding), with the result that the Scottish courts might interpret and therefore apply an Act in a manner different from the English courts.[3] Thus before applying an Act, it is also necessary to examine any cases where the Act has been previously enforced.

Case Law

114 In applying the law, a court may be bound by a previous decision on the matter, this being known as the principle of 'stare decisis'. Judicial decisions are not

---

[1] The commonest example is the crime of incest which is defined by the Incest Act of 1567 (which quotes Leviticus, Chapter 18, verses 6–18).

[2] Although an experiment is presently being examined to see if all statutory measures can be recorded on a computer.

[3] As happened recently in some very important provisions concerning driving while under the influence of alcohol.

only important for interpreting statute, but also stating the common law. A prior decision is a precedent when there was raised, argued and decided in it some issue of law as applicable to a certain set of facts which is the same issue as arises in the present case in relation to a different set of facts of the same general kind. What is important is the raising of the same issue of law, thus there can often be lengthy argument as to whether or not the present case raises the same issues as the previous one. Some prior decisions are binding (i.e. they must be followed) whereas others are only persuasive. As a general rule, a court is only bound by the decision of a superior court, hence the High court is bound by any decisions decided on appeal, and the sheriff court is bound by decisions of the High Court. Otherwise decisions are persuasive only, and need not be followed as authoritative, hence the High Court is not bound by a previous decision of the High Court. Similarly, decisions of English courts may sometimes be persuasive. About 5% to 10% of decisions by the courts are published and there is no official series of law reports. While an unreported decision may be referred to, it will not have the same force as a reported decision.

Apart from interpreting statute law and stating the common law, the High Court of Justiciary has 'an inherent power . . . to punish . . . every act which is obviously of a criminal nature'. In practice, this is probably confined to the condemnation of any new way that may be discovered of committing a recognised crime. For example in a case in 1926, the accused took a motor car without the owner's consent, intending to return it later—i.e. without any intention of stealing it. The court held that this was a criminal offence, although it was not contrary to any statute or common law.[4]

Text Books

115 Legal text books are a useful source of law in so far as they collect all the statute and case law and put it in a logical order. Unfortunately a text book can quickly be rendered out of date by subsequent legislation or case law. As a general rule, text books are persuasive only, and not binding. If the author is dead, the book becomes more authoritative on the grounds that a living author may always wish to alter his work. Certain text books known as 'institutional writings' have more weight, especially if not contradicted by subsequent cases. These books were all written at the end of the 18th and beginning of the 19th centuries.

Custom

116 Except for commercial customs, custom may now be disregarded as a source of modern law.

Application of Criminal Law

117 It therefore follows that the criminal law of Scotland is not clearly defined. While some earlier writers stated that the whole law could be summed up in one short sentence—'Thou shalt do no wrong', the law is more specific than that. Lord Justice General Clyde did however say 'It would be a mistake to imagine that the criminal common law of Scotland countenances any precise and exact categorisation of the forms of conduct which amount to crime. It has been pointed out many times in this court that such is not the nature or quality of the criminal law of Scotland'[5]

[4] Strathern v Seaforth 1926 JC 100. In 1930, this was made a statutory offence.
[5] McLaughlan v Boyd 1934 JC 19.

Apart from statute law, common law offences are ill defined. There is no authoritative definition of murder. Many types of conduct may be considered as an attempt to pervert the course of justice and the crime of breach of the peace covers a very wide range of conduct varying from drunken behaviour to offences of an indecent nature. Occasional writers on Scots law mention crimes and offences, but in fact both terms have the same meaning, although 'offences' are sometimes defined as breaches of the statutory law.

Since many criminal offences depend on common law, it follows that there are no fixed penalties for such offences. The maximum penalty for a criminal offence will therefore depend on the maximum powers given to the court in which the offence is tried. All statutory offences are limited to the penalties prescribed by the statute, but only the maximum penalty is specified, not the minimum.

Scots criminal law is therefore very flexible and easily adapted to meet changing circumstances, and in applying the penalty, the court is left with a very wide discretion.

While much of criminal procedure depends on statute, a great deal is also founded on common law as defined by case law. As a general rule, rules of procedure tend to be more clearly defined, and where interpretation is necessary, this is usually judged on the standard of fairness to the accused.

3. Organisation of Courts of Criminal Jurisdiction[1]

118 In Scotland, the courts of first instance are the Justice of the Peace Courts, Burgh Courts, Police Courts; the Sheriff Court; the High Court of Justiciary.[2] The only appeal court is the High Court of Justiciary sitting as such. Criminal proceedings are described as 'Solemn' when the trial takes place before a jury, otherwise they are known as 'Summary'.

Justice of the Peace Courts, Burgh Courts, Police Courts

119 These courts deal with minor offences, and the distinction between them is fairly technical. The Justice of the Peace Court deals with offences committed in the county, but outwith the territorial jurisdiction of any Burgh or Police Court. The judges are Justices of the Peace, who are lay magistrates (i.e. not requiring legal qualifications) and the quorum of the court is two justices. The Burgh or Police Courts deal with offences committed in particular burghs (i.e. towns or cities). The single judge is a lay magistrate (being a member of the town council)[3] While such courts have lay magistrates, the clerk of court and the prosecutor are both legally qualified. In May 1975, these courts will be replaced by District Courts for which the judges will be lay magistrates.

Apart from any statutory exceptions, the maximum penalties which such courts may impose are 60 days imprisonment, or a fine not exceeding £50. Since common law offences do not have a fixed penalty, and even an offence such as breach of the peace may be tried in any criminal court, it follows that the common law offences tried in such courts are ones where in the first instance the prosecutor estimates that the offence does not merit a penalty in excess of the maximum powers of the court. Further, by statute,[4] such courts are specifically excluded from dealing with any of the following offences:

(a) Murder, culpable homicide, robbery, rape, wilful fire-raising, or attempt at wilful fire-raising;

(b) Stouthrief,[5] theft by housebreaking, or housebreaking with intent to steal;

(c) Theft or reset of theft, falsehood, fraud or wilful imposition, breach of trust or embezzlement, all to an amount exceeding £25;

[1] For comparison with France see paras 7–13.
[2] There are also special courts for dealing with juveniles.
[3] Except in the case of Glasgow which has a full time judge known as a stipendiary magistrate, who is legally qualified.
[4] Summary Jurisdiction (Scotland) Act 1954, Section 4.
[5] Robbery or theft aggravated by housebreaking.

(d) Any of the offences specified in the last foregoing paragraph or any attempt thereat where the accused is known to have been previously convicted of any offence inferring dishonest appropriation of property;

(e) Assault whereby any limb has been fractured or assault with intent to ravish or assault to the danger of life, or assault by stabbing;

(f) Uttering forged documents or uttering forged bank or banker's notes, or offences under the Acts relating to coinage.

The Sheriff Court[6]

120 The sheriff court has both civil and criminal jurisdiction, but we are concerned here only with the latter. For the purpose of criminal jurisdiction, Scotland is divided into sheriffdoms, or sheriff court districts, which do not necessarily correspond to counties, as for example the county of Lanarkshire, which in addition to the sheriff court at Glasgow, has sheriff courts in Hamilton, Airdrie and Lanark. Other sheriff courts may serve more than one county, depending on the density of population and amount of business. The sheriff court districts will all be reorganised in 1975. The sheriff court has competence to deal with all criminal offences except those that may only be tried in the High Court, namely treason, murder, rape, incest, deforcement of messengers and breach of duty by magistrates. The sheriff court has both solemn (trial by jury) and summary (trial by single judge) jurisdiction. The accused has no choice as to which type of trial shall be adopted.

The sheriff summary court has the general power to impose a fine of up to £150; to ordain the accused to find caution for good behaviour for any period not exceeding twelve months and to an amount not exceeding £150, such caution being either in lieu of or in addition to a fine, or in addition to imprisonment; and to award imprisonment for any period not exceeding three months, unless the accused is convicted of a second and subsequent offence inferring dishonest appropriation of property (or attempt thereat) or a second or subsequent offence inferring personal violence, when the maximum period of imprisonment is six months. In the case of certain statutory offences,[7] the court may be empowered to award a longer sentence of imprisonment.

In solemn proceedings before a jury, the court may award a term of imprisonment not exceeding two years. If on conviction, the court thinks (in a case involving a common law offence) that the offence merits a more severe sentence, it has the power to remit the case to the High Court for sentence, in which case it will be dealt with in the High Court as if it had originally been tried there. The High Court will not re-hear the evidence but will rely on a summary thereof given by the prosecution and defence, together with any pleas or evidence in mitigation adduced by the defence.

The cases heard in the sheriff court are therefore those statutory offences[8] where the penalty, being limited by statute, falls within the competence of the court, or common law offences, which in the first instance are judged by the prosecutor not to merit a penalty in excess of the powers available to the court. Thus the procurator

[6] In the 12th century, the Normans introduced the shire-reeve, who was an officer of the king with judicial, administrative and military functions. For such purposes, he required his own shire-reeve court.

[7] Such as assaulting a police officer contrary to the Police (Scotland) Act 1967.

[8] A large volume of these offences concern breaches of the road traffic law, or regulations dealing with motor vehicles.

fiscal (the prosecutor in the sheriff court) who has a complete discretion in deciding whether an offence should be taken in the Summary Court, or whether proceedings should be commenced in such a way as to lead to trial by jury, or in the High Court,[9] plays an important role in effectively deciding the maximum penalty which can be imposed for a particular offence.

High Court of Justiciary

121 The High Court of Justiciary is the highest criminal court in Scotland and deals exclusively with criminal cases. All trials are before a jury and a single judge. In theory in an important case, instead of a single judge, there is provision for two or three judges, but such a course is seldom adopted in practice. The High Court is based in Edinburgh, but the court goes on circuit to various towns, the commonest being Glasgow, Stirling, Oban, Inverness, Aberdeen, Dundee, Perth, Dumfries, Jedburgh and Ayr. Because of the volume of business there are frequently extra circuits in Glasgow, with two judges each holding a separate court.

As noted above, the High Court has exclusive jurisdiction to deal with treason, murder, rape, incest, deforcement of messengers and breach of duty by magistrates. Apart from that it deals with all offences which in the opinion of the prosecutor merit a sentence in excess of two years imprisonment.

High Court as an Appeal Court: the Court of Criminal Appeal

122 This is the only appellate court in Scotland, and sits in Edinburgh. Appeals may be taken from any court, including the High Court itself, to the Court of Criminal Appeal which consists of three or more judges.[10] Appeals may be based on law or fact. The court will not re-hear the witnesses, nor consider fresh evidence and its verdict is final.[11] The prosecution has no right of appeal in cases where the trial is by indictment (i.e. before a jury).

[9] While the procurator fiscal initiates proceedings in such a way that they may ultimately be tried on indictment, such a decision is subject to review by the Lord Advocate—see para 195.

[10] In the case of H.M.A. v Kirkwood 1939 JC 36, 13 judges sat.

[11] For more details re Appeals, see para 231 et seq.

4. Persons Responsible for the Administration of Justice

The Legal Profession—the Judiciary—the Prosecutor—the Police.

Legal Education

123 The law degrees awarded by the Scottish Universities are the Bachelor of Laws (LL.B.) and Bachelor of Laws with Honours (LL.B. Hons.), the former having a three year course and the latter a four year course. Persons intending to practice law will probably study little other than legal subjects.[1] In addition, there are various post graduate degrees. The courses are designed with the concurrence and approval of the Faculty of Advocates and the Law Society of Scotland (the governing body for solicitors) so that candidates wishing to enter either branch of the legal profession may do so after practical training only, and without the need for further academic examinations, provided that certain prescribed subjects have been taken in the university degree.

The Legal Profession

124 There are only two branches of the legal profession—the advocate and the solicitor. Each branch of the profession has exclusive rights and duties. While an individual may move from one branch to the other, no one may belong to or practise simultaneously in both.

Advocates

125 The advocate specialises in the presentation of the case in court, advising on complicated issues of law (and in civil cases, is responsible for the drafting of the written pleadings). Apart from the accused in person, only an advocate has the right to plead before the High Court of Justiciary. The governing body is the Faculty of Advocates, the principal officer of which is the Dean. All advocates are based in Edinburgh, but have the right to appear in any court, anywhere in Scotland. There are no local Faculties or local advocates attached to individual courts. Provided the candidate has the required educational qualifications (usually a LL.B. degree with approved subjects), he may be admitted as an advocate after twenty-one months' apprenticeship in a solicitor's office followed by a period of about nine months' pupillage (called 'devilling') with a practising advocate, and on paying the requisite fee. An advocate will be known as a junior counsel, until he decides to become a Queen's Counsel, when he is known as a senior counsel. Since a Q.C. must be assisted by a junior counsel and his fees are

---

[1] Formerly the degrees were Bachelor of Law (B.L.), and Bachelor of Laws (LL.B.), the latter being preceded by the student having an M.A. or B.A. degree. Under the present system a candidate not wishing to practice law may include in his degree various subjects of a non-legal nature.

higher, an advocate will not become a Q.C. until he has acquired a certain experience, skill and reputation. Not all advocates become Q.C.'s, the decision being left to the individual advocate, although the appointments are formally made by the Queen on the recommendation of the Lord Justice General.[2] Each advocate works on his own behalf, partnerships or fee sharing being forbidden.

An advocate may not be instructed direct by a client, but only through the offices of a solicitor. Hence while an accused may chose a particular advocate by requesting his solicitor to instruct him, in practice, the accused has no choice, this decision being taken by his solicitor. Furthermore in conducting the case, the advocate is completely independent and may act according to his own discretion and judgement, regardless of the wishes of his client, although it is usual and advisable to consult the client before taking any drastic step. The client is of course free at any time to dismiss his advocate and request that another be employed, or as sometimes happens in criminal cases, conduct his own case in person.[3] An advocate is not liable in damages for wrong advice in law, negligence, mistake, indiscretion, error of judgement, or the mismanagement of the case.

In so far as the criminal courts are concerned, all cases in the High Court are defended by advocates and often by Senior Counsel; in the sheriff and jury courts, the appearance of an advocate is quite common, although an appearance by Senior Counsel is not so common as in the High Court; in the sheriff summary court, the appearance of an advocate is fairly uncommon, although defences undertaken by senior or junior counsel are not unknown, especially if the client is of sufficient means, or if the issue raised is of importance.

Solicitors

126 The solicitor is responsible for all legal business where an advocate is not employed. He deals with all matters such as the sale of property, wills, business transactions, taxation, etc. In so far as criminal litigation is concerned, he is entitled to appear in all criminal courts except the High Court of Justiciary, and the majority of cases in the sheriff summary court are defended by solicitors, as are many of the cases in the sheriff and jury court. If the case is conducted in the High Court, or if the solicitor or client desire an advocate in an inferior court, the solicitor will instruct an advocate, in which case most of the preparation for the case will be done by the solicitor, while the actual pleading is left in the hands of the advocate. The solicitor comes into direct contact with the client, as opposed to the advocate who may never see his client until the start of the trial.

To qualify as a solicitor, the candidate must have the necessary educational qualifications—usually an LL.B. degree from a Scottish University, provided the candidate has studied the subjects specified by the Law Society of Scotland, which is the governing body for this branch of the profession. As an alternative it is competent to sit the examinations set by the Law Society of Scotland. Thereafter it is necessary to undergo a period of apprenticeship with a qualified solicitor, though in many instances the apprenticeship may be commenced before the end of the

---

[2] In 1972 there were approximately 300 advocates at the Scottish bar, although all were not in actual practice. Approximately 25% were Q.C.'s.

[3] Occasionally an unscrupulous accused person may dismiss his counsel after any complex legal point has been dealt with, and thereafter conduct his own defence, hoping to gain from the greater latitude allowed by the court to unrepresented accused, or to benefit from the sympathy of the jury.

academic course. The period of the apprenticeship varies from two to five years, depending on the nature and type of academic qualifications, at the end of which the candidate will be admitted as a solicitor. While many solicitors practice in their own names, the majority seek partnerships in small or large firms[4]. If a solicitor is guilty of professional misconduct or is convicted of dishonesty, he is liable to be disciplined by the Solicitors' Discipline (Scotland) Committee which is appointed by the Lord President[5] on the recommendation of the Law Society of Scotland.

There are various small professional societies, some of which have specialised functions, the principal ones being the Society of Writers to the Signet (W.S.), the Society of Solicitors in the Supreme Courts (S.S.C.), the Royal Faculty of Procurators in Glasgow, and the Society of Advocates in Aberdeen (which last is a body of solicitors, not advocates). Each sheriff court district also has its own local Law Society which has certain minor functions. None of these societies is of any relevance when considering the rights and duties of a solicitor before a criminal court.

Legal Aid in Criminal Cases

127 There is an official system for legal aid in criminal cases whereby the expenses of a solicitor or counsel are paid from public funds. Each sheriff court maintains a list of solicitors who are prepared to act in criminal cases. These solicitors work a rota system taking it in turn to act on behalf of accused persons appearing in custody before the court for the first time. As a result all accused persons have the opportunity to be legally represented on their first appearance in custody, an opportunity of which most accused avail themselves. (In 1971, 31,765 accused were given such legal representation.) It is, of course, open for an accused to refuse to be legally represented, or to instruct another solicitor privately. When an accused agrees to be represented by the 'legal aid' solicitor (known as the 'duty solicitor') he has, of course, no choice, having to accept the solicitor who for the time being is on duty. The accused is not required to make any financial contribution and the solicitor's expenses are, within certain limits, met by the state. If the accused is not in custody, or if at his first appearance he pleads 'not guilty' to the charge and the case is sent for trial, he may further apply for legal aid and whether or not this is granted will depend on the accused's financial resources. Should legal aid be granted, the fees due to his solicitor, and in certain circumstances, his advocate will be met by public funds within certain limits. Similar rules apply if the accused is to be tried on indictment. For such purposes, the accused has freedom of choice as to his solicitor.

As a result of this practice, in many of the areas where there are busier courts, there are certain solicitors, who while not dealing exclusively with criminal business, tend to specialise in such cases. While the same situation does not apply to advocates, there are some advocates who have a distinguished reputation for pleading in criminal cases.

By such a system of legal aid, an accused person is not only ensured legal representation, but may choose his legal advisor—all at no cost to himself.

The Judiciary

128 In Scotland, unlike certain continental countries such as France, there is no distinct profession of judges, where the candidate undergoes special training then

---

[4] In 1971 there were 3,267 solicitors in practice, of whom 313 were women.

[5] The Lord President is the Senior Scottish judge—see also footnote 6 to para 129.

starts his legal career as a judge. The judges for the various criminal courts are appointed in different ways.

High Court of Justiciary

129 The 'justiciar' was a Norman official, delegated by the king to administer justice and introduced in Scotland about the 12th century. They held courts known as 'ayres' which continued until 1672 when the High Court of Justiciary was founded. The senior judge is called the Lord Justice General, and the next in seniority the Lord Justice Clerk. In addition there are sixteen other judges known as the Lords Commissioners of Justiciary.[6] In theory all appointments to the bench are made by the Queen, but in practice the Secretary of State makes judicial appointments on the advice of the Lord Advocate, except for the two senior posts which are decided by the Prime Minister on the advice of the Lord Advocate. Appointments are always made from practising advocates, and it was not uncommon for the Lord Advocate to nominate himself especially to the post of Lord Justice General. In recent times, one Lord Advocate refused to nominate himself for the judicial bench, and another Lord Advocate nominated a serving judge for the office of Lord Justice General when that post fell vacant in 1972. Whether such a trend will continue in the future remains to be seen. On being appointed, the judge receives the courtesy title of 'Lord'. All appointments are full-time.

A judge formerly retained his post 'aut vitam aut culpam'—i.e. until he died, or unless he committed a flagrant offence. In 1959, a rule was introduced by which judges appointed after that date must retire on reaching the age of 75 years. In 1972, the age of the youngest judge was 48 years, and the average age was 62 years. To remove a judge from office, it is necessary to have the approval of both Houses of Parliament. When a judge retires, he is paid a pension according to his salary and years of service, the maximum being half salary after fifteen years service.

The role of the judge in court is to settle any points of law that may arise; to decide on the merits of the case as presented by the parties thereto; to determine any penalty; and generally to ensure that justice is 'not only done, but seen to be done'. Judges may not be sued for anything done by them while sitting in their judicial capacity.

The Sheriff Court

130 Scotland is divided into sheriff court districts or sheriffdoms, each of which has a Sheriff Principal, who is an advocate. He has no duties as regards criminal business, except for the administration of the sheriff court. The judges proper in the sheriff court are known as sheriffs, and are appointed by the Lord Advocate, from among advocates or solicitors with at least five years' practising experience. The vast majority of appointments are made from the advocate branch of the profession. Some appointments are full time, others are part-time, depending on the volume of work in a particular court. Since the sheriff court deals with criminal as well as civil litigation, and since there is no form of training before appointment this can result in the judge, on taking office in the sheriff court having little experience in one of these branches of litigation. However, appointments are usually made from among persons with a wide knowledge of the law, and in the

---

[6] While the High Court of Justiciary deals exclusively with criminal matters, the same judges also sit in the Court of Session, which is the highest civil court. In the Court of Session, the Lord Justice General is known as the Lord President.

busier courts in particular, many of the sheriffs are Senior Counsel. The sheriff has the power to appoint honorary sheriff substitutes, either laymen or lawyers, partly as an honour, and partly to assist with the work in case of need. An honorary sheriff, whether or not legally qualified, has the same powers and duties as a full-time sheriff, and although it is unusual for a layman to act as a sheriff for trials, this can happen, and such sheriffs frequently sit on the bench dealing with accused persons appearing in court in custody for the first time.

The rôle of a sheriff in court, and his conditions of service are similar to those of a judge in the High Court, except that his status is lower. The Secretary of State for Scotland may remove a sheriff from office on the grounds of inability or mis-behaviour if he receives a report to that effect from the Lord President of the Court of Session and the Lord Justice Clerk. In practice, a sheriff guilty of misconduct or of committing a criminal offence may be asked to resign by the Lord Advocate, an invitation which would never be refused. A sheriff may not be elected to parliament, nor may he act directly or indirectly as an agent for any candidate for any election in his jurisdiction.

Justice of the Peace, Burgh and Police Courts

131 The judges in such courts are all part-time, and mostly, composed of persons with no legal qualifications, the main exception being Glasgow where the stipendiary magistrate is full-time and legally qualified. As noted above, such courts have a legally qualified clerk of court, who is usually a local solicitor acting in a part-time capacity. While the judges are left to decide on verdict and sentence, they will normally consult the clerk on any legal issue or points of procedure that arise.

The Public Prosecutor

132 Prior to 1587, most prosecutions were left in the hands of the injured party, although the King's Advocate, otherwise known as the Lord Advocate usually joined the prosecution for the king's interest partly in order to preserve law and order, and partly out of financial interest as any fines went to the royal treasury. The instigation of criminal proceedings was however in the hands of the victim. In 1587, the Lord Advocate was empowered by an Act of Parliament to instigate criminal proceedings 'although the parties be silent or would otherwise privily agree'. This power of the Lord Advocate to prosecute without the concurrence of any private party made him the master of the instance, giving him an almost absolute right to decide who should be prosecuted, and, in the absence of legal provision to the con-trary, in which court the case should be tried. The Lord Advocate is responsible for and directs all public prosecutions in Scotland. He is assisted by the Solicitor General for Scotland and seven Advocate Deputes. The Lord Advocate and the Solicitor General are known as the Law Officers of the Crown, and the Advocate Deputes as Crown Counsel.

The Lord Advocate

133 The Lord Advocate and the Solicitor General are appointed by the Queen on the recommendation of the Prime Minister. They are selected from among the leading senior counsel, and since they are political appointments, change office every time there is a change in government. The Advocate Deputes are advocates appointed for this task by the Lord Advocate. While it was normal practice for them also to change office whenever a new Lord Advocate was appointed, a recent Lord Advocate on taking office, although of a different political party from his predecessor, continued to employ the same Advocate Deputes. Whether this is a unique occurrence, or will establish a precedent for the future remains to be seen. Advocate Deputes are not prohibited from continuing to deal with civil cases.

The Crown Agent; Crown Office

134 The Lord Advocate has a permanent staff, known as the Crown Office, which is headed by the Crown Agent. All these officials are permanent civil servants, with the same conditions of service as other branches of the British civil service. Since the staff are permanent, they do not change with each Lord Advocate. Appointments to Crown Office are made from the procurator fiscal service, which the Lord Advocate has the responsibility of administering as well as directing. Much of the routine administration, together with the giving of advice and instructions devolves on the staff of Crown Office. They also act as instructing solicitors to Crown Counsel in appeals before the High Court.

The Procurator Fiscal

135 The procurator fiscal is the prosecutor in the sheriff court, although his duties range much further. The office of procurator fiscal was known in the 16th century when he was an officer employed by the sheriff with the duty of collecting fines imposed by the court. Such fines were paid into a fund known as 'The Fisk', and the procurator fiscal appeared at the trial just before sentence was imposed. While the sheriff acted both as prosecutor and judge in his own court, the prosecuting duties were taken over by the procurator fiscal by the time of the 17th century. The sheriff still retained the power to investigate offences and take statements from witnesses but the procurator fiscal also gradually took over these duties, although he was still required to report the results of his investigations to the sheriff. By the middle of the 19th century, the procurator fiscal became responsible to the Lord Advocate, rather than to the sheriff. In 1927 the appointment of procurators fiscal was placed in the hands of the Lord Advocate and since then all procurators fiscal and their deputes have been whole-time civil servants.[7] Today the procurator fiscal is completely independent of the sheriff.

Career Structure in the Procurator Fiscal Service: Conditions of Service

136 All procurators fiscal, being full-time civil servants have the same general conditions of service as other branches of the British civil service. Applicants for the procurator fiscal service must be qualified as a Scottish solicitor or advocate. Formerly the applicant had to be aged between twenty-six and thirty-five years, but these rules have recently been waived. When a vacancy occurs in the service, it will be advertised and applicants will be subjected to a short interview by a civil service board, consisting usually of the Crown Agent, several senior civil servants, a senior procurator fiscal and a professor of law. The purpose of the interview is to assess the candidate's character, personality and suitability for the job. The board will then report to the Lord Advocate, who alone has the right to appoint a procurator fiscal. The procurators fiscal are attached to each sheriff court and the whole service is divided into grades, depending on the volume of work in each court. The offices of Glasgow and Edinburgh are given special grades, thereafter there are six

---

[7] Apart from a few part-time procurators fiscal in remote country districts who are solicitors in private practice.

posts classed as 'A' grade, twelve as 'B' grade and twelve as 'C' grade. A procurator fiscal may have depute assistance depending on the grade and pressure of work. In Glasgow the procurator fiscal has two assistant fiscals, four senior deputes and sixteen deputes; in Edinburgh the procurator fiscal has one assistant fiscal, one senior depute and five deputes; the 'A' grade procurators fiscal each have two or three deputes; the 'B' grade fiscals each have at least one depute, some having more. Altogether there are thirty-two procurators fiscal and fifty-six deputes. In recent years the number of deputes employed has continued to increase with the volume of work.[8]

137 Deputes are placed on two gradings and promotion to the second grade will be considered if the depute has six year's experience (less in exceptional cases), reached the age of thirty-two years and his standard of work is satisfactory. A person entering the service will first be appointed as a depute. Although no special training is required before entry, the procurator fiscal is responsible for guiding and assisting his deputes, who must obey his instructions. When a promotion vacancy occurs, it will be circulated throughout the service and any serving fiscal may apply. Candidates considered suitable for the post will be subjected to a short interview by a board, the composition of which depends on the seniority of the post. For the senior posts, the Lord Advocate and the Crown Agent usually sit on the board. As with initial entry, only the Lord Advocate may make an appointment, which he will do after hearing the results of the board. Promotion to a senior post would seem, by present practice, to be barred to anyone over the age of fifty-eight years. Until recently, the procurator fiscal was only required to make an annual report to Crown Office concerning deputes on the lowest grade, but this practice has now been extended to cover all members of the procurator fiscal service. The contents of the report which are confidential, not even being known to the subject of the report, cover all aspects of a fiscal's duties and his general relationship with other staff and the public. The reports are studied should the applicant apply for promotion.

All procurators fiscal must retire on reaching the age of sixty-five years. On retiral, they are paid a capital sum and an annual pension calculated according to their final salary and years of service. Pensions are reviewed regularly, as are salary scales, in particular to ensure they keep abreast with the cost of living. Apart from salary, no other allowances are paid to a procurator fiscal. Since all posts are full-time, there is a prohibition on undertaking any other form of professional practice or paid remuneration except for minor fees received in respect of academic or similar work, which must first be sanctioned by Crown Office. Procurators fiscal must not act as political agents or stand as candidates in any political elections; nor assist in any way at any elections. A procurator fiscal must live within his district (although this rule is not strictly enforced). When a procurator fiscal requires to leave his district for more than a brief period, he must, before doing so, report the fact to Crown Office. Any procurator fiscal guilty of breach of discipline or improper conduct may be dealt

---

[8] While the 'C' grade procurators fiscal do not have deputes, they usually arrange for a local solicitor to assist during holiday periods, etc. While such solicitors are called 'deputes', they are part-time only, and not in the same category as the deputes above discussed. The figures quoted refer to the position in 1972. On 1st January 1975, when Scotland is to be divided into six Sheriffdoms, each Sheriffdom will have a Regional procurator fiscal who will have certain administrative duties over the other procurator fiscals in the Sheriffdom.

with by the Lord Advocate, whose powers include dismissal.[9] In addition, he is bound by the terms of service applicable to all British civil servants.

138 Unlike the Lord Advocate who is answerable only to parliament in respect of the discharge of his duties, and who may not be sued, the procurator fiscal may be found liable in damages to anyone he has prosecuted, if it can be shown he has acted maliciously or without probable cause. In practice such actions are exceedingly rare, and as far as is known, none has ever been successful.

Prosecutors in the Criminal Courts

139 Before turning to consider the exact duties of the procurator fiscal, it is necessary to specify the prosecutors in the various courts:

High Court. In the High Court, whether sitting as a trial court, or an appeal court, only advocates have a right of audience. The prosecution case is conducted by one of the Advocate Deputes, although in cases of exceptional importance, this may be done by the Solicitor General, and even by the Lord Advocate in person (this last course being most unusual in modern times).

Sheriff Court. The procurator fiscal (or his depute). In theory, one of the Crown counsel is always available to conduct the prosecution in complicated or serious cases, but in practice this is seldom if ever done.

Justice of the Peace, Burgh, Police Courts. Prior to May 1975, the prosecutor was a local solicitor acting in a part-time capacity and employed by the local authority.[10] Such prosecutors were not subject to the control of the Lord Advocate.[11] When these courts are replaced by District Courts in May 1975, in many instances, the responsibility for prosecuting will be given to the procurator fiscal. Until such time as procurators fiscal are appointed to all district courts, local prosecutors will be appointed as before, with the exception that they will be subject to the control of the Lord Advocate.

Powers and Duties of the Procurator Fiscal

140 The procurator fiscal is subject to the direction of and control by the Lord Advocate, who issues general instructions in a Book of Regulations to all procurators fiscal concerning the conduct of their duties. In addition, from time to time the Lord Advocate issues instructions concerning specific matters by means of Crown Office circulars. The advantage of this system is that it promotes a high degree of uniformity of procedure and practice. The Lord Advocate may also issue instructions concerning the conduct of any particular case. Such instructions however do not derogate from the important functions of the procurator fiscal, who has been described as 'central to the criminal administration of Scotland'. A summary of his powers and duties may be given as:

(1) The responsibility for investigating all criminal offences committed in his district. In the first instance most inquiries are made by the police, who report the results to the procurator fiscal. He will direct what further steps

---

[9] A procurator fiscal may only be dismissed from his post upon a report by the Lord Justice General and Lord Justice Clerk to the Lord Advocate. In practice, however, such a situation would probably be met by the Lord Advocate asking the person concerned to resign.

[10] Except in Glasgow where a full time prosecutor is employed.

[11] Who may however instruct the police to report certain classes of offences competent for such courts direct to the procurator fiscal of the sheriff court.

(if any) should be taken and has the power to issue instructions to the police. In certain instances he may also take charge of the inquiry from the moment when the offence was discovered.[12] He may also examine any witnesses and must do so in all cases to be tried on indictment.

(2) The responsibility for investigating all sudden, unexpected or suspicious deaths.[13]

(3) The conduct of the prosecution of all cases taken in the sheriff court (either on summary complaint or trial on indictment before a jury). This includes a discretion as to whether or not to prosecute, and in the first instance, in the absence of any statutory provision, a discretion as to whether or not an offence should be placed before the summary court, or tried on indictment. (Although before a case may be placed before the court on indictment, the instructions of Crown Counsel must be obtained, so that a decision by the procurator fiscal to place an accused on indictment is subject to review);[14] in the course of the trial he has a discretion to abandon the proceedings permanently or temporarily,[15] which has the effect of terminating the trial; if the accused is convicted, the procurator fiscal may move the court not to sentence the accused, which is binding on the court.[16]

(4) In High Court cases, the procurator fiscal investigates and prepares the case for trial (including examining all the witnesses); attends to the preliminary procedural steps and first calling of the case in court; assists Crown Counsel at the trial, where he acts as the 'instructing solicitor'.

(5) Deciding in the first instance whether or not an appeal should be taken against any verdict in the sheriff summary court (although this decision is subject to confirmation by Crown Counsel) and drafting answers against any appeal lodged by the accused in the sheriff court (whether summary or indictment).

(6) Presenting evidence at all Fatal Accident inquiries.

(7) Investigating all fires and explosions where there is substantial damage or suspicious circumstances, and investigating all other unusual or suspicious occurrences.

(8) Investigating complaints made against the police, especially where there is a suggestion that a police officer has been guilty of a criminal offence.

(9) Investigating 'Ultimus Haeres Estates'—i.e. where a person dies intestate leaving no known heirs, and the estate is due to fall to the Crown.

(10) Dealing with all articles found as 'Treasure Trove'—i.e. if anyone finds treasure or articles of antiquarian interest, it is his duty to notify the procurator fiscal.

(11) At a local level, to give legal advice concerning criminal matters to the police, Customs and Excise, the Post Office, government departments and officials and a large number of official and semi-official bodies and persons on whose behalf the procurator fiscal conducts criminal proceedings.[17]

[12] For further detail see para 163—'Preliminary inquiries'.
[13] For further detail see para 165.
[14] For further detail see para 195.
[15] By deserting the case 'simpliciter' or 'pro loco et tempore'—see para 199.
[16] See para 208.
[17] While in smaller offices the procurator fiscal will perform all of these duties, in the larger offices with several deputes, it is not uncommon to work a rota system.

General Attitude of the Prosecutor

141 The qualities required by the prosecutor are thoroughness, courage, fairness, and most of all, impartiality. In court he must be candid and frank. He must not withhold evidence or knowingly misquote the substance of a document, a witness's testimony, an opposing argument, a text book or a decision. He has a primary duty not of securing a conviction but of assisting the court and trying to secure that justice is done. He must not press the prosecution case unduly. 'His function is to assist the jury in arriving at the truth. He must not urge any argument that does not carry weight in his own mind, or try to shut out any legal evidence, that would be important to the interests of the person accused. It is not his duty to obtain a conviction by all means; but simply to lay before the jury the whole of the facts which compose his case, and to make these perfectly intelligible and to see that the jury are instructed with regard to the law and are able to apply the law to the facts. It cannot be too often made plain that the business of counsel for the Crown is fairly and impartially to exhibit all the facts to the jury. The Crown has no interest in procuring a conviction. Its only interest is that the right person should be convicted, that the truth be known, and that justice should be done'.[18] For the Crown to persist in a charge in the knowledge of the existence of reliable evidence proving the innocence of the accused which is concealed from the accused would 'constitute a violation of every tradition observed by the Crown Office.[19] Although the Crown has no duty to discover a line of defence, once it knows of one it is its duty not to conceal it. The Crown frequently makes such evidence available to the court or the defence. It is normal practice for the Crown to cite all the witnesses and lodge all the productions, whether or not in favour of the Crown case, or even apparently irrelevant, so that such evidence will be available to the defence at the trial, should the defence wish it placed before the court. At the trial, if the prosecutor does not actually lead such evidence, he will at least 'tender' it to the defence. Furthermore, while the defence has the right to cite witnesses for the trial, the prosecutor will frequently agree to cite such witnesses on behalf of the defence, a citation from the prosecutor being more efficacious. To illustrate the unbiased attitude of the prosecutor, in the case of H.M. Advocate v Harrison,[20] where the accused was charged with murder, but sought in his defence to establish that he was only guilty of culpable homicide, the prosecutor having examined the results of medical reports on the accused, asked the court to acquit the accused on the grounds of insanity.

Relationship of the Prosecutor to the Judiciary

142 The prosecutor is independent of the judiciary and no judge can compel or recommend or direct him what he should do. He is the 'master of the instance', being entirely responsible for the conduct of the prosecution. The prosecutor does not however have any advantage over the defence. As parties to the case both have equal rights, privileges, duties and status. Both are equally bound to submit to the rulings of the court.

As far as career structure is concerned, the prosecutor is inferior to the judge, the latter always having superior salary, conditions of service and status. In court, the prosecutor must always address the judge as 'My Lord'. Any disrespectful conduct by a prosecutor could render him liable to proceedings for contempt of court.

[18] Kenny—Outlines of Criminal Law (16th ed.) 504–505.
[19] Gordon—Northern Ireland Legal Quarterly Vol. 19 No. 3. September 1968.
[20] 1968 32 J. Crim. L. 119.

A sheriff may be promoted to Lord Advocate. The Lord Advocate may become a judge in the High Court. Although it is competent for a procurator fiscal to become a sheriff, in recent times this has only happened once. The prevailing view appears to be that a prosecutor with long service is unsuitable for judicial office, and lacks experience in civil law (which he would be required to judge in addition to criminal cases). Apart from these few exceptions it is virtually true to say that interchange between the two professions is non-existent.

The Police: Relationship to the Prosecutor

143 Formerly each county, each large town and each city had its own police force, but due to recent amalgamations, many of the smaller forces have disappeared, with the result that now, a single force may cover one or more counties and all the towns therein. This division of forces is purely for administrative purposes, and since the same conditions of service, legal rules and procedures apply to all forces, the police service for practical purposes is a national one. The police of a particular district not only make use of their own knowledge, but may enlist the advice or assistance of experts from other forces. There is close collaboration and liaison between all the police forces.

Each police force is headed by a Chief Constable, and there are various ranks below him, the lowest being the police constable. For administrative purposes only, the police come under the control of the Secretary of State for Scotland. Each police force usually has various specialist sections such as the detective branch (Criminal Investigation Department), road traffic police, crime prevention, etc. Some police forces have sections to deal with drug offences, complicated frauds, and the like, and may have special laboratories, analysts and other experts. Most forces have police surgeons who may be full-time, or a local doctor acting in a part-time capacity. In addition there are various 'crime squads' consisting of very experienced officers who may be called in to investigate serious or complicated cases, sometimes falling within the jurisdiction of various police forces.

The police are bound to comply with any instructions the Lord Advocate may from time to time issue to any Chief Constable. In relation to the investigation of offences, the chief constable must comply with the instructions of the prosecutor.[21] In practice the procurator fiscal frequently gives such instructions and there exists a very close working arrangement with the police. The ultimate responsibility for the investigation of criminal offences lies with the procurator fiscal and not with the police. He is completely independent of the police who are subordinate to him, and subject to his control. The police do however have a certain limited discretion as to which cases they must report to the procurator fiscal. As a general rule the police need only report cases where there is sufficient evidence to justify taking proceedings against a particular accused. If there is doubt as to the sufficiency of evidence, the procurator fiscal will decide. In other cases, the procurator fiscal may order that certain offences need not be reported as he will refuse to prosecute them—for example, although the statutory speed limit in 'built up' areas is 30 m.p.h., most procurators fiscal will not prosecute unless the speed is 40 m.p.h. or greater, hence the police are instructed not to report any offences where the speed is less than 40 m.p.h.

[21] Police (Scotland) Act 1967, Section 17. See also Smith v H. M. Advocate 1952 SLT 286.

The Victim of a Criminal Offence: Private Prosecutions

144 Before leaving the subject of persons responsible for the administration of justice, it is perhaps appropriate to mention briefly the rights given to the victim of a criminal offence. Originally the person injured by the offence or certain of his relatives were entitled to prosecute the offender. This right was gradually eroded as the powers given to the Lord Advocate increased, and in particular by the Act of 1587 which gave the Lord Advocate a title to prosecute regardless of the wishes of the victim. While the victim's right to prosecute was not abolished, it gradually disappeared and he was only entitled to prosecute with the concurrence of the Lord Advocate. In addition a private prosecutor required to pay the costs of the prosecution and risked being sued for damages if the accused was acquitted. As a result private prosecutions today are virtually unknown, and for practical purposes may be ignored.

A person wishing to institute proceedings must first obtain the concurrence of the public prosecutor, which would probably not be given until the latter had investigated the facts of the case. If the public prosecutor refuses to concur, the victim may apply to the High Court. In a case decided in 1909,[22] the court allowed the private prosecution although the Lord Advocate refused to concur. Before instituting proceedings, the private prosecutor is required to show that he is directly aggrieved or injured by the crime or is a person who has a substantial interest in the property involved in it. In 1961 in the case of McBain v Crichton, an office-bearer of a union of boys' clubs, having been refused the concurrence of the Lord Advocate, asked leave of the court to prosecute the seller of a book entitled 'Lady Chatterley's Lover' because it had shocked him personally and moreover he had a special concern with the welfare and morals of young persons. The court refused permission on the grounds that only the Lord Advocate may prosecute as the protector of the morals of a class of persons in the community.

The above rules apply to common law offences. As regards statutory offences, some statutes allow for private prosecution, but generally only if the person concerned can show injury suffered, danger incurred or other substantial interest. Other statutes confer upon specified bodies or officials the right to prosecute, for example local authorities may prosecute parents for not ensuring the school attendance of their children. Such prosecutions are conducted without the concurrence of the public prosecutor, and although they are properly classed as criminal proceedings, they are frequently spoken of as 'quasi criminal'. The prosecution is conducted by the private prosecutor, the public prosecutor having no knowledge of or concern with the action. The number of such cases is small.

Apart from the somewhat theoretical remedy of raising a private prosecution, the victim of a criminal offence may be entitled to raise a civil action against the accused, but unless the latter is a person of substance, or is covered by insurance against the wrong complained of, such actions would often prove fruitless, since even if successful, the victim of the offence would have little chance of recovering any damages awarded to him. To meet this deficiency in part, a scheme was recently introduced for compensation for victims of crimes of violence. Such victims may be entitled to compensation from public funds if certain conditions are met.

[22] J. & P. Coats Ltd. v Brown 1909 SC (J) 29.

5. General Principles of Scottish Criminal Procedure[1]

The Accusatorial System

145 It has been stated that the purpose of criminal proceedings is not so much to obtain a remedy for an injured person as to vindicate and enforce law and order, to maintain minimum standards of conduct, and to prevent and suppress unsocial, immoral or other detrimental conduct by punishing those who have infringed the code of conduct maintained by the criminal law.[2] In Scotland such aims are achieved by accusatorial rather than inquisitorial proceedings. At a criminal trial the evidence is placed before the court by the prosecution and defence and tested by means of rigorous questionning and examination by both parties. It is for the parties to the case to decide what evidence they will produce and elicit from the witnesses. The function of the judge is not to act as inquisitor and inquire into the matter, nor does he take part in the presentation of the evidence. He may not summon other or fresh witnesses or examine the witnesses themselves, apart from sometimes putting a few supplementary questions to clear up a matter on which he is still in doubt. The judge's role is to "preside at a forensic contest between two parties', to ensure that the rules of law are applied and to decide on a verdict (except where there is a jury). He must arrive at a decision on the facts as submitted to him for judgement. Although the following quotation comes from an English case, it also applies to Scotland— 'In the system of trial which we have evolved in this country, the judge sits to hear and determine the issues raised by the parties, not to conduct an investigation or examination on behalf of society at large . . . however a judge is not a mere umpire . . . his object above all is to find out the truth and to do justice according to the law'.[3]

Since the evidence is only fully examined at the trial, it follows that the emphasis is placed on the trial itself, rather than on any pre-trial inquiries. Each party makes his own separate pre-trial inquiries. The inquiries made by the prosecution are certainly both impartial and thorough and will cover any evidence in favour of the accused as well as that against him, but such inquiries by no means give a full picture of the case as neither the police nor the prosecution has the right to examine the accused who at no time may be questioned unless he voluntarily gives evidence at the trial itself. Furthermore the investigation by the prosecution is secret, the results not even being disclosed to the defence. Likewise, the accused is not required to state or reveal his defence until the close of the prosecution evidence at the trial. The purpose of the

---

[1] For France see para 31 et seq.
[2] Walker—'The Scottish Legal System'.
[3] Jones v N.C.B. (1957) 2 W.L.R. 760.

pre-trial inquiries by the prosecutor is to establish whether or not there is sufficient evidence, which if believed by the court, would entitle the court to convict the accused, or at least provide a reasonable case for the accused to answer. The pre-trial inquiries are therefore merely a preparation for the trial itself.

The purpose of the trial is to decide whether or not the accusation brought by the prosecutor is justified. The basic question at issue may be stated briefly as—is there sufficient evidence to prove that a criminal offence was committed, and if so, that the accused is the person responsible. This question is resolved purely by examining the evidence, and not by examining the accused. The prosecution having brought the accusation, must prove it and the accused does not require to prove his innocence or even justify his actions. As the trial takes the form of a contest between the parties, the accused can not be compelled to give evidence against himself. Since the issues must be resolved according to the evidence, the character of the accused is regarded as irrelevant, not being factual evidence. It follows therefore that it is incompetent for the prosecutor to refer in any way to the accused's character unless the accused himself puts his character in issue, or attacks the character of a prosecution witness.[4] There are one or two minor exceptions to this rule, as for example if the accused is charged with reset of stolen property, the prosecutor may lead evidence showing that the accused has previously been convicted of dishonesty; or where a witness accidentally refers to a previous conviction or other imputation against the character of the accused. If the prosecutor fails to observe these rules, the accused may appeal and the conviction will be quashed. While the facts of the case and the evidence are all that may be considered when deciding on verdict, if the accused is convicted, his full background and personality may then be examined by the court when deciding on an appropriate sentence. It would be true to say that the court only judges the facts when deciding on verdict, but judges the man when determining sentence.

Since the court may only consider the evidence as presented by the parties to the case—hence the saying 'Justice is blind'—and may not consider any other facts or evidence, the parties determine the issues for the court to decide. Since however, each party has an interest in the outcome of the case, it is necessary to have rules specifying what types of evidence may be brought before the court, and its method of presentation.[5] The general rule for judging whether or not evidence should be admitted before the court is 'fairness to the accused'.

Hence the system is accusatorial since it is left to the prosecutor to bring an accusation and produce evidence to justify it. The person so accused leaves it to the prosecutor to prove his guilt, and may answer the charges against him by remaining silent, by arguing that the prosecution evidence is not sufficient, by seeking to disprove the prosecution evidence, or by leading defence evidence to rebut that of the prosecution.

The criticisms commonly levelled against the inquisitorial system, which is the alternative, are that the liberty of the individual is infringed and the safeguards given to the defence are negligible when the person accused of an offence may be com-

---

[4] This can often lead to difficulties where the defence seek to put questions to a prosecution witness either to discredit him, or because the nature or conduct of the defence itself is such that it is necessary to raise specific facts which involve imputations on the character of that witness. In such cases the prosecutor may not attack the character of the accused, unless the judge rules that the attack by the defence consists of an attack of a general nature against the whole character of the witness.

[5] See paras 152–153.

pulsorily questioned both before and during the trial; that the course of the trial is largely predetermined by the pre-trial inquiries, such inquiries being secret, not subject to public scrutiny, and therefore not demonstrating publicly that they were performed in a way that was fair to the accused (the so-called 'confessions' which feature prominently in the trials in some communist countries being an obvious example); that since such pre-trial inquiries consider the defence as well as the prosecution evidence, the issues are not only stated, but settled before the trial itself, thus rendering the presumption of innocence of the accused a fiction, rather than a reality.

Onus of Proof: Pleas of 'Guilty': Presumption of Innocence

146 While the onus of proving the accused's guilt lies on the prosecutor, this will be discharged if the accused admits his guilt in court by 'pleading guilty'. An accused may do this when the case first calls in court at what is known as the 'Pleading Diet' or 'First Diet', or when the case later calls in court for trial, or at any stage during the trial itself.[6] When an accused pleads guilty the court will be given a summary of the facts of the case by the prosecutor, and no evidence will be led. If the plea is given during the course of the trial, no further evidence will be led thereafter. When the prosecutor has addressed the court, the defence may make a similar address, commenting on the facts of the case and giving any evidence in mitigation. The accused may plead guilty to the charge as libelled against him, or to part of the charge, or to a reduced charge, or if there is a multiplicity of charges to some of them only. The prosecutor is not compelled to accept a plea of guilty and may refuse to do so if he is not prepared to agree to the version of the facts given by the defence, or if he decides not to accept a plea to a partial or reduced charge, or if the plea involves only one of several charges. In the last case, if several charges are linked together, should the prosecutor accept a plea of guilty to one charge only, he may not make any reference to that charge at the subsequent trial of the remaining charges. (For example if an accused was charged with theft of a knife and assault by stabbing, if the accused pleaded guilty to the theft charge, the prosecutor could not refer to that at the trial of the assault charge, and in the absence of other evidence, might have difficulty in proving that the accused was in possession of a knife at the time of the stabbing.) If a guilty plea is not accepted by the prosecutor, no reference to this plea may be made at the subsequent trial. Once a plea of guilty has been rejected, the plea falls and the prosecutor may not accept it at a later stage in the proceedings unless it is again tendered. The advantages to the prosecutor of a plea of guilty are that he need not proceed to trial, his onus of proof is discharged, and the accused will be convicted (of which there can be no guarantee if the matter goes to trial). The advantages to the defence are that they may obtain some concessions such as a reduced charge, the dropping of certain charges and the possibility of a lighter sentence (the accused being able to maintain in mitigation that he had never sought to deny his guilt and repented of his actions—an attitude which is more difficult to explain if the accused had denied his guilt by pleading not guilty). Occasionally an accused person may plead guilty for the somewhat improper motive of preventing highly prejudicial

[6] In 1971, the total number of summary prosecutions taken in Scotland was 117,408 of which 108,286 were disposed of by pleas of guilty. The total number of proceedings on indictment was 2,831 of which 1,793 were disposed of by pleas of guilty. The corresponding figures for 1970 were: summary prosecutions 106,446—pleas of guilty, 97,596; proceedings on indictment 2,747—pleas of guilty, 1,843.

evidence, or emotive evidence being placed before the court at length and subjected to detailed examination at the trial. Since in a plea of guilty, the facts against him will be merely narrated briefly by the prosecutor, the accused has a better chance of urging a particular explanation or interpretation of these facts on the court, and in a light more favourable to the accused.

'Plea Bargaining'

These factors give rise to a practice which is described in America as 'plea bargaining'. Before the start of the trial the prosecution and defence (if the accused is legally represented) will frequently have a brief discussion of the case in an effort to find if any plea of guilty will be given, each party seeking to know if the other is prepared to make any concessions. Such discussions can not include sentence since that will only be considered by the judge after the plea is given and accepted. As the judge does not and may not take part in these discussions which are held outwith his presence, he will have no knowledge thereof until the plea is tendered in court, nor will the parties have any prior intimation of the judge's views.

If a plea to a reduced charge is accepted by the prosecutor, he is bound by his acceptance to the reduced charge; similarly if he accepts 'not guilty' pleas to some of the charges, he may not later proceed to trial on these charges, his acceptance of the 'not guilty' plea resulting in a verdict of 'not guilty' being recorded. The rule regarding the defence is not so strict in that if the accused tenders the plea by mistake, or due to a misapprehension or misunderstanding, the court has a discretion to allow him to withdraw his plea and substitute a plea of 'not guilty' in which case the matter will proceed to trial as if the 'guilty' plea had never been tendered. The judge is bound by such pleas and has no power to influence, alter, ignore or refuse to accept them. Since the parties determine what issues shall be presented before him, he is bound by the pleas adjusted between the parties.

If a plea of guilty is not given and accepted, the prosecutor must discharge his burden of proof and overcome the presumption of innocence by leading evidence. As noted above he may not examine the accused, unless the latter voluntarily gives evidence at the trial, nor need the accused do anything other than plead 'not guilty'. As also noted, the prosecutor may not put in issue the character of the accused. Apart from any question of prejudice that disclosure of bad character may bring, it is felt that the accused's guilt should be judged merely on the evidence of the particular case, and not on anything he may have done on a previous occasion.

Confessions

147 Even a confession[7] of guilt made by the accused prior to the trial is by itself not sufficient to discharge the burden of proof, overcome the presumption of innocence and entitle the prosecutor to ask for a conviction. He still requires to produce further evidence to corroborate the confession, although in the case of a detailed confession, the amount of corroboration required is minimal.

Presumptions

148 In some circumstances, however, if certain facts are proved by the prosecution, there is a presumption that the accused is guilty unless he gives a reasonable explanation consistent with his innocence or sufficient to raise a reasonable doubt as to his

[7] For fuller details re confessions, see paras 171 and 172.

guilt. If an accused person was proved to be in possession of stolen property shortly after the time of the theft, and there are other criminative circumstances, he will be presumed guilty of the theft in the absence of a satisfactory explanation. In a case of murder, the malice essential to the crime will be presumed where death occurs as the result of a voluntary act by the accused which is intentional and unprovoked. There are one or two other minor statutory provisions of similar import.

Special Defences

149 If the defence put forward a special defence such as self-defence, impeachment, alibi, or insanity the onus lies on the defence to prove it, not on the prosecution to disprove it. But if the defence are unable to prove such a special defence satisfactorily, the accused will still be entitled to an acquittal if his defence raises a reasonable doubt as to his guilt.

Standard of Proof

150 Having considered the burden of proof, it is necessary to consider what standard of proof is required. The prosecutor must prove his case beyond reasonable doubt. If at the end of the case the judge (or jury) have a reasonable doubt as to the accused's guilt, the accused must be given the benefit of that doubt and will be acquitted. This standard does not apply to the defence when the onus is on them, hence in a special defence, the accused need only satisfy the court on the balance of probability that the special defence is true; and if the defence fail to meet even this standard, the accused will still be entitled to an acquittal if his special defence raises a reasonable doubt as to his guilt.

Corroboration

151 'By the law of Scotland, no person can be convicted of a crime or statutory offence, except when the legislature otherwise directs,[8] unless there is evidence of at least two witnesses implicating the person accused with the commission of the crime or offence with which he is charged.'[9] This rule does not mean that two witnesses are required to prove every fact in the case. It is sufficient if one witness is corroborated by facts and circumstances spoken to by others. 'If one man swears that he saw the (accused) stab the deceased and others confirm his testimony with circumstances such as the (accused's) sudden flight from the spot, the blood on his clothes, the bloody instrument found in his possession, his confession on being taken, or the like, certainly these are as good, nay better even than a second testimony to the act of stabbing.'[10] The essential idea of corroboration is that the testimony of one witness whether direct to the actual commission of the crime, or indirect to some circumstance implicating the accused in the commission of the crime is enforced by testimony, direct or indirect of some other witness so that there are concurrent testimonies either to the same or to different facts, each pointing to the accused as the person by whom the crime was committed. All the essential facts of the case, including the identity of the accused (i.e. that the person in the dock is the person implicated in the crime) must be established by corroborated evidence. An exception to this rule is where the accused is charged with two or more offences linked to

---

[8] The statutory exceptions to this rule are very few and of minor importance.

[9] Morton v H.M. Advocate 1938 J.C. 50.

[10] Renton and Brown—Criminal Procedure 3rd edition; Hume ii 384

121

each other by a common method of commission, circumstances and time, each offence being spoken to by one witness only. All offences may be considered as corroborating each other in that taken together they establish a systematic course of criminal conduct. Hence an accused was convicted of nine charges of indecent assault, of which six rested on the evidence of a single witness, the offences being linked by the facts that all the offences were committed by an employer on female employees in his office premises over a period of three years.[11]

As noted above a confession by an accused person is not enough to convict him. It must be corroborated by a witness who saw him committing the crime, or speaking to facts and circumstances implicating him in its commission.

It follows that in some trials whether or not there is corroborated evidence is a matter of law for the judge to decide, or may be a matter of fact (i.e. interpretation of the evidence) for the jury to decide.

Admissibility of Evidence

152 For the evidence to be admitted in court it must be relevant, and it must be competent (i.e. properly obtained). To be relevant, the evidence must relate directly to the facts in issue, or the credibility of the witnesses. Whether or not evidence is relevant will be decided by the judge. Even if the evidence is relevant it will not be admitted if it is incompetent. When evidence has been obtained by irregular methods, the court has a discretion to decide on its admission. In making its decision, the court will consider the gravity of the crime, the seriousness or triviality of the irregularity, the urgency of the investigation (in the course of which the evidence was obtained), the authority and good faith of those who obtained it and the question of fairness to the accused person.[12] For example the court refused to admit documents recovered in the accused's business premises relating to frauds other than the frauds referred to in the search warrant, there being no urgency to excuse the seizing and retention of the documents and it having required an examination lasting several months to discover whether or not they related to any fraudulent matter;[13] on the other hand, the court admitted as evidence a stolen attaché case found by the police accidentally while searching the accused's house, with his permission, in connection with another matter.[14]

The best evidence must always be led. It is necessary if possible, to produce the eye witnesses of actions and the persons who made the statements or the documents. Sometimes this may be impossible, if the person concerned is dead, or the document destroyed. If the death or destruction is proved, then it is competent to adduce witnesses who can prove statements made by the deceased or produce a copy of the destroyed document. Hearsay evidence is therefore not admissible, except in the above circumstances—i.e. where the original witness is dead (or become insane). Another recent exception was in a case where two witnesses identified the accused at an identification parade prior to the trial, but failed to do so at the trial itself. The court admitted the evidence of the police officers to whom the witnesses had identi-

---

[11] Moorov v H.M. Advocate 1930 J.C. 68. It should also be noted that the accused can be convicted on finger-print evidence alone, provided that the finding of the print and the identification of it as the accused's are spoken to by two witnesses.

[12] Walker—The Law of Evidence in Scotland, p. 3.

[13] H.M. Advocate v Turnbull 1951 J.C. 96.

[14] H.M. Advocate v Hepper 1958 J.C. 39.

fied the accused at the parade. Statements made by a witness shortly after the crime may in certain circumstances be admitted to prove the credibility of the witness.

With regard to statements made by the accused, and the evidence of a co-accused, the rules applying thereto will be considered later.[15]

Oral Evidence

153 Both the prosecution and defence may cite witnesses to court. Provided their evidence is admissable, all persons so cited are competent and compellable, and all give evidence on oath (unless the witness is a child, feebleminded, or affirms).[16] With regard to compellability, a witness must answer all relevant questions unless the answer would lead to his conviction for a crime.[17] Any witness who refuses to take the oath, or answer any question, or prevaricates when answering is liable to be convicted of contempt of court. The accused can not be compelled to give evidence, but if he agrees to do so, he must take the oath and is treated as any other witness,[18] and similar rules apply to the spouse of an accused. If the accused fails to give evidence, the prosecutor is prohibited from commenting on such failure.

The court may only consider evidence that has been given verbally at the trial and all real evidence (i.e. documents, maps, clothing, weapons, etc.) must be spoken to by a witness. The only exception to this rule is where the parties jointly agree that certain evidence should be admitted and accepted as proved, or the defence make a unilateral admission to this effect. This is done by submitting a document known as a Minute of Admissions to the court stating precisely what evidence is agreed and therefore admitted without the necessity of calling witnesses or other proof. While the use of such Minutes both in solemn and summary procedure is not uncommon, it is by no means frequent.

Activities of the Press—Publicity

154 All trials must take place in open court to which the public is admitted. It is illegal to exclude the public except if the trial concerns indecent or sexual offences, or where there has been disorderly conduct or intimidation in the court, or in cases concerning national security,[19] or while a witness under the age of 17 years is giving evidence in a case concerning indecency or immorality. Where the court has been cleared because the case concerns indecency, the public should be readmitted so as to be present at the verdict and sentence.[20]

Since the public is admitted to the courts, it follows that the newspapers may report on any court proceedings except that it is unlawful to publish full details concerning 'any indecent matter, or indecent medical, surgical or physiological details being matters or details the publication of which would be calculated to injure public morals'.[21] Similarly, restrictions are made concerning publication of cases concerning juveniles.

[15] See paras 171, 172, 204.

[16] For further detail see para 202.

[17] Violation of professional secrecy is not a crime.

[18] For further detail see para 204.

[19] A procurator fiscal may not suggest the court be 'in camera' in the public interest without the prior authority of Crown Counsel.

[20] McDonald—Criminal Law of Scotland, 5th edition, p. 266. It should also be noted that the above rules do not apply to proceedings where the accused is a juvenile, such proceedings always being 'in camera'.

[21] Judicial Proceedings (Regulation of Reports) Act 1926.

Prior to the trial itself publication of statements regarding matters which are sub judice constitutes contempt of court[22] where the statements are prejudicial or calculated to cause prejudice to any party, or are in any way likely to impede a fair trial. To publish a statement of known facts is not contempt of court, but in practice, the courts tend to interpret the phrase 'calculated to cause prejudice' very widely in order to protect accused persons. The publication of an accused's photograph or statements made about the case by a potential witness constitute contempt to court. 'Indeed the publication of any information relating to a projected criminal trial other than the bare fact of an accused's arrest and committal on a particular charge may well be treated as contempt of court.'[23] The only exceptions to this rule are where the procurator fiscal decides to use the medium of the press or other publicity to trace a person who is either accused, or a possible witness (as a general rule he will not authorise publication of a photograph, unless a dangerous criminal such as an escaped murderer or murder suspect was at large); where the procurator fiscal gives a statement that a named person has been committed on a particular type of crime (in cases of murder or assault where there is considerable public interest, the name of the victim may also be given); where the procurator fiscal informs the Press that a dead body has been found together with any further factual information which does not affect the progress of the investigation or may be prejudicial to the accused. Procurators fiscal are expressly forbidden by the Lord Advocate to give any other information to the Press.[24]

Finally, in certain circumstances, publishing criticism of a judge (known as 'murmuring judges') may be a criminal offence. While criticism of a judge is competent, if it is disrespectful, such as stating that the judge had acted unfairly, that would constitute a criminal offence.

It therefore follows, that while the public and Press have full access to the courts, prior to the trial secrecy concerning the proceedings is observed, so that the case is not 'judged in advance' by the newspapers or the public.[25]

[22] Contempt of Court being a criminal offence.

[23] Gordon—The Criminal Law of Scotland, p. 1020.

[24] See also para 194.

[25] See also paras 35, 55.

6. Institution of Criminal Proceedings[1]

155 In most instances, and certainly in all serious cases, the responsibility for instituting criminal proceedings lies with the procurator fiscal. The exceptions to this rule are few or concern cases of minor importance, and are as follows:

(a) A private individual may seek to raise a private prosecution, but this is so uncommon, that for practical purposes it may be ignored.[2]

(b) A few public officials, and a few public bodies, such as county councils, may be allowed by statute to prosecute a certain type of offence.[3]

(c) The court may punish anyone guilty of contempt of court ex proprio motu if the contempt occurs in the court itself—i.e. during the proceedings in court. Contempt of court in this sense consists of improper conduct in the court, or prevarication or refusal to answer questions by a witness. The court may deal with the offence on the spot without the intervention of the procurator fiscal. If the contempt occurs outside the court, the procurator fiscal will commence proceedings in the usual way.

(d) Cases taken in the Justice of the Peace, Burgh or Police courts are not the responsibility of the procurator fiscal, since the prosecutor in these courts institutes and conducts the proceedings. Such a prosecutor is independent of the procurator fiscal.[4]

(e) In extremely rare circumstances the Lord Advocate might instruct a procurator fiscal to prosecute a particular case where the latter had not personally instituted the initial proceedings—the commonest example being where another procurator fiscal had instituted the proceedings, and on reporting the case to the Lord Advocate, the latter decided that a different procurator fiscal had the sole territorial jurisdiction to proceed, and accordingly he would send the case to the appropriate procurator fiscal with instructions to prosecute.[5]

[1] For comparison with France, see para 36–75.

[2] See para 144.

[3] See para 144.

[4] For details of the cases taken in such courts, see para 119. After 1975, the prosecutor will be the procurator fiscal.

[5] A simple illustration is where an accused is charged with theft in one district and was found in possession of stolen property in another. The Lord Advocate might direct that the accused be charged only with the reset of the stolen property, this being in the second district. There are various other such instances.

156 Apart from the above, the procurator fiscal has the sole responsibility for instituting criminal proceedings, regardless of whether the case will ultimately be taken in the sheriff summary court, sheriff and jury court, or High Court. He also has the responsibility of investigating all criminal offences committed in his district. Offences usually come to his notice in various ways such as a report from the court, from a public body or official, from a private individual, from the Lord Advocate, or from the police, the last being by far the commonest source.

The Court
157 If any court, whether civil or criminal considers that a witness might have committed perjury, it will report the matter to the procurator fiscal so that he may make inquiries and decide whether or not to take criminal proceedings (having made such inquiries, he must then report to Crown Counsel before instituting the proceedings). The court would also report to him any instance of contempt of court which had not been dealt with on the spot. The court may also formally report to him any facts which might constitute a criminal offence and which came to light during the trial of another offence.

Public Bodies and Officials
158 Since apart from the minor exceptions above mentioned only the public prosecutor institutes criminal proceedings, it follows that the procurator fiscal receives reports from a large number of public bodies and officials with requests to prosecute. These include the Department of Health and Social Security, the Post Office, H.M. Customs and Excise, the Companies Office, and all other government departments, the Registrar of Births, Marriages and Deaths, and numerous semi-official bodies such as the Royal Scottish Society for Prevention of Cruelty to Children, etc. On receipt of such a report the procurator fiscal may institute proceedings forthwith, or might instruct the police to make further inquiries. If he decides not to prosecute his decision is usually accepted, but occasionally the official concerned might arrange for the case to be reported to the Lord Advocate who will then instruct the procurator fiscal as to what further action is to be taken.

Private Individuals
159 While the majority of private individuals will make their complaint to the police in the first instance, some may decide to report direct to the procurator fiscal. Such complaints may naturally cover a wide range of subjects, some of them not even connected with the criminal law. If the complaint appears to have some substance, the procurator fiscal will usually make inquiries, either personally, or more usually by means of the police. Whether or not he notifies the complainer of what action is finally taken depends on the attitude of the individual procurator fiscal. Occasionally an individual who is not satisfied with the procurator fiscal's decision may write to the Lord Advocate who will then request the procurator fiscal to send him a report, after which he will instruct the procurator fiscal as to what action is to be taken. Should the complaint not concern a criminal matter, the procurator fiscal in the first instance will usually inform the complainer of this, often advising him to take private legal advice.

One of the commonest grounds for complaint by individuals is a complaint against the actions of one or more police officers. Considering the large numbers of persons with whom the police come into contact, such complaints are relatively few, but nonetheless, they are not uncommon. Some may be trivial, or activated by malice, while others are genuine. All such complaints are dealt with according to special procedure. In the first instance, the procurator fiscal will report the complaint to the Chief Constable who will arrange for a senior police officer from another area to make the initial inquiry. This officer's report will be given to the procurator fiscal who then makes a personal inquiry into the complaint, interviewing at least the complainer and the main witnesses and taking all other necessary steps to investigate the matter, regardless of the contents of the police report. He may not interview the officer against whom the complaint is made, or any other person who appears to be implicated. The procurator fiscal will then send a report together with the statements he has obtained to the Lord Advocate who will instruct what further action is to be taken. In this manner, since the procurator fiscal is completely independent of the police, complaints against the police are given a detailed and impartial examination.

The Lord Advocate

160 Very occasionally a private individual or public body may make a complaint direct to the Lord Advocate, in which case he will probably instruct the procurator fiscal to make inquiry and report back to him.

The Police

161 In Scotland, the majority of criminal offences are reported to the police in the first instance, so it follows that most of the reports received by the procurator fiscal come from the police.[6] As noted above,[7] the police have a certain limited discretion as to which offences they report to the procurator fiscal. In practice they need not report offences where there is clearly not enough evidence to justify taking proceedings against a named individual. Should there be any doubt as to this, the police will report the case for the procurator fiscal's decision. In other instances the procurator fiscal may indicate that certain very minor offences need not be reported, as he will exercise his discretion and refuse to prosecute.[8]

The report submitted by the police usually commences by giving the accused's name, age and address, then gives a draft of the charge which the police think appropriate—viz. 'You did on 1st November 1971 in the house at 10 High Street, Glasgow assault C.D. and strike him with your fists'. There follows either a summary of the evidence by the constable investigating the offence, or more usually the statements obtained from the witnesses[9] by that constable. Thereafter come the statements of any police witnesses, which, where the accused has been cautioned and charged [10] with the offence by the police, will include any reply by the accused. The report will conclude by giving a brief history of the accused, usually contained in a few lines viz.—'The accused is married and has three children. He lives at the address specified and is employed as a labourer earning £20 per week'. If there is any unusual information of specific relevance to the case, that will also be given. Should the case go to court, that will be all the information about the accused available

---

[6] While no accurate figures are available, at a guess, the police are responsible for about 95% of the reports received by the procurator fiscal.

[7] See para 143.

[8] See para 143.

[9] These statements are not signed by the witness.

[10] See paras 170 and 171.

unless after conviction, the accused supplies further detail, or the court requests a full background report on the accused.[11] If the accused has any previous convictions details of these will also be given in the police report. In complex cases where there are many items seized as evidence, the report may also contain a 'list of productions'. The report is signed by the officer who compiled it, who is usually the officer responsible for the investigation. Before being sent to the procurator fiscal, the report is usually checked by a superior police officer, if the reporting officer is a constable. While there is not a standard form of police report, all reports follow the above lines. The statements in the police report are all written in narrative form, having been compiled from answers given to the constable and which are contained in rough form in his police notebook. This notebook is retained by the constable and may be used by him with the court's permission, when he is giving evidence at the trial, either to refresh his memory, or if the credibility of a witness is at issue, to determine the statement made by the witness to the constable.

PRELIMINARY INQUIRIES

162 Since by Scottish procedure the accused always appears in court on an occasion prior to the trial, and on that occasion may tender a plea of guilty,[12] it is convenient to consider the preliminary inquiries in two stages, firstly those before the accused's first appearance, and secondly those after such appearance, but prior to the trial. With regard to the first stage, a further distinction must be drawn between (a) the initial inquiry seeking to establish if an offence has been committed and who is responsible therefor, and (b) the continuation of the inquiry after sufficient evidence has been obtained to justify a particular individual being considered as the accused, a position which will be arrived at either by the police in the course of their inquiry, or by the decision of the procurator fiscal to institute proceedings.

Prior to the First Appearance by the Accused

163 The purpose of the preliminary inquiries is to provide the procurator fiscal with sufficient information to allow him to decide whether or not to institute proceedings, and the form that any such proceedings should take.

As noted above, the procurator fiscal is responsible for the investigation of all criminal offences committed in his district and has the power to issue instructions to the police for this purpose. In practice, in most minor or straightforward cases, the police make the investigation and the first knowledge which the procurator fiscal will have of the offence is when he receives the police report. In serious or complicated cases, the police will normally inform the procurator fiscal either at the outset of the inquiry, or shortly thereafter; in offences such as murder the police will notify him immediately the offence is discovered. As soon as he is informed of the offence, the procurator fiscal takes personal control of the investigation and may attend the scene of the crime, direct what steps should be taken to preserve or obtain

[11] See para 208.

[12] In summary proceedings the accused is given a copy of the charge on a document known as a 'complaint', and on being brought before the court, is asked if he pleads 'guilty' or 'not guilty'. In solemn proceedings he is given a copy of the charge (which need not necessarily be in its final form) on a document called a 'petition'. He appears in private before the sheriff and although he is not asked to plead to the charge, he may indicate that he is willing to plead 'guilty' by notifying the procurator fiscal by means of a 'Section 31 letter'. This is discussed in full detail in paras 186 and 187.

evidence, and generally take all necessary action to ensure that the offence is properly investigated. The amount of discretion left to the police to take independent action will depend on the circumstances of the case, together with the attitude and instructions of the individual procurator fiscal. There is usually a good working relationship between the police and the procurator fiscal, the latter being 'on call' at all times for this purpose.

Use of Experts

164 At this stage of the inquiry, the procurator fiscal may require to decide whether or not expert evidence should be obtained, and although the police may suggest this, the procurator fiscal alone has the discretion in deciding whether or not an expert should be used. Experts may be employed for a wide variety of matters including ballistics, photography, fingerprints, accountancy or financial matters,[13] analysis (which covers a very wide field including blood, stains, earth, wood, paint, etc.), medical matters, and any other sphere in which the procurator fiscal judges it expedient or desirable. The procurator fiscal may have to make such a decision at very short notice, as analysis or examination often becomes increasingly difficult or impossible if time is allowed to elapse. The only minor restriction on a procurator fiscal is that where the expense of such analysis is liable to be considerable, he should obtain Crown Counsel's instructions, this being done by telephone in cases of urgency. While some experts may be police officers, or employed on a full-time basis by the police, the procurator fiscal has complete discretion as to the selection of an expert, usually choosing one who is of wide repute and distinguished in his own field. There is no official list of experts who may be employed. Bearing in mind the need for evidence to be corroborated, the procurator fiscal will usually employ two experts to act jointly. In certain instances, the procurator fiscal may require to obtain a warrant from the sheriff allowing such an expert to be employed. This procedure is really a historical relic from the times when the sheriff was responsible for the investigation of crime. The two commonest examples are where the procurator fiscal wishes to instruct a post mortem dissection, or where expert examination directly concerns a person who may possibly be charged with an offence at a later stage if the procurator fiscal decides to take proceedings.

Post Mortem Examinations

165 With regard to post mortem dissections, this will arise when the procurator fiscal is investigating a sudden unexpected or suspicious death.[14] Should he decide that a post mortem dissection is necessary, which will always be the rule when there is a possibility of criminal proceedings, he will make a formal request to the sheriff for authority to dissect and examine the body, the request being made in writing. No detailed reasons are given for the request, and in practice the sheriff grants the warrant as a matter of routine, by merely appending his signature to the printed form.

Physical Examination of a Suspect

166 Where the examination concerns a person who may possibly be charged with the offence at a later stage, the law is more complicated, and has been altered somewhat by recent judicial decisions. Prior to the accused being arrested, which will

---

[13] An accountant should not be employed without the authority of Crown Counsel.

[14] For full details of such investigations, see Appendix 9.

only be done when there are sufficient grounds for so doing,[15] it is probably advisable to obtain a special warrant from the sheriff before ordering any expert examination of the person of anyone who may ultimately be charged with a criminal offence. The most recent example of this was in the case of Hay v H.M. Advocate.[16] A woman was murdered and bite marks were found on the body. In a routine examination of youths detained in a nearby Approved School, it was found that the teeth pattern of Hay might correspond to the marks. Hay was neither arrested, cautioned or charged, as at this stage there was not enough evidence to justify such a course. The procurator fiscal applied to the sheriff for a warrant to convey Hay to a dental hospital and have impressions, photographs and measurements taken of his teeth. In presenting the application for the warrant, the procurator fiscal stated his reasons for his request, but Hay was neither present or represented at the hearing. The warrant was granted. (At the subsequent trial, Hay was convicted.) The obtaining of such a warrant would prevent the situation which arose in McGovern v H.M. Advocate[17] where it was held that the police did not have the right to obtain nail scrapings from a suspect prior to his arrest, although in a similar case in 1967, namely Bell v Hogg,[18] the court allowed the evidence of rubbings taken from the palms of persons who had not been arrested. Thus while the law is not extremely precise, it will probably be advisable for the procurator fiscal to obtain a special warrant in cases where he wishes an examination, expert or otherwise of any person who has not been arrested, but who ultimately may be charged. If the court holds at the trial that such evidence has been improperly obtained, it will refuse to admit the evidence, which can therefore not be considered.[19]

Closely allied with the power to order expert examination, is the power to order searches and seizure of items liable to be of value as evidence. At the stage of the initial inquiry, where the suspect has not been arrested by the police, because the police have not sufficient evidence to justify an arrest, the general rule is that the police have no power to search a person or a place without a specific warrant to do so granted by the court. In great emergency, however, the police may search without a warrant,[20] and similarly may take possession of any article without a warrant if the owner consents. The court may allow other exceptions, such as where the police are searching a house with the owner's consent, but without a warrant, and find an article relating to an offence other than the one being investigated.[21]

Search and Seizure

167 Warrants to search are usually granted by the court as a matter of formal routine, but must specify the nature of the goods sought and the premises to be searched, a wide and indefinite warrant being illegal.[22] The granting of the warrant

---

[15] See para 169, i.e. where there is sufficient evidence to justify an individual being considered as the accused.

[16] 1968 SLT 334.

[17] 1950 J.C. 33.

[18] 1967 J.C. 49.

[19] See para 152.

[20] H.M. Advocate v McGuigan 1936 J.C. 16; another exception is created by the Official Secrets Acts 1911–1939.

[21] H.M. Advocate v Hepper 1958 J.C. 39.

[22] H.M. Advocate v Turnbull 1951 J.C. 96.

entitles the police to use force to enter the premises if necessary. Such warrants will be granted whether or not at the end of the day criminal proceedings are taken, since, of course, the search may prove fruitless. In practice search warrants are frequently dispensed with by the police obtaining the owner's consent to make the search. Should the owner refuse, the police may keep the house under observation while a warrant is obtained. Furthermore there is the psychological factor in that while anyone is at liberty to refuse the police the right to search his house, and strictly speaking is merely relying on the right conferred on him by law, such a refusal might be regarded with strong suspicion by the police. Another human factor is that in general most people respect and obey the police and the request for consent to search may be framed in such a way that it is difficult to refuse, whether or not the person concerned is aware of his legal rights.

Right to Question Witnesses

168 With regard to the right to question witnesses, the police may question anyone and may ask a witness to come to a police station to give a statement. The witness has the right to refuse to comply with either of these requests, and the police have no power to compel him to do so. The procurator fiscal at this stage in the proceedings may also take statements in person from the witnesses (this statement being known as a 'precognition'), but such a course is unusual, although not unknown, and is sometimes followed in cases of a complicated nature, usually involving some type of fraud, where it is felt that the investigation can be more competently made by the procurator fiscal rather than the police. In order to examine witnesses, the procurator fiscal may cite them to attend his office, if necessary obtaining a warrant from the court to do so.[23] In most cases however, the procurator fiscal will not precognose the witnesses until later in the proceedings.[24]

One of the most important powers given to the police, is the power of arrest.

Arrest

169 A police constable may arrest anyone whom he finds committing or attempting to commit a serious crime; anyone he finds under suspicious circumstances with goods in his possession which the constable knows or believes to be stolen, and for the possession of which the person can not account in any way consistent with his innocence, and if there is a probability that the prisoner will escape if immediate action is not taken; if he is informed by the injured person or by a credible eye witness that any person has just committed or attempted to commit a serious crime and there is a similar risk of escape; if he sees a person committing a breach of the peace or an outrage, or threatening violence and there is a danger that the person may do injury to himself or others if he is not immediately apprehended (in which circumstances the constable is entitled to arrest on direct information from credible eye witnesses); if the constable has statutory power to arrest without a written warrant. Apart from such instances, an arrest should only be made when the constable has a written warrant to do so.[25]

With regard to minor offences, it is not desirable to arrest without a written warrant unless there is a danger of the offence being repeated, or of the accused

[23] Summary Jurisdiction (Scotland) Act 1954 Section 18 (4).

[24] See para 194.

[25] For the issuing of written warrants, see paras 178–180.

person absconding, or doing injury to himself or others. This naturally leaves a great deal of discretion to the individual officer who may always justify his actions by claiming he was of the opinion that one of these conditions applied. In the case of serious crime, the constable may, without a warrant, break open doors and enter premises incidentally to the apprehension of the offender (provided the constable has disclosed his identity, his purpose and been refused entry). The constable may also request the assistance of any individual in the neighbourhood in affecting an arrest—but in practice constables frequently perform their duties in pairs, partly due to the need for corroborated evidence in court.[26] If the accused resists, the constable is entitled to use reasonable force to effect the apprehension.

Effect of Arrest

170 When he has been arrested, either with or without a warrant to arrest, the accused may be detained in a police station, but must be brought before the court on the next lawful day (which excludes Sundays and Public Holidays),[27] although the procurator fiscal may order his release at any time. Hence apart from persons arrested at weekends, the maximum time spent in police custody will not normally exceed twenty-four hours, and is usually much less. An unjustifiable arrest by a police officer might constitute the criminal offence of abduction. It would render the officer liable to disciplinary proceedings and possibly civil damages.

Once the accused has been arrested, he may be searched (although a warrant to search places should still be obtained). He may also be fingerprinted, which may not be done without his consent until he is arrested. Where necessary the accused maybe subjected to a medical examination, provided he consents. Without his consent he may be stripped and observed, the observation going even to the extent of requiring him to exhibit a cut on his hand.[28] Should a detailed medical or similar expert examination be required, this may be done without the accused's consent if a special warrant is obtained from the court to this effect.[29] A statutory exception to this rule concerns driving while under the influence of drink or drugs where it is a criminal offence to refuse to give a sample of blood or urine for analysis.

The accused is entitled to legal advice and representation as soon as he is arrested, and the police will telephone the accused's legal adviser, or seek to contact him by other means at the request of the accused.

On arrest, the police will normally tell the accused the exact details of the charge against him, but failure to do so does not jeopardise future proceedings as the accused will receive a copy of the charge against him from the procurator fiscal prior to his court appearance. Before telling him the charge, the police will caution him as follows—'You are not obliged to say anything, but anything you say will be noted down and may be used in evidence'. This procedure is known as 'cautioning and charging the accused'.

[26] A private citizen who witnesses a crime may arrest the criminal, but if he pursues him to a house, he can not break in and can only watch the house until the arrival of a constable. Certain statutes give selected powers of arrest either to selected persons or to anyone.

[27] Although in cases to be taken before the Police and Justice of the Peace courts the police may liberate the accused if he lodges a sum of money as bail.

[28] Forrester v H.M. Advocate 1952 J.C. 28 at p. 34.

[29] As noted above. See para 166.

Statements by an Accused Person

171 When the accused person has been arrested, cautioned and charged he may not be questioned by the police in regard to any matter bearing upon the offence (with which he has been charged) for the purpose of obtaining information to incriminate him. All that the police may do is note any reply that the accused may make on being cautioned and charged. No inference adverse to the accused may be taken if he does not reply to the charge, but if he chooses to make a reply, such a reply will be admitted as evidence, unless it is clear that the accused misunderstood the nature of the crime with which he had been charged. Should the accused desire to make a voluntary statement in connection with the offence, the statement must be taken in such a way as to exclude any suggestion of interrogation on the part of the police. If the accused has already consulted a solicitor, no statement should be taken until the accused has had an opportunity to have a further consultation with that solicitor. If the accused has no solicitor he should be informed before the statement is received that he is entitled to have the benefit of legal advice.[30] Should the accused nevertheless insist on making a statement, then the statement should wherever reasonably practicable be made to a senior police officer, who if possible has not been directly concerned with investigating the offence with which the accused is charged. Where this procedure is followed, the officer taking the statement will normally commence the written statement by noting that the accused has been advised of his right to legal representation and the words of the caution will be written out in full. This will normally be signed by the accused, who will then write his statement or dictate it to the police officer. When the statement has been written, the accused will read it, make any alterations he desires, then sign the statement. While this practice is well established, not many accused persons desire to make a statement and the percentage of cases in which it occurs is very small.[31] Knowing the very careful scrutiny which the courts will give to such statements, the police will not put improper pressure on an accused to give a 'voluntary' statement. The court must be satisfied as to the fairness of the procedure, the criteria being that the statement was truly voluntary, given without threat or inducement and not elicited by questioning (the police only being entitled to ask questions for the purpose of elucidation).

As an alternative procedure, if the accused in such circumstances desires to give a voluntary statement, the police may bring him before a sheriff who will record it. The accused who follows this course is said to 'emit a declaration'. Apart from the delay occasioned while waiting for a sheriff, such a practice has fallen into disuse, and as far as present practice is concerned, may be ignored.[32] The accused has no right to demand he be brought before a sheriff for this purpose.

It should be noted that the above rules regarding the police power to search, observe and question the accused apply equally where the accused has not been arrested. All that is required is there is sufficient evidence to justify the individual being treated as the accused, whether or not he is arrested, the clearest indication being that the individual who is cautioned and charged must always be treated

---

[30] Failure to advise the accused of this right need not necessarily render the statement inadmissible as evidence. H.M. Advocate v Fox 1947 J.C. 30.

[31] One notable instance where such procedure was used was the case of Peter Manuel, the mass murderer, in 1958.

[32] See also para 183.

as the accused. The procurator fiscal may not interview or question an accused person.[33]

Persons 'Detained Under Suspicion'

172 While the above procedure applies to the police powers of arrest and restricts the right to interview accused persons, the police in practice detain persons under suspicion and question suspects who have not yet formally become the accused. The law on these matters is far from clear. It is established that unless the police arrest an individual (by virtue of a warrant, or in the circumstances above narrated), they have no power to take anyone into custody. Furthermore, while they may invite anyone to attend a police station to answer questions, they can not compel such attendance. In practice however they frequently invite certain persons to attend a police station voluntarily to 'assist with the inquiries'. The way in which such an 'invitation' is put will usually make it virtually impossible for the person concerned not to attend the police station, and although since such attendance is 'voluntary' and the person may leave the police station at any time, he is not for practical purposes a free agent. The person so detained, is sometimes described as 'detained under suspicion'. This phrase is in fact inaccurate since the person detained may not be a 'suspect' in so far as the police are concerned when they question him, although in many instances such a distinction is more technical than real. Since such detention is treated as voluntary attendance, there is no limit to the duration thereof, although it is obviously impractical to detain someone in a police station for several days. There is no record kept of such detentions, hence no accurate detail may be given. Furthermore since the person is voluntarily in the police station, there is no such situation at law as 'detained under suspicion' and no legal rules to govern such detention.[34]

With regard to police questioning, it is clear that they may question anyone at the early stages of their inquiry (although they can not compel the person to answer). In such circumstances they may well question the accused, although at that time they have no suspicion that he is the perpetrator of the offence. It is accepted that the replies to any such questions are admissible in evidence against the accused should he later be brought to trial. When however someone becomes seriously suspected of being the perpetrator of the offence, which may occur in the course of his being questioned, the law with regard to the police power to question him further is not settled. In Chalmers v H.M. Advocate in 1954, it was stated that 'a police officer, carrying out his duty honestly and conscientiously ought to be in a position to appreciate that the man whom he is in the process of questioning is under serious consideration as the perpetrator of the crime'. When such a stage was reached, 'further interrogation of that person becomes very dangerous and, if carried too far— e.g. to the point of extracting a confession by what amounts to cross-examination— the evidence of that confession will almost certainly be excluded' (i.e. not admitted as evidence at the trial). The questioning should therefore cease when the person becomes a 'suspect' in the minds of the police. Since this obviously depends to an extent on the attitude and interpretation (and perhaps intellectual honesty) of the individual police officer carrying out the questioning, this is not a fixed standard. An

---

[33] See also para 194.

[34] Since the person concerned attends voluntarily, there would seem to be nothing to prevent him obtaining legal advice or representation.

officer whose suspicions are intentionally or otherwise slow to arouse might well continue the questioning beyond the point deemed advisable by another. Since the questioning is usually in the presence of two officers (for the purpose of corroboration) both officers require to agree at what moment the person became a 'suspect'. This is why the term 'detained under suspicion' is false, since the person detained may technically not be a 'suspect'.

It can be argued that when the police decide to caution someone (that he is not obliged to say anything, but anything he does say may be used in evidence), then at that stage he must be a suspect in the mind of the police. Thus after a caution has been administered, no further questions are permissible and only a voluntary statement by the accused may be admitted as evidence. This argument is, however not in accordance with subsequent judicial decisions, where the accused was cautioned by the police then subsequently questioned by them, the replies to the questions being admissible. Such evidence was admitted by the courts in Brown v H.M. Advocate decided in 1966, Miln v Cullen decided in 1967, and H.M. Advocate v Ashington in 1968. In Brown v H.M. Advocate it was stated 'the police have a right and indeed a duty to make investigations and to question people in order to find out whether and by whom a crime has been committed, and for the purpose of conducting these investigations, to interrogate persons who may be involved . . . It is not possible ab ante to lay down the precise circumstances in which answers given to the police, prior to a charge being made, are admissible . . . this is so much a question of the particular circumstances of each case . . . But the test . . . is simple and intelligible . . . has what has taken place been fair or not'? In Miln v Cullen, it was stated 'Fairness to an accused person . . . is not a unilateral consideration. Fairness to the public is also a legitimate consideration, and in so far as police officers in the exercise of their duties are prosecuting and protecting the public interests, it is the function of the court to seek to provide a proper balance to secure that the rights of the individual are properly preserved while not hamstringing the police in their investigation of crime with a series of academic vetoes which ignore the realities and practicalities of the situation and discount completely the public interest'.

It therefore appears that there are no rules regarding the police power to question a suspect, the only test being fairness to the accused. Provided the police do not induce or intimidate the suspect into making a statement, or attempt to obtain a confession by cross examination (which may be capable of various interpretations), any replies made to police questioning will be admitted in evidence. As one writer puts it from the police viewpoint 'an officer is faced with choosing between the prospect of a reprimand from his superiors for failing to obtain information, and that of a reprimand from the court for acting improperly'.[35]

Action Taken by the Procurator Fiscal at the Conclusion of the Initial Inquiry

173 After the initial inquiries are complete the procurator fiscal must decide whether or not to take proceedings. If he decides to do so, then depending on the circumstances of the case, he may require to decide the nature of the charge, the form the proceedings should take and the means by which the accused should be brought before the court.

[35] Gordon—'Institution of Criminal Proceedings in Scotland', Northern Ireland Legal Quarterly, Vol. 19, No. 3. September 1968.

Discretion of the Procurator Fiscal to Order 'No Further Proceedings'

174 If the alleged offence contravenes certain statutes, the procurator fiscal may not institute proceedings without the previous authority of Crown Counsel. The particular statutes concerned are few in number and contravention thereof is relatively uncommon. In theory with regard to indecent offences, the procurator fiscal should not proceed without the prior instructions of Crown Counsel (except in the most minor charges), but in practice, this rule is frequently ignored. When a case is reported for prosecution by a government department, the procurator fiscal should refer it to Crown Counsel if he decides not to prosecute, but again in practice this rule is not always observed, although sometimes the procurator fiscal may discuss the case with the local official of the government department concerned, before deciding to take no further proceedings. In proceedings under the Trade Descriptions Act, the appropriate government body must be notified before proceedings are instituted. A charge of perjury must be referred to Crown office before the institution of proceedings. In cases where the Lord Advocate has ordered the procurator fiscal to make particular inquiries, the results of these inquiries will usually be referred to the Lord Advocate who will decide whether or not to prosecute. In any case of doubt or difficulty or where there are special circumstances the procurator fiscal should refer the matter to Crown Counsel for their decision.[36] Such a course however is exceptional and as a general rule the decision will be taken by the procurator fiscal. Naturally whether or not a case is referred to Crown Counsel will depend on the circumstances and, to an extent, the attitude of the individual procurator fiscal. It should be noted, that as a general rule, the views of the victim of the offence are ignored, and even where these are expressed, are regarded as being of little consequence.

The above restrictions only fractionally affect the power given to the procurator fiscal to decide whether or not to institute proceedings. Before making such a decision he must of course satisfy himself that the facts ascertained constitute a criminal offence and that there is sufficient evidence to justify proceedings. He does not require to judge the credibility of the evidence, but bearing in mind the rules regarding corroboration and admissibility of evidence, the question of sufficiency often depends on an interpretation of fact and law. It follows also, that the procurator fiscal must ensure there is no legal bar to the taking of proceedings, such as lack of jurisdiction, or a statutory offence being time barred.[37] Assuming that there is sufficient evidence, and there are no legal bars, the procurator fiscal has the sole discretion, in the first instance, in deciding whether or not proceedings should be taken. In particular the police, the victim of the offence or the court can not influence his decision. If he decides not to prosecute, he does not require to give reasons for or justify his decision. The commonest factors which will influence his decision are

---

[36] A typical example would be where offences were committed by 'strikers', the victim being the employer. If the procurator fiscal thought that the taking of proceedings might inflame the strikers and lead to a worsening of the situation, he would refer the matter for Crown Counsel's decision.

[37] Certain proceedings under the Road Traffic Acts may only be taken if the accused is warned of such a possibility by the police at the time of the offence, or by the procurator fiscal within fourteen days of the offence—1972 Road Traffic Act, Section 179. For more discussion re legal bars to proceedings, see para 191.

(a) that the offence is not of sufficient importance to be made the subject of a criminal prosecution, (b) if he suspects that information has been given out of malice or ill-will, a fact which may or may not be directly disclosed by the police when making their report, and a fact which will always be considered when the complaint has been made direct to the procurator fiscal by the complainer. (c) whether there is sufficient excuse for the conduct of the accused person to warrant no proceedings being taken against him.

In 1971, the total number of cases reported to full time procurators fiscal in Scotland was 147,008, out of which 13,005 (i.e. 8%) were marked 'No further proceedings'. The police normally only report cases where they estimate proceedings are legally competent, and some of the cases marked 'no further proceedings' may be accounted for by the fact that the procurator fiscal disagreed with the police view. While the number of such cases can not be distinguished in the above statistics, the figures do illustrate to some extent the degree to which the procurator fiscal exercises his discretion. In this sphere, the procurator fiscal may be said to be acting as a judge, rather than a prosecutor.

Effect of decision not to prosecute

175 A decision by a procurator fiscal to take no further proceedings is an administrative one, hence if proceedings are subsequently taken (if the decision is reviewed), such a decision can not be founded on as a plea of 'res judicata'. If further evidence comes to light, the procurator fiscal can change his mind, although in practice police inquiries will usually cease following on the fiscal's decision. Any person aggrieved by the decision not to prosecute may always raise the matter with the Lord Advocate who may instruct the procurator fiscal to report to him. Thereafter, the Lord Advocate will make the final decision as to whether or not to prosecute. Such a course, although extremely uncommon, is not unknown. Should the accused be in custody following on his arrest, the procurator fiscal will order his liberation when he decides to take no further proceedings. On occasions, where the case is of a trivial nature, he may issue the accused with a formal warning or instruct that this be done by a senior police officer.

If the Procurator Fiscal decides to prosecute, he must decide on the charge

176 While in most instances, the police will already have drafted a charge, the procurator fiscal will require to revise it and he is not bound by the police charge. For example he may alter a police charge of attempted murder to assault, or vice versa. Similarly he is not bound to take proceedings against the person designated as the accused by the police. He may substitute a different accused or take proceedings against additional accused. The procurator fiscal alone decides who will be prosecuted and on what charge, in the first instance. If the accused has previous convictions, the procurator fiscal will decide which ones to 'libel' against him, and the court may only take cognisance of the convictions so 'libelled'.

Form of Proceedings

177 Having decided to prosecute a particular individual on a particular charge, the procurator fiscal must then decide whether the proceedings should be taken in the summary court or on indictment before a jury.[38] In some instances, the procurator fiscal has no discretion in this matter. If the offence falls within the exclusive juris-

[38] Whether or not the case is sent for trial in the High Court or before a sheriff and jury is decided by Crown Counsel—see para 195.

diction of the High Court (treason, murder, rape, incest, deforcement of messengers and breach of duty by magistrates) the procurator fiscal must bring the accused before the court (i.e. the sheriff in private) by means of a document known as a 'petition'. On the other hand, certain offences are restricted by statute, or because of the statutory penalty to the summary court, in which case the procurator fiscal will bring the accused before the court by means of a document known as a 'complaint'. Apart from such cases where the form of proceedings is fixed by law, the procurator fiscal has a wide discretion in deciding whether the case should be tried by solemn or summary proceedings. The importance of this decision is that if he decides to adopt summary proceedings, any penalty ultimately imposed can not exceed the powers of imposing penalty given to the summary court,[39] thus the procurator fiscal decides the maximum penalty that may be awarded. The summary court can not refuse to try the offence and no judge can influence or direct the procurator fiscal in making this decision. When, however, the procurator fiscal decides that the case should be tried on indictment, he will further investigate the case then report the matter to Crown Counsel who will either confirm his decision or order summary proceedings.[40] When the procurator fiscal has decided on summary proceedings, he may not review his decision and later change to solemn, except in special circumstances, where the case has not called in court.[41] This would usually occur where the accused was charged with a further more serious offence to be tried on indictment and it was decided that both cases should be dealt with at the same time. Where, however, the procurator fiscal has initially decided to proceed by means of solemn procedure, the case may be reduced to summary proceedings at any time prior to the start of the trial. The accused person has no right to decide which method of proceedings shall be followed.

In making his decision, which arises in all common law offences, the procurator fiscal will take into account the gravity of the offence, which is the main consideration. He will also require to consider any previous convictions applying to the accused, since these will be considered as aggravations by the court when deciding on penalty. The question of penalty is therefore the second consideration to be taken into account. Thus a very minor assault charge might be taken on indictment where the accused has a bad criminal record and has very recently been convicted of assault, although a more serious charge may be taken on summary complaint if the accused has no previous convictions. There are no definite predetermined rules applicable and apart from the above considerations, the matter depends on the circumstances of each case and the way in which the individual procurator fiscal chooses to exercise his discretion. When the gravity of the offence itself does not preclude summary proceedings, an unofficial factor which may occasionally influence some prosecutors in 'borderline' cases is the sentencing policy of the judge—as for example in the case of an accused charged with breach of the peace and having numerous previous convictions; if on previous occasions or in identical cases, proceedings have been taken on indictment, and the sheriff has repeatedly indicated his views by imposing sentences less than the maximum available in the summary court (since only the maximum and not the minimum penalties are prescribed by law) a procurator fiscal may decide that solemn procedure would not be justified bearing in mind the public expense, inconvenience and lengthy proceedings involved.

[39] See para 120.
[40] Or order 'no proceedings'—see para 195.
[41] Or possibly where the case has called, but the trial has not commenced.

Such considerations are however of minor importance when examining the general question of how the prosecutor exercises his discretion. It follows that since the initial decision by the procurator fiscal can pre-determine the maximum penalty to be imposed, in this sphere also, he is acting as a judge, rather than a prosecutor. In 1971, of the cases in which proceedings were taken by procurators fiscal, 117,408 were dealt with by means of a summary complaint, and 2,831 were dealt with on indictment. (The corresponding figures for 1970 are 106,446 summary complaints and 2,747 solemn proceedings.)

Method of Bringing the Accused Before the Court
(a) Solemn proceedings
178   The final decision which the procurator fiscal will have at this stage in the proceedings is how to bring the accused before the court.

In solemn proceedings, the procurator fiscal has no choice of action. He must lodge a document known as a petition with the sheriff. The petition sets forth, where the particulars are known, the name, age and address of the accused person, states the criminal charge against him and requests warrants (i.e. the sheriff's authority) to arrest the accused and bring him before the sheriff for examination,[42] to search his person and premises and place where he is found and to open lockfast places, to cite witnesses for precognition and production of evidence; after examination to commit the accused for further examination or until liberated in due course of law.[43] If the accused's name is unknown, the petition may set forth that 'a man to the petitioner unknown' (giving such a description as will suffice to distinguish him), has committed the offence. With regard to the charge, the date must be specified (although there is an implied latitude of three months or more, depending on the circumstances); the place must be specified at least in such a way as to show that the court has territorial jurisdiction; the facts must be specified in such a way as to constitute a criminal offence and give the accused notice of the charge against him. Since the facts of the case have usually not been fully investigated at this stage of the proceedings, the charge on the petition may differ from the charge ultimately appearing on the indictment; nevertheless, it should set forth the above details as clearly as possible, this being of special importance if the accused indicates he is willing to plead guilty before the indictment is drafted.[44] The sheriff normally grants the petition (by signing it) as a matter of form. There is no formal hearing, nor is the procurator fiscal asked to justify his request—'Such petitions, being presented by responsible officials are assumed to be well founded'.[45]

If the accused has already been arrested without a warrant, the same form of petition is still presented and the procedure is the same as if the accused had been arrested in terms of the warrant. Should the accused not have been arrested, the warrant gives the police authority to do so. Occasionally the procurator fiscal may give the police instructions as to how the arrest is to be enforced, such as allowing the accused an opportunity to present himself at a police station by arrangement, rather than being arrested on sight. It will be noted, that in addition to the power of arrest, the sheriff also grants warrants to search the accused and premises, and for

[42]   See para 183.
[43]   See para 185.
[44]   See para 186, Section 31, letters.
[45]   Renton and Brown—Criminal Procedure, 3rd edition, p. 31.

the procurator fiscal to cite witnesses for precognition. On arrest, the police officer will inform the accused of the charge against him, if need be letting him see the warrant. He will then caution the accused and note any reply. As the subject of the warrant is clearly designated as the accused, the police have no power to question him.[46] The accused must be brought before the court as speedily as possible and may be detained until this can be effected. He is also entitled to immediate legal advice. The police will bring the accused to the court where the warrant was issued and submit a report to the procurator fiscal who will arrange for the accused to be brought immediately before the sheriff in private. Prior to this appearance, the procurator fiscal will serve a copy of the petition on the accused, who will be legally represented at his appearance before the Sheriff.

(b) Summary proceedings

179 In summary proceedings, the procurator fiscal prepares a document known as a complaint which 'runs in his name'—i.e. it states 'The Complaint of John Smith, Procurator Fiscal . . .' and is signed by him. As with a petition, the complaint will specify the accused's name, age, address and give details of the charge against him. Where a statute has been contravened, reference must be made thereto. A list of any previous convictions which the procurator fiscal seeks to libel will be attached to the copy served on the accused, but not on the principal copy for use by the court. In a statutory offence, a note of the maximum penalties laid down by the statute will also be appended. If there are several charges, all may be libelled on the same complaint, and charges may be libelled as alternatives to each other.

Summary warrants

180 Having prepared the complaint, the procurator fiscal has a choice of action. Where the accused, having been arrested, is in custody and is brought to the court by the police, the procurator fiscal will serve a copy of the complaint on the accused and place him before the court forthwith. If the accused has not been arrested, the procurator fiscal must decide whether to apply for a warrant for his arrest, or alternatively to cite him to attend.[47] While there is no legal rule to bind the procurator fiscal in this choice, it being left entirely to his discretion, normally where the accused has a fixed place of abode, is usually law abiding and the offence is minor, the procurator fiscal will cite him to attend in the first instance. Should these conditions not apply, or should the accused fail to attend in answer to the citation, the procurator fiscal will apply for a warrant to arrest the accused. The complaint with the request for a warrant to arrest the accused (and if desired to search for and seize evidence) will be given to the sheriff, and, as with petition warrants, the request will be granted as a matter of routine, by the sheriff appending his signature. The procurator fiscal will pass the warrant to the police, usually issuing instructions to them at the same time as to whether the warrant is to be enforced, or the accused given an opportunity to surrender himself. If the latter course is adopted, the police will inform the accused that they have a warrant for his arrest, but that if he presents himself at a police station at an arranged time, the warrant will not be enforced until

[46] See para 171.

[47] There is also a special procedure whereby the procurator fiscal may apply for a warrant to cite the accused, but this procedure is very uncommon and is used mainly to commence proceedings formally when the time limit for taking them has practically expired.

then. Should the accused fail to keep such an arrangement, or if no such instructions are given by the procurator fiscal, the police will enforce the warrant, arresting the accused whenever and wherever he may be found. As with petition warrants, the accused will be cautioned and told of the charge against him. Being clearly designated as the accused, he may not be questioned by the police, who may only note any reply he makes to the charge.[48] The accused must be brought before the court not later than the course of the first lawful day (i.e. excluding Sundays and public holidays) after his arrest, and may be detained by the police until this is done. On arrest, the accused is entitled to legal advice. The police will bring the accused to court and submit a report to the procurator fiscal who will place the accused before the court the same day. Prior to this appearance, the procurator fiscal will ensure a copy of the complaint is served on the accused (although by law this is not strictly necessary) and the accused will have a further opportunity to have legal advice.[49]

Summary cited cases

181 Where the procurator fiscal decides to cite the accused to attend court, he has a choice of two methods. Either he may have the complaint served on the accused by the police or he may post it to the accused by registered post or recorded delivery. When the first method is adopted, the police will return an execution of service to the procurator fiscal, or report if they have been unable to trace the accused. If the complaint is served by post, the Post Office will return the complaint to the procurator fiscal immediately if they are unable to deliver it. The procurator fiscal will then instruct the police to trace the accused. Service is effective if the complaint is served on the accused personally or left for him at his dwelling place or place of business with some person resident or employed there. The accused must be given a minimum of forty-eight hours notice of his appearance in court, and in practice, is usually given at least two weeks. If the procurator fiscal is unable to effect service of the complaint, he will instruct the police to trace the accused, and if this be fruitless, he will either drop the proceedings or obtain a warrant for the accused's arrest. Should service apparently have been effected, but the accused fail to appear, the procurator fiscal will normally request the court to adjourn the case while he sends a further intimation to the accused, or if the complaint has been served by post, he may decide instead to have it re-served by the police. If the accused still fails to appear, the procurator fiscal must decide whether to request a warrant for the accused's arrest, or to drop the proceedings, either temporarily until the accused is traced, or permanently. A warrant to arrest is seldom requested in cases of minor importance.

Procurator Fiscal does not interview the accused

182 Before passing to the next stage in the proceedings, it should be noted here that at no time does the procurator fiscal interview or even see accused persons. When the police arrest an accused and bring him to court, the procurator fiscal merely receives the police report, the accused remaining in the cells in the court building. When the procurator fiscal is deciding whether or not to take proceedings, and the form that such proceedings should follow, he does so only on the basis of the police report and any other information he receives from them. The first time

[48] See para 171.
[49] See para 127.

that the procurator fiscal sees the accused is when he appears before the sheriff in private (on petition) or in the summary court (on a complaint).

First Appearance by Accused: Solemn Procedure

183 The first appearance by an accused person being dealt with by solemn procedure is when he is brought before the sheriff on the petition. The proceedings are in private, so the only persons present will be the sheriff, the sheriff clerk (i.e. the clerk of court), the procurator fiscal (or his depute), the accused and his legal adviser and the necessary police escorts. By Section 17 of the Criminal Procedure (Scotland) Act 1887 the accused prior to his appearance must have access to a solicitor, who is entitled to have a private interview with the accused previous to his appearance and to be present thereat. If necessary, the proceedings may be adjourned to allow this to be done. When the accused appears before the sheriff, that latter should in theory read the charge over to him, but this is seldom done as the accused will have received a written copy in advance, and will have discussed the charge with his solicitor. Thereafter in theory the accused may be examined and if he answers, he will be said to 'emit a declaration'. In practice he is never questioned, and seldom makes any declaration. The historical basis for such proceedings is as follows. Originally the accused could not be examined or give evidence at his trial, so that it was impossible for him to answer the charge or the evidence against him. At his first appearance on petition, the sheriff could inform the accused, for example, of the general line of evidence to be adduced against him at his subsequent trial, and invite him to explain how a plea of innocence could be consistent with such evidence.[50] The accused would be told that he was not bound to answer any questions put to him, and any answers would be written down and might be used as evidence at the trial. If he failed to answer or to emit a declaration, such failure would also be noted, and could be commented on at the trial. The sheriff thus acted to some extent as a 'juge d'instruction', his function being inquisitorial. The accused's answers were embodied in the form of a declaration which was then read over to him and signed by him. It was also signed by the sheriff and by others present. Though there is some doubt on the matter, it is probable that the procurator fiscal, although present had no right to question the accused. In 1887, as above mentioned, the Criminal Procedure (Scotland) Act gave the accused the right to legal advice and representation, with the result that accused persons increasingly declined to emit any declaration. In 1898, the Criminal Evidence Act allowed the accused to give evidence on his own behalf at the trial, so that it was no longer important that the accused should give his version by emitting a declaration. Finally in 1908, the Summary Jurisdiction (Scotland) Act stated that if an accused intimated he did not desire to emit a declaration 'it shall be unnecessary to take one before committing him for trial'. As a result of these three Acts, it is now almost unheard of for an accused to emit a declaration, and he is never questioned by the sheriff, although the sheriff still has the power to do so.

In the very exceptional case where an accused today makes a declaration he must be warned that it may and probably will be used in evidence against him and that he may either answer or refuse to do so. No temptation or inducement must be given, as the declaration should be completely voluntary. The accused is not put on oath, and it is incompetent to say, for example, that it would be better for him to be candid

---

[50] At this period, the sheriff had an opportunity to examine all the evidence prior to the examination. In practice today, all he sees is the charge contained on the petition.

and tell the truth. A declaration must not be taken unless the accused is in sound mind and sober. The declaration will be reduced to writing by the sheriff clerk. Any declaration can be produced by the prosecutor at the trial, and while in theory he may refrain from so doing, in practice it will always be produced if the defence so request. The main advantage in modern proceedings of emitting a declaration is that the accused may comment on the charge or the evidence, such comment being placed before the court at the trial without the accused giving evidence which would necessarily involve him in being cross examined on all aspects of the charge by the prosecutor.

Judicial Examination

184 At the present moment in Scotland there are two schools of thought concerning the revival of the practice of judicial examination of the accused. Its opponents take the view that as the accused is entitled to the presumption of innocence, and is 'required to become an antagonist in a contest in which the State is the challenger, he is therefore . . . no longer a participant in the community's investigation of crime', having the right to remain silent and reserve his defence until he is aware of the evidence to be led against him. There are, however, many people including eminent Scottish jurists who think that the system of judicial examination should be revived. They argue that notwithstanding the presumed innocence of the accused, since it is in the interests of society that crime be detected and successfully prose-cuted, it is the duty of all citizens to participate in this process, and that he who is suspected of being the culprit, and whose assistance is therefore most likely to be of value, cannot be shielded from this duty. The object of the examination must be to ascertain the truth and not to obtain a conviction. It is suggested that the procurator fiscal should have the right to require the accused to appear before a sheriff and there put to him such further questions as he considers necessary (in so far as they are allowed by the sheriff) and to take note of his answers or his refusal to answer, this being admissible at the trial. The accused should have the right to have his solicitor present, not for the purpose of taking part in the interrogation, but to ensure that his client is treated fairly. The procurator fiscal should be permitted to ask the accused whether he committed the crime, or not, and if the accused denies it, then he should be asked to explain his denial in the light of the evidence. An innocent person would have nothing to fear from such a procedure, which would have the advantage for him of providing an opportunity to explain his position, and also allow any evidence in his favour to be explored with the full resources of the State available to the prosecutor.

There are further reasons for allowing such a judicial examination (or as above described, an examination before a judge by the procurator fiscal). The rights given to accused persons seem much wider than in most legal systems, namely the need for the prosecution to prove its case by corroborated evidence, the right of the accused to refuse to give evidence at his trial which may not even be commented on by the prosecutor, the reality of the principle of the presumption of innocence, and the excellent system of criminal legal aid and full facilities given to an accused to defend himself. Furthermore there is the inability of the police to question the accused, even allowing for the improper practice of detention 'while assisting the police with their inquiries' and the uncertain legal position of any statements made by the accused at this stage. Another factor is the general attitude of the prosecutor, who is not concerned with obtaining a conviction, but only with ensuring that the proper person is brought before the court for trial. His impartiality is incidentally recognised by the 'judicial' status afforded to him when deciding whether or not to prosecute, the form of any proceedings, and the numerous other issues that arise when investigating and prosecuting a criminal offence. Finally consideration must be given to the fundamental purpose of taking criminal proceedings, and in particular whether the rights given to the accused in the contest between him and the prosecutor should be allowed to hinder the investigation after the truth on which all justice must be based, where the silence of the accused may only serve to obscure or at least conceal the truth especially in regard to his relationship to the evidence.

Regardless of how such arguments will ultimately be settled, at the present time, when the accused first appears before the sheriff on petition, he normally remains silent, and his solicitor merely says 'No plea or declaration'. The procurator fiscal will then request the sheriff to 'commit the accused for further examination', which is basically a meaningless phrase, since the accused not having been examined by the sheriff, will not be examined by him at a later stage. Its only effect is that it may prolong by a few days the period during which an accused may be kept in custody before the trial.[51] As an alternative, the procurator fiscal may request the sheriff to commit the accused for trial, but this is usually done eight days later. The sheriff will grant either of these requests automatically, both being virtually meaningless, since in committing the accused for trial, the sheriff has no knowledge of the evidence and the accused does not comment thereon.

Pre-trial Custody

185 Under solemn procedure the accused may be detained in custody or liberated until the date of his trial. With regard to liberation, the only condition that may legally be imposed is that the accused lodges a sum of money as bail to guarantee his future appearances. Very exceptionally a judge may impose some other condition such as surrender of the accused's passport. All criminal offences are bailable except murder and treason, and even in these cases bail may be accepted at the discretion of the Lord Advocate or the High Court of Justiciary.

When the accused is committed for further examination, he may apply for bail and while the sheriff has a discretion to grant the application, in practice he will tend to accede to the procurator fiscal's demands on the matter since only the latter has a knowledge of the circumstances of the case. At this stage in the proceedings, an accused can not appeal against refusal of bail, although the procurator fiscal has the right to appeal if bail is granted. If such an appeal is taken, the accused is detained in custody until the appeal is disposed of in the High Court, which is done as quickly as possible and at least within three days.

When the accused is committed for trial he may again apply for bail, such an application usually being made verbally if the accused is brought to court, or more commonly by a written petition submitted to the sheriff, since the accused is not usually present when committed for trial. An application for bail must be disposed of within twenty-four hours after its presentation to the sheriff, failing which the accused is forthwith liberated. An opportunity must be given to the procurator fiscal to be heard on the application. The sheriff has a discretion as to whether or not to admit the accused to bail. If he does so, the procurator fiscal may appeal to the High Court either as regards the granting of the bail or the amount of the bail. The pro-

---

[51] See para 185.

curator fiscal must notify the accused of his appeal and the accused is detained in custody until the appeal is decided, which must be done within seventy-two hours, failing which the accused is liberated if he lodges his bail. If the sheriff refuses bail, the accused may either appeal to the High Court, or after five days, request the sheriff to reconsider his decision. Should the sheriff still refuse to admit the accused to bail, the accused may again apply to the sheriff after a further fifteen days have elapsed. Once the High Court has refused the accused's appeal, he will not normally make a further application for bail unless new circumstances have come to light, or if the procurator fiscal agrees. Similar rights are given to the accused to appeal against the amount of bail fixed by the sheriff. In fixing the amount of bail, the sheriff, while considering the gravity of the charge, will be mainly concerned with the financial means of the accused, it being regarded as pointless to fix an amount which the accused can not find, since this is tantamount to refusing bail.

In deciding whether or not to grant bail, the presumption of innocence is regarded as irrelevant, pre-trial custody not being indicative of the accused's guilt. When an accused applies for bail on being committed for further examination, the procurator fiscal will not normally oppose the application unless there are circumstances which necessitate opposition in the interests of justice, as for example, where there is evidence indicating the possibility of the accused interfering with the inquiry if released, or where further charges are likely to be brought against him within a short period. Where bail has been opposed, the procurator fiscal will reconsider his decision when the accused is committed for trial. As a general rule the factors considered by the procurator fiscal in deciding whether or not to oppose bail will be the same as those considered by the court when deciding whether or not to refuse it. The procurator fiscal will normally oppose bail if (a) the accused is liable to abscond, or has previously absconded when allowed bail, (b) where the accused has been liberated on bail and is reported for committing a similar offence or serious offence while liberated on bail, (c) if the accused is charged with a serious assault or sexual offence against children or persons with whom he is in close contact, (d) if there is clear evidence that the accused will threaten or intimidate the witnesses if released, (e) where the accused has a criminal record, is obviously carrying on a career of crime and has been released from prison within a relatively short time (e.g. one year) of the offence with which he is presently charged. Normally the procurator fiscal will not oppose bail in cases such as complicated frauds requiring lengthy investigation (since the maximum time an accused may be detained in custody is one hundred and ten days).[52] Where bail has been refused, and the procurator fiscal discovers in the course of his investigations that the case is unlikely to prove at the trial, he will reconsider his opposition to bail. When bail has been fixed, the procurator fiscal will inquire from the sheriff clerk when a week has elapsed as to whether the accused has found his bail. Should the accused not have done so, the procurator fiscal will normally notify the accused's solicitor and at the same time agree to a lesser amount of bail. In practice, once the procurator fiscal has agreed to bail, he will do all that he can to ensure that the accused is released, although it is not known if there is any truth in the rumour that on occasions a procurator fiscal has been known to pay the bail from his own pocket where an unrepresented accused has been unable to do so.

Once the accused is liberated on bail, if he fails to appear for trial, the bail will be forfeit and a warrant taken for his arrest. In certain circumstances however, the

[52] See infra.

145

court may agree to refund forfeited bail to the accused, if it thinks such a course is justified. When an accused is released on bail, he is required to give an address where the indictment may be served on him, such an address being known as the 'domicile of citation'. In many instances this is given as the office of the sheriff clerk (i.e. clerk of court).

When an accused person is detained in custody and is not served with an indictment within sixty days of being committed for trial, he may notify the Lord Advocate that if he is not served with an indictment within a further fourteen days, the prosecutor will be called on to show cause before the High Court why the accused should not be released from prison. Should the court not be satisfied with the prosecutor's reasons, it may order the release of the accused unless an indictment is served on him within three days. If the accused is released by virtue of this provision, the prosecutor may apply for his re-arrest when the indictment is subsequently served.

When an accused person has been detained in custody for eighty days and an indictment having been served on him, he is detained in custody further, then unless he is brought to trial and the trial concluded within one hundred and ten days of the date of his committal for trial on the petition, he is forthwith liberated and may not be prosecuted for the offence with which he was charged—unless the delay is due to the illness of the accused, the absence or illness of an essential witness or any other sufficient cause for which the prosecutor is not responsible, in which case the court may order the accused to be kept in custody for such further period as may seem just. The court may also extend the hundred and ten day period on the motion of the defence, as for example in a complex case where the defence must choose between going to trial before the hundred and tenth day with the defence inquiries incomplete, or extending the period of custody beyond one hundred and ten days and allowing the defence to complete its preparations for the trial.

While the 'sixty day rule' is seldom invoked, the 'hundred and ten day rule' is strictly enforced. Such a ruling places a great deal of pressure on the prosecutor to ensure that the investigation and bringing of proceedings are timeously accomplished.

Accused Persons Wishing to Plead Guilty—'Section 31' Procedure

186 Since in solemn proceedings the accused is not asked how he pleads to the charge until he appears on indictment at the first diet (or pleading diet) shortly before the trial, it follows that he can not plead guilty to the petition. If he is legally represented, he can however instruct his solicitor to write to the Crown Agent indicating his intention to plead guilty. Such a procedure is authorised by Section 31 of the Criminal Procedure (Scotland) Act 1887, hence this letter is known as a 'Section 31 letter'.

When the accused first appears on petition, or at any stage before the service of the indictment, his solicitor may approach the procurator fiscal and give him such a letter for transmission to the Crown Agent. Since the plea may be to the charge as libelled in the petition, it is obviously important that the initial charge has been fully and properly drafted. Alternatively, the plea may be to a partial or reduced charge, or to one or more of several charges. This can give rise to 'plea bargaining' as above described.[53] If the plea is not to the charge as libelled, the decision as to whether or not to accept it lies with Crown Counsel, who will however, frequently follow any recommendations made by the procurator fiscal. On receipt of a Section 31 letter, the procurator fiscal must immediately send it to Crown Office, together with a

[53] See para 147.

summary of the facts of the case. When Crown Counsel so instructs, the accused will then be brought before the court on a shortened form of indictment which does not contain a list of the witnesses or documentary or other productions. The accused's appearance must be not less than four clear days after issuing the notice and in practice it is usually within seven to ten days. A notice of previous convictions which the prosecutor intends to libel is also served on the accused.

When the accused appears in court and pleads guilty, he requires to sign the indictment to this effect. The procurator fiscal gives a summary of the facts, moves the court to sentence the accused and lodges any list of previous convictions. The defence then address the court in mitigation of sentence after which the court will either sentence the accused, or since the proceedings are in the sheriff court, it may decide to remit the accused for sentence in the High Court if the sheriff thinks the offence merits a sentence in excess of two years' imprisonment, or if the crime falls within the exclusive jurisdiction of the High Court.

Occasionally when the case calls in the sheriff court, the accused will change his mind and plead not guilty. If this occurs the procurator fiscal will desert the indictment 'pro loco et tempore' and the case will subsequently proceed to trial as if no Section 31 letter had been given. Should the accused not have been committed for trial previously, his committal on the Section 31 letter will be treated as committal for trial. Since the issuing of a Section 31 letter is clearly contrary to the presumption of innocence, a practice has evolved whereby the latter will not be given until after the accused has been committed for further examination (or for trial) and has been released on bail. In some instances the letter may be given beforehand, but will be post dated and thus not operative until the accused has been liberated. Such a course can not be followed where the accused is not liberated on bail, and since pre-trial custody need not necessarily count towards the ultimate sentence, the Section 31 letter will be tendered by the defence at the earliest possible moment.

First Appearance by the Accused—Summary Procedure

187 When a summary complaint calls in court for the first time the accused is required to state whether he pleads 'guilty' or 'not guilty' to the charge. Such proceedings are in open court to which the public is admitted. The clerk of court will call out the accused's name and when he answers it, the sheriff will usually satisfy himself that the accused has received a copy of the charge against him and that he understands it. The accused's plea to the charge will then be recorded. The accused will always be present in court when he is appearing in custody following on his arrest (or where he has been detained in custody on petition and the charge is reduced to a summary complaint). If he is not in custody, the accused has an option not to appear and to have his plea—whether guilty or not guilty—recorded in his absence. The accused may adopt the latter course by writing to the procurator fiscal, or by instructing a solicitor to appear on his behalf. The accused is notified of this right by the procurator fiscal. Occasionally the accused may instruct a third party to appear on his behalf, in which case the sheriff will satisfy himself that this person has been properly authorised by the accused to act on his behalf. Where the accused is in custody, he will have an opportunity to consult a solicitor prior to his court appearance, and if he is not in custody, he naturally may do so at his own expense or may be granted legal aid for this purpose. It will be noted that the accused is only asked how he pleads to the charge and is not questioned in relation to the offence.

(a) *Accused pleads guilty*

188 When the plea of guilty is tendered to the charge as libelled, the procurator fiscal will normally accept the plea, unless he does not agree with the facts to be adduced by the defence in mitigation. Where he only learns of such facts after the plea of guilty has been recorded, he may request the court to withdraw the plea of guilty and substitute a not guilty plea so that the case may proceed to trial. The procurator fiscal has a discretion as to whether or not to accept a plea of guilty to a reduced or partial charge,[54] but if he refuses to accept such a plea, then a plea of not guilty is entered. Where a plea of guilty is accepted, this is recorded and the procurator fiscal will narrate the facts of the case,[55] after which the accused may address the court in mitigation. The court may then dispose of the case, or adjourn while further inquiries are made, provided that no single period of adjournment exceeds three weeks. If the accused is present, the court may remand him in custody or release him (with or without bail) during the period of adjournment. When the accused is not present the court may not impose a sentence of imprisonment,[56] but must adjourn the case to a later date for personal appearance by the accused; if the sentence is other than imprisonment, the court has a discretion to impose the sentence in the absence of the accused.[57] A summary court may not remit the accused to the High Court for sentence. The court may allow an accused to withdraw a plea of guilty if the same was given as a result of a misunderstanding of the facts or misapprehension as to the law.

(b) *Accused pleads 'not guilty'*

189 When an accused pleads not guilty, in theory the trial may commence immediately except in the case of an accused person who is appearing in court immediately following his arrest and who is entitled to ask for an adjournment of forty-eight hours, or in the case of an accused pleading not guilty by letter. Irrespective of whether or not the case falls within these two categories, in practice the trial will never commence at this stage in the proceedings and the case will be adjourned to a later date for trial. The date must be fixed as the case can not be adjourned to an indeterminate time. The trial should be held as early as is consistent with the just interests of both parties, but will also depend on the volume of work and pressure of other business, and whether or not the accused is to be detained in custody awaiting the trial. Other factors which will be considered are the gravity of the offence, the availability of witnesses, whether or not any of the witnesses are children (and therefore more liable to forget their evidence), the complexity of the case and sometimes any other court commitments of the defending solicitor. When the accused is to be detained in custody, the trial will normally take place in one to four weeks' time, but where the accused is liberated and the case is of minor importance, in some of the busier courts it is not uncommon for the trial to be fixed for a date six to nine months in the future.

The accused may be detained in custody or liberated according to the rules above narrated for procedure on petition. If he is liberated, this may be done with or

[54] See para 147—'plea bargaining'.

[55] In minor cases, such as 'speeding' offences, etc., the narration will be exceedingly brief.

[56] 'Imprisonment' also includes various forms of custodial disposal for persons under the age of 21 years.

[57] For details re penalties, see para 217 et seq., and for appeals, para 231 et seq.

without bail, or the accused may be ordained to appear under a penalty not exceeding £10—i.e. he does not lodge this sum in advance but will be liable to pay it if he fails to appear at the trial.

In 1971, the total number of summary prosecutions taken by procurators fiscal in Scotland was 117,408. In 108,286 instances, the accused pled guilty; in 9,122 instances the accused pled not guilty and the case proceeded to trial.

(c) *Accused neither appears nor tenders a plea*
190 In the event of such an occurrence the procurator fiscal may request that the case be continued without plea (usually for fourteen days) to enable him to notify the accused or re-serve the complaint; or he may desert the case pro loco et tempore and re-serve the complaint; or if the court is satisfied that the accused has been properly cited to attend, it may grant a warrant to arrest the accused on the motion of the procurator fiscal,[58] or in certain restricted cases, the court may proceed to try the offence in the absence of the accused,[59] this course being extremely unusual.

Objections to Proceedings
191 When the complaint first calls in court and the accused (or his solicitor) is present, if the accused has any legal objection to the proceedings, these should be stated before he gives his plea. The objections may be to the competency or relevancy of the complaint, or a plea in bar of trial.

The accused may object to the competency of the proceedings if (i) the court has no jurisdiction to try the offence, either because the offence was committed outwith the territory of the court, or that its gravity exceeds the powers of the court, or that the judge has a personal material interest in the accused or the question at issue; (ii) the charge involves a question of civil right; (iii) there has been an irregularity in prior proceedings; (iv) that proceedings in a statutory offence have not been taken within the time limited by statute for prosecution (as a general rule this is six months, but there are some exceptions where the period is longer). Apart from this provision, prescription does not apply to criminal offences, hence proceedings can not be time-barred.

Objections to the relevancy are mainly that the charge is not in the correct form; that the facts set forth do not constitute a criminal offence; that the charge contains a statement lacking in specification as to time, place or mode of committing the crime charged; or that there is a formal defect with the complaint. There are numerous other such grounds.

Pleas in bar of trial are that the accused is insane at the time of the trial and is unable to plead to the charge or give instructions for his defence. Another plea in bar of trial is res judicata, namely that another court has previously decided that a charge in the same form as the present one is irrelevant, or (more commonly) that the accused has already 'tholed his assize'—i.e. he has already been tried for the same offence. If however after the previous trial an event has occurred which changes the character of the offence, a plea of res judicata will not be upheld (for example where an accused has been convicted of assault and the victim dies after the trial, the accused may still be charged with homicide). A final plea in bar is where the accused claims he was a witness called by the prosecutor to give evidence at a previous criminal trial

[58] See para 181.
[59] For further detail see para 211.

since such a person may not subsequently be charged for an offence with regard to which he has given evidence.

Adjournments

192 Before any plea is recorded, the court has a discretion to adjourn the case to a later date on the motion of either of the parties in order to allow time for further inquiry or for other necessary cause. The period of adjournment should not exceed seven days or on special cause shown, twenty-one days (in fact the phrase 'on special cause shown' is widely interpreted and adjournments for more than seven days are common). The court may adjourn the case more than once. During the period of the adjournment the court may remand the accused in custody or release him with or without bail, or ordain him to appear under a penalty of £10. The commonest reasons for a request for an adjournment being made by the procurator fiscal are that he requires to make further inquiries concerning the charge or the accused (which may include having the accused mentally examined if the procurator fiscal has reason to believe the accused may be suffering from mental illness),[60] or that there are further charges pending against the accused. The accused frequently requests such adjournments to allow him to obtain legal advice, or to make further inquiry before deciding on a plea.

Even after a plea has been given and a date has been fixed for the trial, the court, on the motion of one or both of the parties, or ex proprio motu may adjourn the trial diet to a later date. Such adjournment may also be granted after the trial itself has commenced.

Pre-trial Inquiries: Preparation for Trial

193 After the accused has appeared for the first time either on petition or summary complaint, the procurator fiscal is required to prepare the case for trial, provided of course that the accused has not pleaded guilty by Section 31 letter (petition) or on the first calling of the case in court (summary complaint). The preparation for the trial varies considerably depending on whether the case is to be dealt with by solemn or summary procedure.

(a) *Solemn procedure*

194 Once the accused has been fully committed for trial, it is the duty of the procurator fiscal to investigate the case fully and prepare it for trial. This includes collecting, examining and verifying all the available evidence, and must be effected with the utmost dispatch. The full investigation must be completed and reported to Crown Office within thirty days of the accused's committal, failing which the procurator fiscal must give reasons for the delay.[61] As will be noted later, this procedure covers cases to be tried in the High Court and before a sheriff and jury. All investigations are carried out in private and are secret. Any procurator fiscal or member of his staff who directly or indirectly communicates or makes public any part of the pro-

---

[60] When the procurator fiscal requests an adjournment to have the accused mentally examined, he will normally request that the accused be detained in custody (which in effect means the prison hospital) or in certain circumstances in a mental hospital. The procurator fiscal will then instruct one or two psychiatrists to examine the accused and report to him before the case next calls in court.

[61] In 1971, 2,057 cases were precognoced by procurators fiscal in Scotland; the figure for 1970 is 1,795.

ceedings or the contents thereof will be guilty of a breach of duty and possibly liable to prosecution under the Official Secrets Acts 1911–1939. Furthermore the Press are effectively prohibited from publishing any details.[62] The rights of the defence will be considered later.

In making his inquiries, the procurator fiscal has the power to order the employment of experts, to instruct searches and seizure of evidence, and to direct the police all as above mentioned, most of these steps usually having been taken before the accused is committed for trial.

The procurator fiscal has the power to examine witnesses and the statements obtained are called 'precognitions'. This power is conferred by the sheriff in the petition warrant. The procurator fiscal may cite witnesses to attend his office for the purpose of precognition and a witness is liable to arrest if he fails to attend. Very occasionally the procurator fiscal will bring a witness before the sheriff for precognition, in which case the witness will be put on oath before being questioned by the procurator fiscal. If the witness refuses to answer questions, the sheriff may commit him to prison. Normally however, witnesses are examined informally by the procurator fiscal in his office and are not put on oath. No person other than the procurator fiscal, a member of his staff and the witness may be present. (Although if the witness happens to be in custody, a police escort may occasionally be there for reasons of security.) The accused is not entitled to be present or to be represented at the examination, nor is he later entitled to see the precognitions. The examination usually commences with the procurator fiscal noting the witness's name, age, occupation and address. Thereafter he will question the witness, being careful not to lead him or put words in his mouth. If he suspects the witness is lying or withholding evidence, he will cross examine the witness. There are no rules for the form or content of the questions, or for the conduct of the questioning. While there seems to be no reason why witnesses giving conflicting evidence should not be confronted, this is never done, possibly because of the time factor, or because the resolving of such conflicts is usually left until the trial. It is not uncommon for the procurator fiscal to make a general suggestion to a witness that he must be lying or mistaken since other witnesses disagree with his evidence. The same comments apply to reconstructions of the crime, although rather than visit the scene of the crime, extensive use is made of photographs. There is no limit to the number of times a witness may be examined. When questioning a witness the procurator fiscal should seek to bring out any evidence in favour of the accused as well as evidence against him.

The procurator fiscal may not examine the accused, and since the latter is not required to reveal his defence, it follows that at this stage the procurator fiscal is also precluded from investigating the defence or examining any defence witnesses. In practice, the procurator fiscal will usually try to investigate any line of evidence which he estimates may be taken by the defence. With this restriction, he will investigate the case as fully and impartially as possible, as his purpose is not to obtain evidence leading to a conviction, but to ascertain if there is enough evidence which would warrant the case proceeding to trial.

The statement given by the witness will be recorded in narrative form by the procurator fiscal who will also note any comments about the witness which he thinks of relevance. Such comments may be factual, such as that the witness is feeble minded,

[62] See para 154.

or is going abroad, or is related to the accused, or may give the opinion of the procurator fiscal as to the reliability or credibility of the witness. The precognition need
not be read over to or by the witness, who does not sign it. In theory the witness may
ask that his precognition be handed over to him or destroyed before he gives evidence
at the trial. The general consensus of legal opinion is that at the trial, the contents of
the precognition may not be put to a witness who departs therefrom, in order to
discredit him. Should the procurator fiscal examine a witness who is not called to
give evidence at the trial and against whom proceedings are subsequently taken as
an accused, the contents of the precognition can not be used against him. If however,
the witness is examined on oath before the sheriff, and a precognition obtained, he
can not afterwards be charged with the crime. Except for precognitions given on
oath, no proceedings for perjury are competent.

The procurator fiscal will also make a somewhat cursory investigation of the
accused's background in so far as any information is available or appears relevant
to the charge. Frequently this does not go beyond the few lines contained in the
police report (saying whether the accused is married or single, has a fixed place of
abode and is employed), together with any previous convictions.[63] If the accused is
charged with murder, the procurator fiscal will always instruct an expert to examine
him as to his mental condition, otherwise such an examination will only be ordered
where the procurator fiscal has reason to believe the accused may be suffering from
mental illness.

The statements of the witnesses together with any background information will be
bound in book form, this being known as 'the precognition', and sent to Crown
Counsel with a covering report by the procurator fiscal. The report may be formal,
or may draw attention to any points of difficulty or worthy of particular attention.
It is becoming an increasing practice for procurators fiscal to include their views or
recommendations as to what further action should be taken.[64]

Decisions by Crown Counsel

195 Crown Counsel will then decide what disposal should be made of the case,
their instructions being binding on the procurator fiscal. Since there exists a close
working relationship between Crown Counsel and the procurator fiscal, Crown
Counsel may discuss the case with the procurator fiscal before the decision is taken,
or alternatively if this is not done, the procurator fiscal may occasionally contact
Crown Counsel to query the decision. In cases of special importance or complexity,
Crown Counsel may consult the Solicitor General or the Lord Advocate. It is also
understood that Crown Counsel may sometimes seek the advice of the Crown Agent
and members of his staff. In deciding what action to take, Crown Counsel will normally be guided by the same principles as affect the procurator fiscal when he is
considering whether or not to prosecute, and the form that such proceedings should
take.[65] The following instructions may be given (a) that the procurator fiscal should
make further inquiries, usually along specific lines, (b) that no further proceedings
should be taken, in which case the accused will be released if in custody, (c) that the

---

[63] Much more detailed information may be sought after the accused is convicted, but this
will not be obtained by the procurator fiscal.

[64] An exception to this rule concerns murder cases where the results of the preliminary police
inquiry will be sent to Crown Counsel before the case is precognosed.

[65] See paras 174 and 177.

accused should be prosecuted on a specific charge in the sheriff summary court, in which case the procurator fiscal will serve a complaint on the accused, (d) that the accused should be prosecuted on indictment before a sheriff and jury, in which case the procurator fiscal will draft the indictment and serve it on the accused, (e) that the accused should be prosecuted on indictment in the High Court, in which case Crown Counsel will draft the indictment and send it to the procurator fiscal for revisal.[66]

Form of Proceedings Prior to Trial on Indictment

196 All indictments, whether for trial in the High Court, or the sheriff and jury court are at the instance of the Lord Advocate, viz.—'A.B. you are indicted at the instance of X.Y. (name of Lord Advocate), Her Majesty's Advocate, and the charge against you is that you did on 15 May 1972 in the house at 10 High Street, Glasgow occupied by C.D. steal five diamond rings'. The indictment will give the name of the accused, and either his address (being his domicile of citation) or the prison wherein he is detained. The charge must be clearly specified (following the same rules as above described for petitions and complaints). High Court indictments are signed by an advocate depute (i.e. one of the Crown Counsel), but sheriff court indictments are signed by the procurator fiscal 'by authority of Her Majesty's Advocate'. Following the charge, there is a list of the documents and articles which are to be produced as evidence at the trial;[67] thereafter there is a list giving the name and address of each witness who is to be cited by the prosecutor to give evidence at the trial. Where the prosecutor seeks to libel previous convictions against the accused, a list thereof will be attached to the copy of the indictment to be served on the accused, but not to the indictment intended for use by the court. There is no notice of penalties.

The accused is then served with a copy of the indictment, either personally if he is detained in prison, or by leaving it at his domicile of citation if he is on bail. In the former instance service is effected by a prison officer, and in the latter usually by the police. If the domicile of citation is given at the sheriff clerk's office, the sheriff clerk may notify the accused or his solicitor that the indictment has been served, although it is the duty of the accused to keep himself informed of this. At the same time as service, many procurators fiscal will notify the accused's solicitor by letter, often enclosing an extra copy of the indictment for the solicitor's use. Attached to the indictment is a notice citing the accused to appear at the first (or pleading) diet, and thereafter at the second (or trial) diet. The indictment must be served not less than six days before the first diet and the interval between the first and second diets must be at least nine days. The first diet will always be held in the sheriff court, even where the trial is to be taken in the High Court. The accused must be present at both diets. When the case calls in court for the first diet, the accused will be brought from prison; if he is on bail and fails to attend (and the court is satisfied that the accused has been properly served with the indictment), the prosecutor may desert the indictment pro loco et tempore, request the court to declare the bail forfeit and grant a warrant to arrest the accused. As an alternative course the procurator fiscal may ask the court to continue the case to the second diet, this action being taken where the procurator

---

[66] In 1971, the number of cases indicted in the High Court was 211, and the number before a sheriff and jury was 827. In 1970, there were 192 High Court cases and 712 sheriff and jury trials.

[67] The documents and articles themselves being lodged with the clerk of court and thus available for examination by the accused.

fiscal has reason to believe that the accused will be present at the trial diet despite his absence at the first diet. In such circumstances he may also instruct the police to interview the accused and warn him to attend the trial diet.

At the first diet, the accused must state any objections he has to the competency or relevancy of the indictment, or intimate any plea in bar of trial.[68] Once the court has decided such issues, or if there are none, the accused is asked how he pleads. When he pleads 'not guilty' the case is continued to the second diet and the accused is further detained in custody or his liberation on bail continues. If his defence falls within a category known as 'special defences', the accused must give notice thereof at the first diet. Special defences are alibi, insanity at the time of the offence, self defence and impeachment[69] (blaming another named person as the perpetrator of the offence). Should such a defence not be intimated at the first diet, evidence thereof can not be led at the second diet unless the court so allows on special cause being shown and provided intimation was made at least two days before the trial diet. In practice this rule may cause difficulties in cases where the defence has not been timeously lodged, or disallowed by the court, since if the accused gives evidence he may refer to his defence in the course of his evidence. For example, if the special defence of self defence has not been lodged in time, the court can not consider such a plea, but suppose the accused gives evidence and is asked 'Why did you stab A.B.'? to which he answers 'Because A.B. pulled out a knife and I acted in self defence'. The prosecutor may always suggest that since no special defence to this effect had been lodged, the accused must be lying, as he failed to reveal this at the first diet. Regardless of any explanation given (which often takes the form of the accused saying that he told his solicitor, but is not responsible for the latter's actings), the evidence is before the court, regardless of any legal rules.

Where the accused pleads guilty at the first diet the procedure is the same as where such a plea is given following on a Section 31 letter.[70] Should the defence tender a partial plea, the procurator fiscal may sometimes be less disposed to accept it had such a plea been tendered at an earlier stage. He might refer such a decision by telephone to the Crown Office and would certainly do so if the case concerned a High Court indictment. If a full plea of guilty were tendered to a High Court indictment, the sheriff will almost automatically remit the case for sentence to the High Court, and must do so if the offence falls within the exclusive jurisdiction of the High Court.[71]

If an accused refuses to plead, or gives an ambiguous plea, then the plea is recorded as one of not guilty.

It should be noted that all proceedings at the first diet are in open court—i.e. the public is admitted.

Rights and Duties of the Defence

197 Officially, the accused is only informed of the charge against him when he receives a copy of the indictment six days before the pleading diet. Prior to this he

[68] See para 191.

[69] Sometimes called 'incrimination'.

[70] See para 186.

[71] In 1971 of the 2,831 cases in which proceedings were taken on indictment, 1,793 were disposed of by means of a plea of guilty tendered either by a Section 31 letter or at the First (or Second) Diet.

has only received a copy of the petition, and since the charge has normally been drafted before the procurator fiscal has investigated the case fully, it follows that the charge on the indictment might vary considerably from the one on the petition. In practice, however, since all accused charged on petition are legally represented, the defence solicitor will keep in touch unofficially with the procurator fiscal, and may thus learn if the charge on the indictment is going to vary radically from the charge on the petition. Since the inquiries made by the procurator fiscal are confidential, the defence have no right of access thereto, and in particular do not receive a copy of the precognition containing the witness statements. In theory, the defence have no knowledge of the case until six days before the pleading diet when they receive the list of witnesses on the indictment. During this period the defence may interview the witnesses and examine any evidence lodged by the procurator fiscal. If after such inquiries, the defence decide to plead not guilty, they have a further nine days to prepare for the trial. Witnesses have a duty to give statements to the defence if requested, but the defence have no right to cite them for interview or to compel them to give a statement prior to the trial. In practice many defending solicitors employ persons (who are not legally qualified) to visit the witnesses in their homes or other places by arrangement, in order to obtain statements from them. Such persons are known as 'precognition clerks'.[72] While the above rights are the only ones legally given to the accused to enable him to discover the content of the case against him, the procurator fiscal will normally exercise discretion to assist the defence in their investigations. While the minimum time between service of the indictment and the first diet is six days, and between the first and second diets nine days, the procurator fiscal will normally serve the indictment much longer than six days before the first diet, and arrange that the period of time between the first and second diet exceeds nine days (bearing in mind, of course that the hundred and ten day rule for persons in custody may sometimes affect the exercise of this discretion). Most persons charged on petition benefit from legal aid, hence there are no financial restrictions on the defence in making their inquiries. Any further assistance given to the defence will depend on the discretion and attitude of the individual procurator fiscal and his relationship with the defending solicitor. In certain instances at the request of the defence, the procurator fiscal may send an unofficial list of the witnesses prior to the indictment being served. It is also quite normal practice for the procurator fiscal and the defending solicitor to discuss the case prior to the trial, such a discussion covering the main points at issue between them. Sometimes agreement may be reached on certain aspects of the evidence, in which case the defence will accept such evidence by means of a Minute of Admissions, which dispenses with the need to call witnesses in relation to prove that evidence. During such discussions, if the defence have been unable to interview a witness, the procurator fiscal may make known to the defending solicitor the contents of that witness's precognition, and in very exceptional cases, let him see the precognition itself. It is therefore true to say that either because of the legal rights given to him, or because of the discretion of the procurator fiscal, no accused person will come to trial in ignorance of the charge or the nature of the evidence against him. Finally in certain circumstances, the defence may request the court to adjourn the trial diet to a later date to enable them to make

[72] Some procurators fiscal employ similar precognition clerks to investigate cases of minor importance or a straightforward nature, but the witnesses are always cited to the procurator fiscal's office for interview.

further inquiries. Such a course is most unusual. (There is also the right, which is never exercised, to request that the indictment be served after the accused has spent sixty days in custody.)[73]

With regard to the duties incumbent on the defence, apart from the requirement to state any objection to the proceedings and intimate any special defence at the first diet, the accused must give written intimation to the procurator fiscal (for a sheriff and jury trial) or the Crown Agent (for a High Court trial) of any witnesses he intends to examine or any productions[74] he wishes to put in evidence at the trial, unless such witnesses or productions are already listed on the indictment. Such intimation must be made at least three days prior to the trial, but if made at a later stage the court has a discretion to allow the witnesses to be examined, if need be adjourning the case to allow the prosecutor time to make further inquiries. While the prosecutor is entitled to object to any witness of whom timeous intimation has not been made, in practice he does not always do so, especially if the defence have unofficially acquainted him with the nature and content of the evidence to be led. Where the defence lodge a list of witnesses, the procurator fiscal may have little opportunity to precognose them before the trial, but he will invariably instruct the police to interview them and lodge the statements with him prior to the trial. Since however the prosecutor may be unaware of the full nature of the defence, it may be difficult to interview the witnesses in regard to a particular line of evidence. If the accused intends to attack the character of the person he is charged with injuring, he must give advance notice to the prosecutor and the court of his intention.

In considering the nature of pre-trial inquiries, it is obvious that a great deal depends on the relationship between the procurator fiscal and the defending solicitor, which often resolves on a question of personalities. If one of the parties insists rigidly on all the formalities being strictly obeyed while revealing nothing at all of his own case, this is liable to provoke a reciprocal attitude in the other. Similarly a lack of trust, or an attempt to conceal vital evidence when adjusting a plea prior to the trial is liable to preclude any close co-operation between the parties. It must, of course, be borne in mind that the main purpose of pre-trial inquiries is to prepare for the trial which takes the form of a contest between the parties. The inquiries are not designed to be an exhaustive search after the whole truth, nor to prejudge the issues. Only at the trial itself will all the evidence be fully and impartially examined and the issues decided.

Pre-trial Inquiries and Preparation for Trial

(b) *Summary proceedings*

198 When the accused has tendered a plea of 'not guilty' at the first calling of a summary complaint, it is unusual for the procurator fiscal to make any further inquiries. While in theory he may precognose witnesses, direct the police to make further inquiries, etc., he usually proceeds to trial on the statements of the witnesses furnished by the police, on which he based his decision to take proceedings on a summary complaint. All that the procurator fiscal will normally do is to cite all the prosecution witnesses to attend at the trial. If, however, some new evidence comes to light between the first calling and the trial diet, he will investigate it usually by means of the police.

[73] See para 185.
[74] If the defence are unable to obtain possession of articles in the hands of a third party, they may petition the High Court to order that such articles be handed over.

With regard to the rights and duties of the accused, he will have full notice of the charge against him on the complaint. Since the complaint does not contain a list of witnesses or productions, the accused has no official knowledge of the content of the evidence or the witnesses who will be called against him at the trial. To remedy this, a practice has developed whereby the procurator fiscal will furnish the defence with the names and addresses of his witnesses should the defence request this be done, making it clear that all the witnesses on the list need not necessarily be called to give evidence and that additional witnesses not on the list may be adduced to give evidence. As a condition of furnishing such a list to the defence, the procurator fiscal will request that the defence provide him with a list of any witnesses to be called for the defence. Although this practice is authorised by the Lord Advocate, it is not sanctioned by any legal provision, so that failure to follow the practice by either party can not be founded on at the trial. As in solemn proceedings, the procurator fiscal and the defending solicitor may discuss the case and the nature of the evidence in advance of the trial. and at such discussions the procurator fiscal might disclose the nature of a witness's statement. The defence normally have adequate time to investigate the case and prepare for trial since the period of time between the first calling of the case and the trial diet is normally longer than the period between the first and second diets in solemn proceedings.[75] Whether or not the accused has legal aid will depend on his financial circumstances, but he will not be prevented from preparing his case because of lack of funds. If the defence is one of alibi, the accused must notify the prosecutor with particulars of time, place and witnesses to prove it, prior to the first witness for the procurator fiscal being called to give evidence at the trial. If necessary, the procurator fiscal may request an adjournment to investigate the alibi. Should notice of the alibi not be given until a later stage in the trial, perhaps because an accused who is not legally represented has no knowledge of this procedural rule, whether or not the court admits the evidence rests with the discretion of the judge, who may frequently be influenced by the attitude of the prosecutor. In most cases, if not all, the procurator fiscal would not object in these circumstances since a successful objection would preclude the evidence and might result in the conviction of an accused who is in a position to prove his innocence.

Apart from a defence of alibi, and any unofficial undertaking to intimate his witnesses to the procurator fiscal, an accused is not required to give notice of any defence witnesses or productions. Hence the first knowledge which the procurator fiscal or the court might have of them is at the trial itself when the defence case is opened after the close of the prosecution one. The defence have the right to cite witnesses to the trial, but if such a witness is on the unofficial prosecution list, the accused may merely confirm that he will be cited by the procurator fiscal. In some instances the procurator fiscal may agree to cite defence witnesses to court to ensure their attendance, although at the trial he will leave it to the accused to call the witnesses to give evidence. In certain areas the police will cite witnesses for the defence, failing which this is done by an official called a sheriff-officer.

[75] See para 189.

7. Proceedings in Court: Trials

199 All criminal trials being at the instance of the prosecutor, if there are several trials arranged for the same day and at the same time, it is for the prosecutor to decide the order in which they are taken. Several trials may be arranged for the same time because of the pressure of business on the courts. By this arrangement, if one trial cannot proceed because of the absence of the accused, or the accused pleads guilty, or because the court adjourns it on the motion of one of the parties, the court can proceed immediately to the next trial. Should all the cases be going to trial, then an informal timetable is sometimes arranged to suit the convenience of the witnesses and defence lawyers. A criminal trial commences with the clerk of court calling the name of the accused. If he fails to answer to his name, then normally the prosecutor will move for a warrant for his arrest, no fresh diet of trial being fixed. When the accused is arrested subsequently and brought before the court, the same procedure will be followed as if the case were calling at the pleading diet for the first time. Should the accused again plead 'not guilty', a new trial diet will be fixed and the accused probably detained in custody. There are very limited provisions for trial in absence,[1] and apart from such minor exceptions, all procedure at the trial must be in the presence of the accused and the prosecutor. If the accused appears he will be asked again how he pleads to the charge. In the event of him pleading guilty, the case will be disposed of in the same way as if he had tendered such a plea at an earlier stage. The accused may plead guilty at any stage in the proceedings, hence if he does so after some of the evidence has been led, the plea will prevent the leading of further evidence if accepted by the prosecutor. In solemn proceedings, if the plea of guilty is tendered after the jury is empanelled, the judge will formally direct the jury to find the accused guilty 'in terms of his confession', and the jury will formally and unanimously find him guilty.

Prior to the accused being asked how he pleads, the defence should make any objections to the competency or relevancy of the proceedings or raise any bar to legal proceedings if such matters have not been dealt with at the first diet—for example, if the accused were detained in custody beyond one hundred and ten days, this would be the proper moment to raise such an objection. The majority of such preliminary pleas will have been disposed of at the first diet. Where there is more than one charge or one accused on the same indictment (or complaint), the defence may request the court to order that each be tried separately. Unless the prosecutor agrees to such a request the court will decide thereon by the general

---

[1] See para 212.

rule of fairness to the accused. Similar considerations apply if a motion is made to conjoin separate offences or accused into the one trial. It is also competent to amend the wording of the charge at any time prior to the verdict unless such amendment alters the character of the offence charged. The accused may request the court to adjourn the trial if the charge is so amended.

As a general rule, the court has a discretion to grant an adjournment of the trial to a later date whether or not the trial has commenced. In solemn proceedings however, adjournments for more than a few hours are seldom granted before the verdict is given. As a result, both the prosecutor and accused will ensure all their respective witnesses are present before the trial commences, and if an essential witness is absent, will move the court to adjourn the case prior to the start of the trial. In summary procedure such a request is often made by both parties, having agreed on this course in advance, in which case the court will usually grant the adjournment as a formality. Either party has the right to object to a request by the other for an adjournment, and the court will decide each case on its merits. When an adjournment is granted, it must be to a specified day.

Should the court refuse to grant an adjournment on the motion of the prosecutor, or where some difficulty of a more serious matter arises preventing him from proceeding with the trial, the prosecutor may desert the case, unless the jury is sworn (solemn procedure) or if he has begun to lead evidence (summary procedure). In theory the prosecutor requests the court to desert the diet, and the court can refuse to do so, but in practice no court will ever refuse such a motion. The diet may be deserted in two ways. By deserting the diet 'pro loco et tempore', the trial can not proceed further, but it is open to the prosecutor to commence fresh proceedings at a later date, unless in the case of a statutory offence if it is time-barred. The prior proceedings will not act as res judicata in relation to the subsequent ones. When the prosecutor deserts the case 'simpliciter', this has the same effect as a verdict of not guilty, in that no subsequent proceedings may be taken. After the trial has commenced the prosecutor may at any time accept the accused's plea of not guilty and invite the court to return such a verdict. The prosecutor will adopt this course where he is satisfied that there is not enough evidence to justify proceeding further or where the evidence clearly demonstrates the accused's innocence. When this is done, no subsequent proceedings are competent.

Solemn Procedure
200 The rules governing trial on indictment are virtually the same whether the case is called in the High Court or before a sheriff and jury, except that in the former case the prosecutor is an advocate depute, and in the latter the procurator fiscal.

After the accused has tendered his plea of 'not guilty' and if there are no preliminary objections etc., the jury is selected by ballot. The sheriff clerk for each county is required to keep a General Jury Book containing the name and designation of all persons who qualified to serve as jurors and who reside in the county. Every person who is not specially exempted, and who is between the ages of 21 years and 60 years is liable to jury service if he owns land to the value of £5 per annum or is worth at least £200 in goods and possessions. Persons specially exempted include Peers (i.e. members of the House of Lords); judges; advocates; solicitors; professors; physicians and surgeons; and police officers. Women are not exempt from jury service unless pregnant or suffering from another 'feminine complaint or ailment'. It will be noted that persons with previous convictions are not excluded, regardless of the gravity thereof. The Clerk of Justiciary (for a High Court trial) or the sheriff clerk (for a sheriff and jury trial) will prepare a list[2] of thirty jurors taken from the General Jury Book, for each trial. This list gives the names, occupations and addresses of each juror, and should contain an equal number of men and women. After the indictment has been served on the accused, he is entitled to be given a copy of the list, but in practice this is never requested. The prosecution and defence each receive a copy of the List of Assize immediately before the jury is ballotted. The jurors are cited to attend the court for the trial, and failure to attend without reasonable excuse may be visited with a fine. Prior to the judge coming on the bench, the clerk of court will confirm that all the jurors on the list are present, although if one or two are absent the trial may still proceed. The names of the jurors are written on separate slips of paper and the thirty slips are folded and placed in a large glass urn which is prominently displayed. When the jury is empanelled, the clerk of court draws the names from the urn until fifteen jurors have been selected. The prosecutor may challenge up to five jurors without giving any reason, but in practice he never exercises this right. Each accused has a similar right to five peremptory challenges and thereafter may challenge any other juror on special cause shown, the causes being infamy, insanity, deafness, dumbness, blindness, minority (i.e. under the age of 21 years), relationship or enmity on the part of the juror. There is also provision for either the prosecutor or defence to apply that the jury should be composed of men or women only. A female juror may apply to the judge to be exempted because of the nature of the evidence or the issues to be tried. In practice the defence frequently object to several jurors by means of their right of peremptory challenge. While no reasons are given, and the exercise of this right obviously depends on the individual accused and his legal representative, it is sometimes possible to guess at the reasons for an objection—for example, an accused charged with theft from a shop is liable to object to any shopkeeper who is called for jury service. The jurors are not subject to any examination prior to the peremptory challenge, and objections on special cause are very rare.

Occasionally a juror who has a pressing business or personal engagement, if not exempted in advance by the clerk of court will arrange with the defence that they will object to him if his name is ballotted. When more than one trial is to be disposed of at a sitting, the same jury may serve for all the trials with the consent of the prosecutor and the accused.

Once the jury is ballotted, the clerk of court reads aloud the charge in the indictment. The judge may also direct that written copies of the charge be given to the jury. The clerk of court then asks the jury to stand and each juror to raise his right hand and administers the following oath—'You fifteen swear by Almighty God, and as you shall answer to God at the great Day of Judgment, that you will truth say and no truth conceal, so far as you are to pass on this assize.' The jurors answer collectively 'Yes'. If a juror objects to the oath on the grounds that he has no religious belief, he may affirm instead. After the oath (or affirmation) has been administered, the clerk of court will read over to the jury any special defence and may at this stage also read any Minute of Admissions. The jurors resume their seats and any persons on the

[2] Known as the 'List of Assize'.

list who have not been empanelled are excused further attendance at the court unless they are required for subsequent trials.

Duties of the jury

201 The jury is described as 'master of the fact', which means that it alone decides which facts are held to be proved and which witnesses are to be believed. If there are any legal issues, including whether or not there is sufficient corroborated evidence, the jurors must apply the law as directed by the judge. On the question of corroboration, the judge may say 'If you believe the evidence of A. then together with the other evidence, there is sufficient corroboration, but if you do not believe A. then I direct you that there is not sufficient corroboration to entitle you to convict.' The jury thus decides issues of credibility and interprets the evidence. In deciding whether or not the accused is guilty, a jury may only convict if it is satisfied beyond reasonable doubt as to the accused's guilt. During the conduct of the trial, a juror may, with the judge's consent, question any witness (or the accused if he gives evidence), but this right is never exercised. Apart from being given a copy of the charge, or hearing it read over, the jurors will have no prior knowledge of the case, especially in view of the restrictions on publicity placed on the Press. In most instances they will not even know the nature of the case until after the charge is read to them. It is not normal for the judge to inform the jurors of their duties prior to the hearing of the evidence, although he will do so before they retire to decide on their verdict.[3] By custom neither the prosecutor nor the defence makes any opening speech, although there is no legal rule to prohibit this being done.

As a result, after hearing the charge, the jury proceeds to listen to the evidence without any prior instruction as to its legal duties or without any idea of the relative importance of different aspects of the evidence. With regard to the latter, it rests with the parties in presenting their cases to ensure that the evidence is properly placed before the jury, although it is not until their closing addresses, after all the evidence has been heard, that the parties have an opportunity to address the jury and comment on the relevance or importance of a particular piece of evidence. Since the trial takes the form of a contest between the parties, it follows that during the examination of the witnesses, each party may tend to emphasise any point in his favour by drawing it to the attention of the jury, while at the same time attempting to minimise any point against him. Because the party may be unaware of exactly what answer a witness may give to a particular question, great skill must be exercised in the framing of the questions and the order and timing thereof, so that a maximum advantage may be drawn from the witness's evidence. For similar reasons, it is essential to appreciate at what stage to cease questioning the witness. None of these rules derogate from the obligation on the prosecutor to place all the evidence before the court, whether or not it is in his favour, but he also has a duty to ensure that the public interest is properly represented, so that the extent to which he uses such tactics may often depend on the methods employed by the defence. It follows therefore that a prosecutor opposed by an unrepresented accused may present his case differently than if the accused is represented by senior counsel. The jury thus hear the evidence from the witnesses according to the manner in which each party decides to present his case. It is for

[3] See para 206.

these reasons that the accusatorial system is sometimes accused of being theatrical.

After the jury is sworn, no communication on the subject of the trial between a juror and any person can be permitted. The jurors sit in special seats at the side of the court apart from the judge, the parties, the witnesses and the public. They do not, however, sit on a raised level like the judge. If the trial is adjourned from one day to another, it is not necessary that the jury should be secluded during the adjournment.[4] Should a juror be taken ill during the conduct of a trial, then the trial may continue if the parties agree provided that there are at least twelve jurors. There is also provision for substituting a fresh juror in such circumstances, but in practice this situation never arises, and the trial normally continues with fourteen jurors if one becomes ill or dies.

The factors in favour of and against the use of the jury system in Scotland are the same as in France,[5] except that since sentence and any mitigating or aggravating factors are considered separately from the verdict, since the judge alone decides on sentence, and since the powers of sentencing given to a judge are very wide (neither the maximum nor minimum penalties being laid down for common law offences and no minimum penalty being specified for statutory offences), it is believed that the sentence which must follow a verdict of guilty is not a matter which has much influence on the jury when considering its verdict.

The role of the judge at the trial has already been considered.[6] He does not have the power to call witnesses or to determine the order in which they are heard. He leaves the examination of the witnesses in the hands of the parties to the case, except for occasional questions to clear up any ambiguity. Even if a witness is on the prosecution or defence list, the judge has no power to insist that such a witness be heard. He must accept the case as presented by the opposing parties regardless of his personal views.

Oral evidence—general rules

202 As noted above[7] the court may only consider evidence if presented orally and even items of evidence, for example such as sketch plans, or a bloodstained weapon, may only be examined if spoken to by the witnesses who made or found them. It is not competent to dispense with the attendance of a witness and in his place read a statement made earlier to one of the parties. The only exception to this rule is where the witness is dead. Each party to the case cites his own witnesses and a witness failing to attend is liable to be arrested and punished. When witnesses attend court for a trial they are kept out of the court room in a special room set aside for this purpose. While the female witnesses are kept separate from the male, it is not the normal practice to keep the prosecution and defence witnesses apart. Once a witness has given evidence, he requires to remain in court unless he is allowed to leave by the judge. Since the judge may recall a witness at a later stage to clear up any ambiguity, the judge will exercise great discretion in deciding whether or not to release a witness from further attendance. Where a witness is

---

[4] Formerly when capital punishment was a legal penalty, juries in such trials were normally given special overnight accommodation in an hotel.

[5] See Appendix 1.

[6] See para 145.

[7] See para 153.

allowed in error to remain in court prior to his giving evidence, his evidence may still be admissible if the judge so allows, provided that the witness has not been unduly influenced by what has taken place in his presence and that no injustice will result from his examination. The only exceptions to this rule are that the accused in person, his solicitor and in certain circumstances expert witnesses (if specially permitted by the court) may all give evidence despite being in court throughout the prior proceedings. All persons may be cited by the prosecutor to give evidence except the accused or his spouse.[8] A person who was insane at the time of the offence may not be cited. Children may be called to give evidence if they have sufficient intelligence to understand the obligation to speak the truth, there being no age limit. A child aged three and a half years has given evidence. The prosecutor conducting the case may not give evidence. A witness may only be examined in solemn procedure if his name is on the list of witnesses, although the accused may be allowed to call a witness not on the list if the court consents and the prosecutor does not object.

Every witness called to give evidence must take the oath unless he is a child, feebleminded or affirms. The judge tells the witness to raise his right hand and repeat the following oath—'I swear by Almighty God and as I shall answer to God at the great Day of Judgment, that I will tell the truth, the whole truth and nothing but the truth' (the words . . . 'and as I shall answer to God at the great Day of Judgment'—may be omitted). If the witness is a child or feebleminded, he will be warned by the judge to tell the truth. Should the witness refuse to take the oath on religious grounds, he may affirm instead—'I do solemnly sincerely and truly declare and affirm that I will tell the truth, the whole truth and nothing but the truth.' The above rule applies to the accused if he elects to give evidence in his defence. Refusal to take the oath or to affirm will be punished as contempt of court. A witness telling lies on oath commits the crime of perjury.

A witness must answer every question put to him unless the answer would lead to his conviction for a crime, or unless the court refuses the question to be put. Any witness failing to answer a question or prevaricating may be found guilty of contempt of court. The court may disallow a question if it is put merely to insult or annoy the witness, or if it is irrelevant. Either party may object to the questions put to a witness by the other. As a general rule the character of a witness may not be inquired into unless it affects his credibility.[9]

The form and content of the question is also important. A 'leading' question is one which suggest the answer desired—hence a witness should not be asked 'Was A.B. present?'; but 'Who was present?'; not whether he formed certain impressions, but what impressions he formed. Unfortunately if a leading question is put and objected to, the damage is usually done even if the question is subsequently rephrased. No question should be put which usurps the function of the court, thus if the case involves a road accident, a witness may not be asked who was to blame. A witness may not refresh his memory by use of notes unless made at the time and the judge so agrees.

---

[8] In three instances the prosecutor may call the spouse to give evidence, viz: where the spouse is the victim of the offence; if the offence is bigamy; or if the offence involves bodily injury to or incest with a child or young person. In each case the spouse is a competent witness, but only in the first can the spouse be compelled to give evidence. See also para 204.

[9] See para 145.

Presentation of the Prosecution Case

203 The trial commences with the prosecutor calling his first witness. After he has taken the oath, the witness is asked his name, age, address and occupation. The prosecutor will then question the witness about his evidence, and in so doing may not use leading questions unless the defence does not object. Usually no such objection is taken if the witness is giving evidence of a formal nature or if the defence is not disputing the content of the evidence. If however the witness gives evidence which is damaging to the prosecution case, or is hostile to the prosecutor, the latter may suggest to the witness that he is mistaken, unreliable or untruthful, and may ask the court not to believe the witness. It is competent to ask a witness if he has been intimidated. In order to discredit a witness, the prosecutor may put to the witness any previous statements made by him, unless such a statement was made on precognition. Should the defence object to any question put by the prosecutor, the judge will rule on the objection and either party dissatisfied with the ruling may subsequently appeal.

When the prosecutor has finished questioning the witness—this being known as examination in chief—the defence has the right to question him. This is called cross examination. The purpose of cross examination is to test the witness's veracity and accuracy, and to bring out any points on which he has not been questioned and which may favour the defence case. The witness may be examined by means of leading questions in cross examination. If the defence intends to lead evidence which contradicts that of the witness, questions should be put to this effect, this being known as laying a foundation in cross examination. Such questions sometimes give the prosecutor his first intimation of the nature of the defence to the charge. Failure to cross examine a witness does not mean that the defence necessarily accepts his evidence, although such failure may be subject to later comment. If two witnesses are both speaking to the same evidence, it is improper practice to fail to cross examine the first, then cross examine the second. As a general rule, a witness after giving his evidence may not be recalled. Thus if he is on both the prosecution and defence lists, he must be questioned by the defence in cross examination, and can not be recalled as a defence witness at a later stage in the trial. The prosecutor may request permission to recall a witness before, but not after, he has closed his case. If the judge recalls a witness at a later stage to clarify any ambiguity, and fresh evidence emerges as a result of such questioning, the prosecution and defence are entitled to put further questions in relation to the fresh evidence.

After the witness has been cross examined, the prosecutor has the right to re-examine the witness in regard to any new matter elicited in cross examination and which was not the subject of questions in examination in chief. When the prosecutor has concluded his re-examination, if any, the witness leaves the witness box and may not be questioned further unless recalled in the instances above described. In particular if the accused or a subsequent witness gives contradictory evidence, he may not be recalled for the purposes of confrontation with the subsequent witness or accused.

If at any time while a witness is being questioned, either of the parties objects that the content of the evidence is inadmissible[10]—as opposed to objecting to the form of the question—the court will require to decide thereon. Since it is often

[10] See para 152.

impossible to decide whether or not the evidence is admissible without hearing the evidence itself, and since it would be improper for the jury to hear the evidence should it be declared inadmissible, when such an objection is taken, the jury is asked to retire, and the evidence is heard outwith its presence, at the conclusion of which the parties will present their arguments for and against allowing the evidence to be admitted at the trial. Whether or not the evidence is allowed by the judge will depend on how it was obtained and whether it is relevant. The judge will then give his ruling, which is capable of being subsequently appealed. This procedure is sometimes called a trial within a trial. If the judge rules that the evidence is inadmissible, no reference may be made thereto when the jury returns, but if the evidence is allowed, it must be heard again, this time in the presence of the jury.

The prosecutor may call the witnesses on his list in any order he sees fit, but may not call witnesses on the defence list. Where it is clear that an individual is also involved in the commission of the offence, but is not presently on trial, the prosecutor is sometimes required to decide whether or not to call him as a witness. If he judges there is sufficient evidence, he will not call such a person to give evidence, since by so doing he renders that person immune from prosecution in regard to the offence for which he has given evidence. The prosecutor is thus required at this stage in the proceedings to judge whether or not he has produced sufficient evidence to satisfy the jury as to the accused's guilt. Occasionally he may decide not to call such a witness in the knowledge, or hope, that if he fails to do so, the witness will be called to give evidence by the defence, which does not confer an immunity against subsequent proceedings.

When the prosecutor has called his last witness, he formally announces to the court that he has closed the prosecution case. This is an important decision, for by closing the case he is precluded from leading any further evidence. He does not address the court or the jury at this stage in the proceedings. Should there be any witnesses on his list whom he has not called to give evidence, he will tender them to the defence—i.e. make them available to the defence should it wish to call them.

Presentation of Defence Case

204 Once the prosecutor has closed his case, the defence must decide what action to take. The defence may announce that it is leading no evidence, in which case the prosecutor proceeds to address the jury. Alternatively the defence may decide to lead evidence on behalf of the accused, either by calling the accused himself to give evidence or by calling other witnesses. When the accused decides to give evidence, he should do so before any other defence witness, although failure to observe this rule does not render his evidence inadmissible. If he fails to give evidence, such failure may not be commented on by the prosecutor. In calling witnesses, or the accused, the defence is bound by the same rules as applied to the prosecutor when presenting his case, so that if the accused gives evidence, at the conclusion of his examination in chief, he may be cross examined by the prosecutor on all aspects of the case. Should the defence intend only to challenge one aspect of the evidence, in deciding whether or not to call the accused it is necessary to balance this against the right of the prosecutor to cross examine. Because of this the defence sometimes seeks to argue at the end of the prosecution case that there is not sufficient evidence to justify the judge allowing the case to be considered by the jury. This results in another 'trial within a trial', and the defence will only be required to lead evidence if the judge allows the case to continue. While this practice is quite common, the proper time to make such a motion is at the conclusion of the prosecutor's speech to the jury (i.e. after the defence case has been closed). The danger of making such a motion earlier, is the psychological effect on the jury, who, if they learn of the nature of the defence request and that such a request has been refused, may feel that in the opinion of the judge, the accused is guilty.

The accused person may give evidence without giving notice to the prosecutor and his name need not be on the defence list. If the accused desires to call his spouse, the spouse's name must be on the list. The prosecutor may not comment on the failure of an accused to call his spouse as a witness. If there is more than one accused, one co-accused can not call the spouse of another and the evidence of a spouse called by one co-accused is not evidence for or against another. Where there are several accused, one co-accused can not call another to give evidence. If a co-accused decides on his own behalf to give evidence and if each accused puts forward a separate defence, the evidence of each accused is evidence against but not in favour of the other, thus at the conclusion of his examination in chief, he may be cross examined by his co-accused in so far as the latter is incriminated by his evidence. For example if A and B are driving separate motor cars which collide, and both are charged with careless driving, if A gives evidence in the course of which he blames B, then B may cross examine A. Such cross examination precedes the cross examination by the prosecutor. Where however, several accused make a joint defence—(i.e. one that is common to all), if one accused gives evidence, such evidence is admissible both in favour of and against his co-accused and there is no right to cross examine unless the evidence incriminates the co-accused.[11] If one of the co-accused has pled guilty at an earlier stage in the proceedings, he may be called as a witness either by the prosecutor or defence. Should one accused wish to call another to give evidence (and the case against the other has not been disposed of) the only way this can be accomplished and the other competently compelled to give evidence, is for the first accused to request the court to separate the trials, so that both accused are not tried jointly.

The presentation of the defence case follows the same rules as that of the prosecution. The accused and his witnesses are called by the defence, examined in chief, cross examined by the prosecutor and re-examined by the defence. Since the accused is not required to reveal his defence in advance, it is often only when the accused gives evidence, that the prosecutor becomes fully aware of the accused's answer to the charge. This gives the defence an element of surprise not available to the prosecutor whose witnesses are intimated in advance of the trial to the defence to enable it to learn the content of the prosecution evidence. The prosecutor is not allowed to lead further evidence after the accused gives evidence, having no right to a proof in replication. After the last witness has been called for the defence, the accused closes his case.

Closing Addresses

205 When the defence case is closed, the prosecutor has the right to address the jury, a right which is always exercised. While there are no rules as to the form

---

[11] The Law of Evidence in Scotland" by Walker at p. 384.

of the speech, the prosecutor usually mentions that the accused is presumed innocent and that the burden of proving his guilt lies on the prosecution. He will then review the evidence suggesting to the jury the way in which it supports the prosecution case. He may comment on the defence evidence, but may not comment on the failure of the accused or his spouse to give evidence. He normally concludes by requesting the jury to convict the accused. He will not make any reference to sentence.

The defence may then address the jury, and always does so after the prosecution. At this stage they may request the judge to withdraw the case from the jury and find the accused not guilty on the grounds of insufficiency of evidence, this course resulting in a 'trial within a trial'. Unless the accused is representing himself, he does not address the jury in person. The defence may comment on the evidence, and usually end by asking the jury to acquit the accused.

Address by the judge

206 The judge addresses the jury after the defence. 'The primary duty of the presiding judge is to direct the jury upon the law applicable to the case. In doing so it is usually necessary for him to refer to the facts on which the questions of law depend. He may also have to refer to the evidence where controversy has arisen as to its bearing on a question of fact which the jury has to decide. But it is a matter very much in his discretion whether he can help the jury by resuming the evidence on any particular aspect of the case.'[12] He will inform the jury about the presumption of innocence, the burden of proof and the need for corroboration. He will also tell the jurors that they must be satisfied 'beyond reasonable doubt' as to the accused's guilt before they convict him. Where evidence for the prosecution has been given by an accused disposed of an an earlier occasion, or a person involved in the offence but called as a witness instead of being prosecuted, the judge will direct the jury to give special scrutiny to such evidence before accepting it. He will then instruct the jury that it has a choice of three verdicts, viz.—guilty, not guilty and not proven.

Verdict

207 While the jury may give its verdict at once, it is normal for the jury to retire to consider it. On retiring, the jurors enter a room which is then locked. No one may enter or leave the room until the jury has decided on their verdict. The first thing the jury will do is elect a foreman. The jury may request the judge to allow it to examine any of the items produced as evidence and this is normally allowed. Should the jury require further direction as to the law, the court will be re-convened to allow the judge to do so. There are three verdicts available to the jury: guilty, not guilty or not proven. A verdict may be unanimous or by majority—i.e. a verdict of guilty must have at least eight votes. When the jury announces its verdict the foreman merely states whether it was unanimous or by majority, not having to specify any majority. While the verdict of guilty is self evident, it is necessary to distinguish between not guilty and not proven. Since the onus of proof lies on the prosecutor to produce a sufficiency of corroborated evidence, the jury may find that the prosecutor has failed to prove his case, hence the verdict is not proven, as for example if the case rested on the evidence of two witnesses, one of whom

---

[12] Hamilton and others v H.M. Advocate 1938 J.C. 134 at p. 144 per L. J. G. Normand.

was not believed by the jury Such a verdict differs from not guilty which may be otherwise expressed as saying that the jury finds the accused innocent. While at the end of the day the difference is purely technical and both have the same legal result, there is a slight psychological difference in that an accused found not guilty leaves the court without any slur on his character, whereas a certain stigma always attaches to a verdict of not proven. Since that is the only effective difference between the verdicts, many people advocate the abolition of the not proven verdict.

The verdict must be consistent with the indictment, and if there is more than one charge, the jury must consider each charge separately; if the verdict ignores a charge, this is held to be an acquittal. The verdict must also be unambiguous. The jury may find the accused guilty of part of the charge only, or of a lesser charge, even although the latter is not specifically libelled, hence for example an accused charged with theft may be convicted of reset. When the jury has decided on its verdict the court re-convenes and the foreman announces the verdict. The judge may ask the jury to make any amendment or give any explanation should the verdict require it. The verdict is then recorded by the clerk of court who reads it to the jury, confirming with them that the record accurately notes the verdict.

If the verdict is not guilty or not proven the accused is immediately dismissed.

Sentence

208 When the verdict is guilty, the prosecutor must move the court to pass sentence on the accused. Although the jury is not concerned with this aspect of the case, its function being terminated, the jurors remain in the jury box. If the prosecutor fails to move for sentence, then the accused can not be punished. While such a course is uncommon, it is sometimes followed if the indictment contains several charges of varying degrees of gravity. The prosecutor may occasionally not move for sentence in relation to a minor charge, leaving the court free to consider only the serious ones. In theory, this right given to the prosecutor permits him, where he disagrees with the verdict, to prevent the imposition of any penalty, but in practice he would never exercise his right for this purpose. When he moves for sentence the prosecutor merely says 'I move the court for sentence,' but does not give any views as to what the appropriate sentence should be. Occasionally, he may comment on the gravity or prevalence of the offence, or alternatively suggest that the court might deal leniently with the accused. While the judge is free to ignore such remarks, he may often be influenced by them. If the accused has any previous convictions, the prosecutor will give a list of them to the judge, provided a copy has previously been served on the accused.

The defence will then make a plea in mitigation of sentence, and the plea may include evidence as to the good character of the accused. This may be done by reading testimonials, reports etc. or by calling witnesses as to character. The prosecutor is entitled to comment or examine such witnesses if he believes the evidence to be untrue. The court then has a discretion to adjourn the case for any period not in excess of three weeks 'for the purpose of enabling inquiries to be made or of determining the most suitable method of dealing with the case.'[13] During an adjournment, the accused may be detained in custody or liberated. The inquiries are usually made by trained social workers and the results are embodied

[13] Criminal Justice (Scotland) Act 1949, Section 26.

into a document called a social enquiry report. The report will deal with the accused's parentage, upbringing, education, family background, any relevant medical history and any other information about the accused or the offence which would be useful to the court in determining sentence. All these facts are given in the form of a summary, but the report may go further than a 'dossier du personnalité' in that it often concludes by making positive recommendations as to sentence. The court may also order that the accused be physically or mentally examined during the period of adjournment. When the court re-convenes after such adjournment, the jury will not be present. The court will consider the results of the inquiries and may then proceed to sentence the accused, or order a further adjournment. When the court is considering any social enquiry or medical reports, both the prosecutor and defence have a right to comment thereon. Usually the prosecutor does not do so unless there is any inaccuracy, as by tradition the prosecutor does not concern himself with sentence.

Once the judge is satisfied, with or without an adjournment, that he has all the information he requires, he will pass sentence on the accused.[14] The sentence is always announced in open court, and in solemn proceedings the accused must always be present. The sentence must be consistent with the law and with the charge; if a period of imprisonment is imposed, the length must be stated clearly and unambiguously; if a fine is imposed this must also be clearly stated, and the accused must either pay it immediately, or make arrangements with the judge concerning payment. Any sentence of imprisonment will commence to run from the date of its pronouncement, unless the court specifically allows it to be back dated from the day when the accused was taken into pre-trial custody. Should the accused be convicted of several offences, the judge must state whether the terms of imprisonment imposed for each offence are to run consecutively or concurrently, and the same rule applies if the accused is already in prison serving a sentence previously imposed. In sheriff and jury cases, the sheriff may remit the accused to the High Court for sentence.[15]

Neither the jury in giving its verdict, nor the judge in determining sentence is required to give reasons for their decisions. When he has passed sentence, the judge does not notify the accused concerning his rights of appeal.

Recording of proceedings

209 All solemn proceedings are recorded in full by a shorthand writer who notes verbatim everything that is said. He usually sits on the bench beside the judge and prior to the start of the trial takes an oath to perform his duties accurately. If the case is adjourned for sentence, the shorthand writer does not attend the adjournment diet. In the event of an appeal, his notes, or a portion of them will be extended in full for examination by the Appeal Court.

Summary Procedure

210 Since the rules for procedure are the same in the sheriff summary court, the police courts and Justice of the Peace courts, there is no need to distinguish between such courts when considering summary trials.

The trial commences with the clerk of court calling the accused's name. As

[14] For a note re penalties see para 217 et seq.
[15] See para 186.

noted above, if the accused fails to answer, the prosecutor will normally move for a warrant for the accused's arrest and a warrant will be granted if the judge is satisfied that the accused has had proper notification of the trial diet. Should the judge not be so satisfied, the trial will usually be adjourned to a later date and the accused will be notified of the new diet of trial.

Trial in absence

211 Where, however the accused is charged with a statutory offence for which a sentence of imprisonment can not be imposed in the first instance,[16] the Summary Jurisdiction (Scotland) Act 1954 provides that 'the court may, on the motion of the prosecutor and upon proof that the accused has been duly cited or has received due intimation of the diet where such intimation has been ordered, proceed to hear and dispose of the case in the absence of the accused.' The initiative thus rests with the prosecutor in deciding whether or not to make such a motion and while the use of such procedure is not unknown, it is fairly uncommon.

Examination of the witnesses and general procedure

212 When the accused answers to his name and is not legally represented, the judge will usually ensure that the accused has had an opportunity to obtain legal advice. He will frequently advise the accused of the legal procedure to be followed at the trial. Provided there are no legal objections to the proceedings, the trial will continue with the prosecutor calling his first witness, there being no jury in summary trials. The rules for obtaining the evidence from the witnesses, and for the presentation of the prosecution and defence cases are the same as in solemn procedure. A witness who fails to attend court, or who refuses to take the oath (or affirm) or to produce documents in his possession or refuses to answer any question which the judge allows, may be found guilty of contempt of court and punished with a fine of £25 or up to twenty days imprisonment. It is also contempt of court if a witness in answering questions, is held by the judge to be prevaricating—i.e. showing a 'manifest unwillingness candidly to tell the whole truth, fencing with questions in such a manner as to show reluctance to disclose the truth, and a disposition to conceal or withhold it.' When such a situation arises, the judge may punish the witness on the spot, but more commonly he will order that the witness be detained in custody until the conclusion of the trial when the matter will be dealt with. On occasion, the prosecutor may move the judge to find a witness guilty of prevarication although in most instances the judge will do so ex proprio motu. Since the witnesses in most summary trials are not precognised in advance by the prosecutor, the trial proceeds on the basis of the statement given by the witnesses to the police. Should a witness depart from his statement to the police and should the prosecutor (or defence) have reason to believe that the witness is lying or prevaricating, it is competent to ask the witness if his evidence differs from his original statement and to read the statement to him. This is merely done in order to discredit the witness, since only the statement made under oath at the trial may be considered as evidence. A statement made to the police prior to the trial may not, as a general rule, be considered as evidence.

Since there are no official lists of witnesses either for the prosecution or the defence, either party may call anyone (except the accused or the prosecutor in

[16] —i.e. where imprisonment can only be imposed as an alternative to non payment of a fine.

person) to give evidence. Hence the prosecutor may even call a witness who has been cited to court by the defence. As in solemn procedure, evidence such as plans, bloodstains etc. is only admissible if accompanied by oral evidence. Therefore, for example, in the trial of a person charged with driving in excess of the speed limit, where the offence has been detected by means of radar, the prosecution require to call witnesses to prove how the radar device functions and to its accuracy, in addition to proving that the accused committed the offence.

As there is no jury, if either party objects to the competency or admissibility of a line of evidence, there is no need for a 'trial within a trial.' The judge will decide the issue on the spot either upholding or rejecting the objection. Where it is necessary for him to hear the evidence before deciding on its admissibility, he will do so, and if he then decides that it should not be admitted, he will merely ignore it when deciding on his verdict. It is felt that a judge has the ability to ignore inadmissible evidence even although he has heard it, whereas a jury might be unable to exclude such evidence from their thoughts even if directed to do so. At the conclusion of the prosecution case, the defence must decide, as in solemn procedure, whether or not to lead any evidence.

Closing Addresses

213 When the defence case is closed, the prosecutor, then the defence will address the judge, the defence always having the last word. Since there is no jury present, the addresses tend to be much shorter than in solemn procedure. In simple cases, the prosecutor may merely say that there appears to be sufficient evidence to convict and ask the judge to do so. This part of the trial is much more informal than a jury trial, and it is not un-common for the judge to ask the prosecutor or the defending lawyer to state his views with regard to certain parts of the evidence. As a result a debate may ensue with both parties addressing the court several times, although the defence has the right to speak last. It is then left to the judge to decide on his verdict, since in the absence of a jury, there is no need for the judge to 'sum up' the case. He requires to decide on both the facts and the law.[17] His verdict will usually be given immediately although in very complicated cases, he may adjourn for a few minutes or even days to consider his verdict.

Verdict and Sentence

214 If the verdict is not guilty or not proven, the accused is discharged. Should the accused be found guilty, the prosecutor will give the judge a list of any previous convictions applicable to the accused, and if the offence is contrary to a statute, a notice giving the penalties for the offence as specified by the statute. Copies of the list and notice must have been given to the accused in advance and this is usually done by attaching them to the copy of the complaint when it is served on him. While the prosecutor may address the court on sentence, he seldom does so other than perhaps stating that in his view the offence is serious or trivial, or mentioning any other factor relevant to disposal of the case.[18] The defence will then address the judge in mitigation of sentence and the same rules apply as in solemn procedure.

[17] See para 145 for the duties of the judge.

[18] In the Justice of the Peace and police court, the prosecutor occasionally suggests a specific sentence, but this is never done in the sheriff court.

The judge then announces the sentence, or adjourns the case for further inquiries to be made as above described.[19] The accused in a summary trial may not be remitted to another court for sentence. Where the judge is considering a custodial disposal of the case it is quite common, and in some cases it is mandatory, for him to consider background reports on the accused before imposing such a sentence

Record of Proceedings

215 No formal record is kept of the proceedings at the trial other than the complaint, the plea, a note of any documentary evidence produced and the conviction and sentence or other finding of the court. Any objections taken to the competency or relevancy of the complaint or proceedings, or to the competency or admissibility of evidence shall, if either party desires it, also be recorded. Most judges keep personal notes of the proceedings which they may consult if there is an appeal, but such notes are not available for consultation by the parties.

In conclusion, it should be noted that although the procedural rules must always be followed, since there is no jury present and the subject matter of the trial is of less importance, there is a greater degree of informality in the conduct of a summary trial which can usually proceed much more expeditiously than a jury trial.

Parking offences dealt with administratively

216 Before leaving summary procedure it should be mentioned that certain types of parking offences are dealt with administratively by the local authorities who employ officials known as traffic wardens to note such offences. The accused is given an opportunity of paying a fixed monetary penalty to the local authority without the need for court proceedings or judicial involvement. It is only if he fails to pay the penalty, that criminal proceedings will be instituted against the accused in the normal way.

[19] See para 208.

8. Penalties

217 Under Scots law, the maximum penalties for statutory offences are fixed by the statute creating the offence, and for common law offences by the maximum powers given to the various courts of criminal jurisdiction. The minimum penalties are never fixed. Before deciding on a penalty the court may adjourn the case to make background inquiries about the accused, provided no single adjournment exceeds three weeks. The inquiries may concern any aspect of the accused's previous life and a report is usually submitted by a trained social worker, the report being known as a social enquiry report. In addition the court may obtain medical or psychiatric reports.[1] In considering sentence the court will examine all this information, supplemented if necessary by verbal submissions from the defence and prosecution, or by verbal reports from the social worker. As a result of the great latitude given in deciding on penalty and the full information about the accused, the court is well placed to ensure that the penalty is appropriate to the individual accused. Naturally where the court decides in the first instance merely to impose a fine or make a lesser disposal, it will not normally request full background information about the accused. Once the penalty has been imposed, it is enforced immediately and the prosecutor is in no way concerned with this aspect of the procedure.[2] Should, however, the accused appeal either against sentence or conviction, enforcement of the penalty may be delayed until the appeal is decided. The following is a brief summary of the penalties available to Scottish courts.

Death
218 The death penalty is now only available for treason, so that for practical purposes it has ceased to exist. The method of execution is by hanging and only the High Court of Justiciary may impose this penalty. The Queen has the power to issue a reprieve, in which case the accused would serve a sentence of life imprisonment.

Imprisonment
219 In the absence of statutory restriction, the maximum powers given to the courts for dealing with common law offences are as follows: High Court—life imprisonment; sheriff and jury court—2 years imprisonment; sheriff summary

---

[1] In the case of juveniles and young persons additional reports are obtained regarding the most suitable disposal of the case. There are other special rules for dealing with juveniles.

[2] Except in certain instances where he requires to notify the appropriate authorities where the accused is employed in particular occupations such as nursing, schoolteaching, etc.

court—3 months imprisonment and in certain instances six months imprisonment;[3] Justice of the Peace, Burgh and Police Courts—sixty days imprisonment.

With regard to life imprisonment which is the sole penalty for murder, the sentence does not run for the natural life of the accused who may be released at any time on the instructions of the Secretary of State for Scotland. Prior to the abolition of the death penalty for murder, the average detention of persons sentenced to life imprisonment was seven to eight years, but since all murderers are now sentenced to life imprisonment it is too early to say what the average length of detention will be. When a determinate period of imprisonment is imposed, the prisoner is entitled to a remission of up to one third of his sentence if he behaves while in prison. In addition he is entitled to request his release on parole after he has served one third of his sentence, such a request being considered by a specially constituted parole board which decides each case on its merits. These provisions do not however apply to short sentences of imprisonment. All sentences date from the day on which they are imposed unless the court otherwise orders. If an accused has been detained in custody awaiting trial, the court has a discretion to back date the sentence to when the accused was first taken into custody. Alternatively, if the accused is currently serving a term of imprisonment when a further term is imposed, the court can order that the further term shall only start to run on the expiry of the present term. When the accused is convicted of several offences at the same time, the court may impose a sentence of imprisonment for each offence and must order whether the sentences have to run concurrently or consecutively, provided that if ordered to run consecutively, the aggregate does not exceed the powers of sentencing of the court—hence where an accused was convicted in a police court with five offences and was sentenced to twenty days imprisonment in respect of two charges taken together, and twenty days imprisonment in respect of each of the remaining three charges, the sentences to run consecutively making an aggregate of eighty days, the sentence was quashed on appeal, and a period of sixty days substituted.

Since the accused is always present when a sentence of imprisonment is imposed, he is taken into custody and transferred to prison immediately. The provision regarding summary trials in the absence of the accused does not apply if the offence carries a sentence of imprisonment. Where an accused has pled guilty by letter and the court decides to impose a sentence of imprisonment, the court will adjourn the case, ordering the accused to appear in person at the adjourned diet. If the accused is liberated pending an appeal and should the appeal court confirm the sentence of imprisonment, the appeal court will issue a warrant ordering the accused's arrest and transfer to prison.

No court of summary jurisdiction may impose imprisonment on a first offender of or above the age of twenty-one years unless the court is of the opinion that no other method of dealing with him is appropriate.[4] The court will normally only come to this opinion after it has obtained a social enquiry report dealing with the accused.

Fines
220 In the absence of statutory restriction, the maximum powers given to the courts for imposing fines in relation to common law offences are as follows:

---

[3] See para 120.
[4] First Offenders (Scotland) Act 1960.

High Court and Sheriff and Jury Courts—unlimited; Sheriff Summary Court
—£150; Justice of the Peace, Burgh and Police Courts—£50. The High
Court has the power to impose a fine in addition to imprisonment. When
a fine is imposed in a court of summary jurisdiction and the accused is
present, the court may order him to be searched and any money found on
him may be taken towards payment of the fine, unless the money does
not belong to the accused or the loss thereof would prove more injurious to his
family than his imprisonment (for non-payment of the fine). This situation is
however exceptional and the general rule is that a summary court must allow time
for payment of a fine unless the accused does not ask for time to pay, or fails to
satisfy the court that he has a fixed place of abode, or the court is satisfied 'for any
other special reason' that no time should be allowed. The reason for disallowing
time to pay must be stated. As the alternative to non payment of a fine is imprisonment, it frequently occurs that where an accused is convicted of several offences
and is sentenced to imprisonment on some, but fined in respect of others for which
a sentence of imprisonment is not competent, the accused will not ask for time to
pay the fines and ask the court to impose the period of imprisonment for non
payment, since both terms of imprisonment are usually ordered to run concurrently.

The length of time allowed for payment of the fine rests with the discretion of
the court, but a minimum period is seven days. In deciding the length of time the
court will consider the amount of the fine and the financial resources of the accused,
hence when the accused is present in court when the fine is imposed, he will
normally make verbal submissions as to the time to be allowed. Should the accused
have pled guilty by letter, the court will consider any submissions contained in
the accused's letter, and in these cases the sheriff clerk will write to the accused
telling him of the amount of the fine and the time allowed for payment. As an
alternative to allowing time to pay the fine, the accused is entitled to request that
he should pay the fine by regular instalments of such amount and at such times
as the court sees fit, and the court must inform the accused of this right.

All fines must be paid to the clerk of court. In the event of non payment of the
fine, or an instalment thereof, the accused will be cited to attend court again, or a
warrant for his arrest may be issued. When he appears before the court, he will
be asked why the fine has not been paid and the court will further inquire into
his means—hence the court is colloquially called the 'Means Enquiry Court.' The
prosecutor is not present at these hearings. At the end of the hearing, the court
may allow the accused a further opportunity to pay the fine or may impose an
alternative period of imprisonment. An alternative is always given in solemn
proceedings at the time when the fine is imposed, and may also be given at the
same time as the fine in a summary court if the accused is present and the court,
having regard to the gravity of the offence or to the character of the accused or
for other special reason, decides that it is expedient that the accused should be
imprisoned without further inquiry in default of payment. Whether the alternative
period of imprisonment is imposed at the same time as the fine, or at a later date
by a 'Means Enquiry Court,' the alternatives are as follows:

A fine not exceeding £2 -   -   -   -   -   7 days imprisonment
A fine exceeding £2, but not exceeding £5   -   14 days imprisonment
A fine exceeding £5, but not exceeding £20   -   30 days imprisonment
A fine exceeding £20, but not exceeding £50 -   60 days imprisonment
A fine exceeding £50   -   -   -   -   -   90 days imprisonment

These periods of imprisonment are the maximum that may be imposed and there is no rule preventing thee court from imposing a shorter period if it thinks fit. Where part of a fine has been paid, the court may only impose an alternative of imprisonment in relation to the unpaid balance of the fine.[5] The court may also at any time order that the accused be placed under supervision (usually by a social worker) for the purpose of assisting and advising the accused in regard to payment of the fine.

In conclusion it should be noted that when an accused is convicted on indictment of a statutory offence for which the statute provides no other penalty but imprisonment, the court may impose a fine instead of imprisonment if it thinks such a course is appropriate. The fines that may be imposed are as follows:

Imprisonment not exceeding 3 months   -   -   fine not exceeding £100
Imprisonment exceeding 3 months but not exceeding 6 months   -   -   -   -   -   fine not exceeding £200
Imprisonment exceeding 6 months but not exceeding 1 year   -   -   -   -   -   fine not exceeding £400
Imprisonment exceeding 1 year   -   -   -   such fine as the court may in its discretion decide.

There is a similar provision for accused persons convicted on a summary complaint where a statute stipulates no penalty other than imprisonment.

Caution

221 As an alternative to any other penalty, a sheriff summary court can order the accused to lodge a sum of money known as caution as a surety for his good behaviour for twelve months following the date of conviction. The maximum sum is £150. The accused may be allowed time to find the caution and failure to find it will be treated in the same way as non payment of a fine. Should the accused be of good behaviour, the money will be refunded to him at the end of the period, but if he commits a further criminal offence during the period, the procurator fiscal will move the court to forfeit the caution. When an accused person applies to the sheriff clerk for return of the caution, his application is passed to the procurator fiscal who will normally instruct the police to submit a report concerning the accused's behaviour during the previous twelve months. A similar provision applies to the Justice of the Peace, Police and Burgh Courts, but the period is limited to six months and the amount to £50. Caution may be imposed in lieu of or in addition to a fine.

Probation

222 Any court may place any accused, regardless of the offence with which he is convicted (except murder), on probation for a period of up to three years. The accused must agree to be placed on probation and to abide by any conditions which the court imposes. There are few limits on the number and type of conditions which a court may impose, which may include a condition that the accused undergo medical treatment[6] if there is medical evidence that this is desirable. During the

---

[5] The court may also order that a fine may be recovered by civil diligence—i.e. the accused's possessions, or some of them are seized and sold, the proceeds of the sale being used to meet the fine. This is usually only done when the accused is a company or other corporate body, and is most uncommon where the accused is a private individual.

[6] The length of medical treatment may not exceed one year.

period of the probation the accused is under the supervision of a social worker whose instructions he must obey. Failure to do so, or to follow any condition of probation, or commission of a further offence will result in the accused being brought again before the court which may then dispose of the case by fining the accused up to £20 and allowing the probation to continue, or by varying any condition of the original probation order, or by disposing of the case as if the accused had not been placed on probation.

Admonition
223 A court may in its discretion dismiss any accused convicted of a criminal offence by merely admonishing him. An admonition is a warning to the accused and incurs no other penalty.

Absolute Discharge
224 If the court is of the opinion that having regard to the circumstances including the nature of the offence and the character of the accused that it is inexpedient to inflict punishment on him and that a probation order is not appropriate, it may make an order discharging the accused absolutely. This course is sometimes followed where the accused is only 'technically' guilty of the offence.

Forfeiture
225 When an accused is convicted, the court may order the forfeiture of any instruments or other articles found in his possession and used or calculated to be used in the commission of the offence of which he is convicted. Such items are seized by the clerk of court who will later arrange for their sale or destruction.

Medical treatment
226 Where there is medical evidence that the accused is suffering from some form of mental illness, the court may make an order confining the accused to hospital where the appropriate treatment may be given. A similar provision exists where the accused is found to be insane and unfit to plead to the charge.

Driving offences
227 Where statute so provides, a court may order that an accused convicted of certain road traffic offences be disqualified from driving motor vehicles.

Deferred sentence
228 Sometimes a court instead of passing sentence, will defer sentence for a fixed period. This differs from probation in that the accused's consent is not necessary, he is not supervised and at the end of the period the accused must again appear before the court to be sentenced. The court will frequently impose conditions which the accused must obtemper during the period of deferment. While one condition is that the accused must be of good behaviour, there is no limit to the number or type of other conditions. A common condition is that the accused must make restitution to the victim of the offence. The sentence that is ultimately imposed on the accused will depend on the extent to which he has followed the conditions imposed. While this disposal is not frequent in serious crimes, in minor crimes of dishonesty it is often the easiest way of ensuring that the victim is repaid and that the accused does not profit by his offence.

It should be noted that deferred sentence differs from a suspended sentence (which can not be imposed in Scotland) in that in the former case the sentence is not determined until the end of the period of deferment, whereas in the latter a sentence is pronounced and only its enforcement is suspended.

Expenses
229 No expenses may be awarded either for or against the accused (or the prosecutor).

Pardons: Indemnities
230 A pardon may be granted by the Queen on the advice of the Secretary of State for Scotland. The granting of pardons is extremely rare and usually only occurs to rectify a miscarriage of justice where evidence subsequently comes to light demonstrating the innocence of an accused who has been convicted.

When the Secretary of State for Scotland is requested to advise the Queen to exercise the prerogative of mercy in respect of any person convicted on indictment, he may, if he thinks fit and whether or not an appeal has been heard, refer the whole case to the High Court acting as an Appeal Court which will then dispose of the case as if it were being heard on appeal. Alternatively if he desires the assistance of the Appeal Court on a particular point in the case, he may refer that point to the Court for their opinion.[7]

Very occasionally an indemnity against prosecution may be granted, the commonest example being an undertaking not to prosecute any persons illegally in possession of firearms provided the same are surrendered to the police before a specified date.

---

[7] Criminal Appeal (Scotland) Act 1926, Section 16. See also Appendix 10 hereof.

9. Appeals and Review

While all appeals are decided by the High Court of Justiciary sitting as the Court of Criminal Appeal[1] the form of the appeal depends on whether the decision appealed against was given in a solemn or summary court.

Appeals in Solemn Proceedings

231 An accused person convicted on indictment whether in the High Court or by a sheriff and jury, may appeal against his conviction on any ground of appeal which involves a question of law alone. This would arise if the accused claimed that the indictment was irrelevant or incompetent; where inadmissible evidence had been wrongfully admitted by the trial judge, or competent evidence had been wrongfully excluded; if the trial judge had misdirected the jury or mis-stated the law.

An accused may also appeal, (a) on any ground of appeal which involves a question of fact alone or (b) on any ground of appeal which involves a question of mixed law and fact or (c) on any other ground which appears to the Appeal Court or to the judge who presided at the trial to be a sufficient ground of appeal. Before any of these types of appeals can be taken, the accused must either obtain leave of the Appeal Court to appeal or a certificate from the judge who presided at the trial that it is a fit case to appeal. If an appeal is taken on questions of fact, or mixed fact and law, the Appeal Court will only examine the case with a view to deciding whether or not there was enough evidence to justify a verdict of guilty; the court is not entitled to examine the evidence to see if it is capable of a different interpretation. The court 'can allow an appeal only when, after considering all the relevant facts and circumstances which are disclosed in the case, they come to the conclusion that the case against the appellant has not been proved with that certainty which is necessary in order to justify a verdict of guilty.'[2]

With leave of the Appeal Court, the accused may also appeal against the sentence, (unless it is one fixed by law—e.g. life imprisonment is the only competent sentence for murder). A sentence may only be appealed against if the accused claims that it is incompetent or excessive.

Notice of appeal, or application for leave to appeal must be made by the accused within ten days of conviction (or sentence, if the appeal is against sentence), the notice being given to the Clerk of Justiciary. The appropriate forms are in the possession of prison governors who make them available to any accused wishing

[1] See para 122.

[2] Renton and Brown, 3rd edition, p. 151.

to appeal, and he will forward any notices or applications to the Clerk of Justiciary. Occasionally the Appeal Court may allow an appeal to be lodged after the expiry of the 10-day period. The accused must also notify the Crown Agent of his appeal. The grounds of appeal must be specified at the same time although the Appeal Court may allow the grounds to be amended at a later stage. An accused who has been sentenced to imprisonment is entitled to apply to be released on bail pending the outcome of his appeal, but such liberation is seldom granted. Any time spent in custody prior to the determination of the appeal is reckoned as part of the sentence.

At the hearing of the appeal the accused is entitled to be present in court, unless the grounds of appeal involve a question of law alone, when only his advocate will be present. The accused may present written arguments for the court's consideration but if he does so, he may not present additional verbal submissions unless the court so allows. The prosecutor (represented by an advocate depute) may make oral submissions in answer to the appeal. The judge who presides at the trial must furnish his notes and a report of the case which will not be disclosed unless the Appeal Court so orders. Since all proceedings of trials on indictment are recorded by a shorthand writer, a transcription of his notes, or any relevant parts thereof may be obtained for consideration by the Appeal Court.

The Appeal Court may, if it thinks it necessary or expedient in the interest of justice (a) order the production of any document or other thing connected with the proceedings, (b) order any witness who would have been compellable at the trial, to attend and give evidence whether or not the witness was called at the trial, such evidence being taken by a judge or other person appointed by the Appeal Court, and the statements so obtained being available for consideration by the Appeal Court.[3] New evidence alone will not allow the court to grant the appeal unless the court is satisfied that a reasonable jury having heard the old and new evidence would have acquitted the accused. The court may also receive the evidence of any witness who was competent, but not compellable at the original trial (i.e. the accused or his wife). If the appeal involves prolonged examination of documents or accounts or any scientific or local investigation which can not conveniently be conducted before the court, it can order a special commissioner to inquire and report. The court may also appoint any person with expert knowledge to act as assessor to the court where such special knowledge is required for the proper determination of the case.

At the conclusion of the hearing, the court may allow the appeal and quash the conviction and sentence. Alternatively the court may refuse the appeal, in which case it has the power to increase the sentence and may even impose a sentence of more than two years imprisonment when the indictment was tried in the sheriff court. It also has the power to reduce the sentence. This power to review the sentence applies whether the appeal was taken against conviction or against sentence. If the court thinks that the accused has been improperly convicted of one part of the indictment, but properly convicted of another, the court may set aside the verdict of the jury and substitute a verdict of guilty as it judges appropriate. Similarly, where the accused has been convicted of an offence and the jury could have found him guilty of some other offence, and on the finding of the jury it appears to the appeal court that the jury must have been satisfied of facts which

[3] See Appendix 10.

proved him guilty of that other offence, the court may substitute for the verdict found by the jury a verdict of guilty of that other offence.

At any time after a note of appeal or application for leave to appeal has been lodged, it may be withdrawn by the accused on lodging a note of abandonment. An appeal is also held to be abandoned if no appearance is made by the accused or his legal representative at the hearing of the appeal. If a ground of appeal on law alone appears to be frivolous or vexatious, the court can dismiss the appeal without a full hearing.

It will be noted that the above rules relate to appeals by the accused only, the prosecutor having no right of appeal. In theory, if the court dismisses an indictment on the grounds of irrelevancy or incompetency or on other grounds of a similar nature, the prosecutor may appeal by a method known as advocation, but since in practice this course is never adopted it is not necessary to consider here the rules for this type of appeal.

Appeals in Summary Proceedings

232 The rules governing appeals from a summary court are the same whether the decision appealed against was given in the Burgh, Police, Justice of the Peace or Sheriff Courts. In practice there are two methods of appeal available—stated case and bill of suspension.

Stated case

233 An appeal by stated case is competent against the relevancy or competency of the complaint, any irregularity in procedure or any alleged error of the court on a point of law (such as admitting improper evidence etc.). The appeal must be taken on grounds of law, not fact, and where the accused was legally represented at the trial objection must have been taken at the trial. An appeal can also be taken on the ground of incompetency, or corruption, or malice or oppression, or if the accused has been misled as to the true nature of the charge against him or been prejudiced in his defence on the merits, and a miscarriage of justice has resulted thereby.

Unlike solemn procedure, the prosecutor has the same rights of appeal as the accused. The party wishing to appeal must apply to the clerk of court within ten days of the decision appealed against, or notify his application at the time when the decision was made. Where the former course is adopted, as is usually the case, the clerk of court must notify the opposing party. If the appeal is taken by the accused, he must lodge a sum of money known as 'caution' to meet any fine imposed and the expenses of the appeal; should he fail to do so, the appeal will not proceed.[4] A procurator fiscal will not normally mark an appeal without the prior consent of Crown Counsel. If the accused is in custody, the court may grant him interim liberation pending the decision on the appeal and a request by the accused to be so liberated must be decided within twenty-four hours. Should the accused be dissatisfied with the amount of caution, or the court's decision to refuse to liberate him, he may appeal forthwith to the High Court whose decision is final. Should the accused be granted interim liberation then abandon his appeal, the court which imposed the original sentence will issue a warrant for his arrest and imprisonment until the sentence has been served.

[4] Although the court may dispense with caution.

When an application for a stated case is made, the clerk of court must prepare a draft stated case within ten days (or within five days of the caution being found). The form is contained in the Summary Jurisdiction (Scotland) Act 1954 2nd Schedule, part VI. The stated case gives a narrative of the proceedings including the details of the charge. It does not relate what each witness said at the trial, but gives a summary of the facts held by the court to be proved. It must also give any objections to the admission or rejection of the evidence, the grounds for the court's decision and any other matters necessary to be stated for the information of the Appeal Court. The stated case usually concludes with the question 'On the facts stated, was I entitled to convict (or acquit) the accused?' Where a specific legal issue is to be raised, it should be put in the form of a question of law.

A draft of the stated case must be sent to both parties to the case. Since in summary trials no full record is kept of the proceedings, the parties to the appeal may suggest adjustments to the draft stated case. Intimation of such adjustments must be made to the judge and the other party within thirty days of receipt of the draft stated case. If the appellant fails to do so (or fails to intimate he has no adjustments to propose) within this time limit, he is deemed to have abandoned his appeal. The procurator fiscal always advises Crown Counsel of any adjustments proposed by him or the accused. Occasionally a sheriff may hold an informal hearing at which both parties are present to discuss any proposed adjustments, but whether or not he accepts any adjustments to the draft stated case lies within his discretion, and he may if he wishes ignore them all.

Within fourteen days after the latest date on which any adjustments are received, the judge must issue the stated case in its final form and the clerk of court must send it to the appellant, who in turn serves a copy on the other party. If he fails to serve a copy to the other party and to lodge the principal with the Clerk of Justiciary (i.e. the clerk of the High Court) within ten days, he is deemed to have abandoned his appeal. In any event, the appellant may abandon his appeal at any time prior to the case being lodged with the Clerk of Justiciary. Once the case has been lodged, the High Court will fix a date for the hearing of the appeal. At the hearing, the court will not hear objections which have not been made the subject of questions of law in the stated case unless such objections are of so serious a character as to indicate fundamental nullity in the proceedings. The prosecution will be represented by an advocate depute and the defence by the accused in person, or more commonly by his advocate. Both parties submit verbal submissions for the court's considera-tion. In disposing of the appeal, the court has the following powers: to affirm, reverse or amend the decision of the inferior court; to impose a fine instead of imprisonment where imprisonment has been awarded; to reduce the period of imprisonment; to reduce any fine; to remit the case back to the inferior court to be amended (in order that additional facts or questions of law might be stated) and thereafter on the case being amended and returned, to deliver judgment thereon; to remit the case to the inferior court with their opinion; where an appeal against an acquittal is sustained, to convict and sentence the accused, or to remit the case to the inferior court with instructions to convict and sentence the accused (the accused being bound to attend any diet fixed by the inferior court for this purpose); to remit to any fit person to inquire and report in regard to the facts and circumstances of any appeal, and thereafter on considering such a report, to pronounce judgement; to award such expenses (i.e. of the appeal) as the court thinks fit. In addition, the court has power to amend any conviction or sentence and to pronounce such other judgement or sentence as it thinks expedient.

Since the court is thus restricted to considering the case and the evidence as contained in the stated case, the appeal does not take the form of a re-trial, although both parties are represented. It also follows that if one party appeals, it is not necessary for the other party to lodge a counter appeal. Should an appeal be taken by an accused in any case where the prosecutor is not prepared to oppose the appeal, the prosecutor may intimate that he consents to the conviction and sentence being set aside, either in whole or in part. The case will then be considered by a High Court judge either in court or in chambers, and such judge after hearing the parties, if they desire to be heard, may set aside the conviction either in whole or in part, or may refuse to set aside the conviction in which case the appeal will be disposed of in the normal way in due course.

Bill of Suspension

234 This is a means of appeal which is only available to the accused, and not the prosecutor. It is used where the accused claims that the decision of the court was illegal or improper. Should the accused be in custody, he may be liberated until the appeal is decided. This type of appeal should properly only be used where there has been an irregularity in procedure, or irregularity or oppressive conduct on the part of the judge or prosecutor; if it involves a question of law based on the facts of the case, the correct type of appeal is by stated case.

The merits of the conviction can not be reviewed, hence a bill of suspension may not be used to claim that the verdict was contrary to the evidence. It may however be used to appeal against the decision of a trial judge in admitting or rejecting certain evidence. As with stated cases, where the accused was legally represented at the trial, proper objection must have been taken at the time. It may however also be used if the appeal is taken on the grounds of incompetency, or corruption, or malice or oppression. As a result, if an accused has plead guilty to the charge and there is therefore no dispute on the facts, he may appeal against sentence by means of a bill of suspension on the grounds that the sentence is harsh and oppressive.

There is no time limit for bringing a bill of suspension, but it should be done as soon as possible. As a general rule, a delay of a few months is fatal, but in one exceptional case[5] a delay of four and a half years was allowed.

The procedure begins with the accused lodging the Bill of Suspension with the Clerk of Justiciary (i.e. the clerk of court of the High Court). The Bill narrates the charge and the sentence, claiming that the conviction and sentence were imposed 'most wrongously and unjustly', giving the reasons for this claim, and requests the court to set aside the conviction or sentence or both. A copy of the Bill is served on the prosecutor.

If the court decides to liberate the accused until the appeal is decided, it may require him to lodge caution. Should this be done, and the accused fail to appear at the hearing of the appeal, he will be deemed to have abandoned the appeal. When the procurator fiscal is served with a copy of the Bill, he will draft answers to it which he will send, together with a statement of the facts of the case to Crown Counsel. The latter will decide whether or not the Bill is to be opposed, and if so, the final form of the answers for the prosecution. The court will then set a date

---

[5] Muirhead v McIntosh 1890 2 White 473.

for the hearing of the appeal at which both parties may make verbal submissions to supplement their written ones.

As a general rule, at the hearing the court will not consider the facts of the case, but if it requires some further information about the evidence, it can remit the sheriff to make further inquiry and report. At the conclusion of the hearing the court can suspend the sentence and order repayment of any fine; refuse the appeal and re-commit the accused to prison (if such was the original sentence); amend the conviction and sentence and remit the case to the inferior court with instructions, if necessary.

Alteration of Sentence by a Summary Court

235   Although appeals by way of stated case or bill of suspension are the methods by which a case is reviewed by the High Court, there is a limited provision allowing the court which passed the sentence to review it. A summary court may alter or modify any sentence provided imprisonment has not followed, but can not increase the sentence.[6] Thus if the accused is sentenced to imprisonment, but has not left the court to be taken to prison, the court can modify the sentence. Alternatively, if the accused has been fined, the court can reduce the fine or allow a longer time for payment. If the accused has been disqualified from driving, the court can remove the disqualification.

This procedure is often used either where the accused has pled guilty by letter, or was not legally represented at the original hearing. In such instances it may happen that certain facts in mitigation of sentence were not placed before the court, or were not properly put. The accused will usually consult a solicitor, who in the first instance may request the judge to consider the case further, such procedure being used as an alternative to a bill of suspension claiming that the sentence was oppressive. Since the accused need not be present at such a hearing, the judge frequently arranges an informal hearing for the solicitor to submit his arguments as to why the sentence should be modified. The prosecutor will also be present and may comment on the accused's arguments. Should the judge refuse to modify the sentence, the accused may still appeal by means of a bill of suspension.

[6] Summary Jurisdiction (Scotland) Act 1954, Section 57.

Appendix 1. The French Jury System

See paras 10 and 88

Prior to 1832, the jury was only allowed to decide matters of fact and pronounce on the guilt or innocence of the accused. The judges decided any legal issues and imposed sentence after the jury returned a guilty verdict. The main disadvantage lay in the fact that since French law specifies the minimum (as well as maximum) penalty for every offence, the jurors, while not officially concerned with sentence, were always aware of what a guilty verdict would entail. This gave rise to instances where juries would return a verdict of not guilty merely because jurors felt the offence did not merit the penalty prescribed by law. In 1832, juries were allowed to declare whether or not any mitigating circumstances existed, and so to a very limited extent determine the sentence. By a law passed in 1908, the president of the court was allowed to enter the jury room during its deliberations to indicate and discuss the probable penalty in the event of a verdict of guilty. The president could not, however, bind the two 'assesseurs' so that the court could award a penalty other than that predicted by the president.

In 1932, a further law, while leaving to the jury the power to decide on the verdict, allowed it in the event of a guilty verdict, to deliberate with the judges on the sentence. Experience showed however, that while this remedied one defect, the verdicts by juries were not always satisfactory in that juries could be swayed by emotional factors or advocacy and in some cases gave verdicts which were themselves inconsistent, or were contrary to the evidence. Difficulty was also experienced in complicated cases.

To overcome this difficulty a change was made in 1941, whereby the judges retired with the jury to decide on both the verdict and the sentence. At the same time the number of jurors was reduced from twelve to six, but this number was increased to seven in 1945 and nine in 1958. Jurors are selected from a list prepared annually and must be thirty years of age or older, be literate and have full civil rights (which are withdrawn on conviction of certain serious offences). The verdict may be unanimous or by majority—at least eight persons voting for guilty, hence the opinion of the lay jurors outweighs that of the judges. (Details of how the verdict is reached are given in paras 93 and 94 dealing with the cour d'assises). If the verdict is guilty, sentence is then decided by a simple majority (see para 94) within the legal limits.

It is felt that this solution, while allowing the jury its independence, permits the judges to counteract any ignorance, inexperience or bias on the part of the jurors, and assist them to interpret the evidence in complex cases. (The judges still retain the power to settle any legal issues). Similar systems exist in Germany and Italy.

CP-O

That the independence of the jury still exists is illustrated by the verdicts in many 'crimes passionnels' of which a typical example is the case of Jean Berdold (Cour d'assises de la Moselle, 1972). The accused, who was aged 60 years, and had no previous convictions was charged with the murder of his wife. The facts were that his wife had been suffering from cancer since 1961, was always in extreme agony and was dying. The accused killed his wife by suffocation, then reported the matter to the police. In his confession, he said that he could not stand to see her suffer any longer. The facts were not in dispute at the trial, and the prosecution suggested that while finding the accused guilty, the jury might consider a minimum penalty such as two years' suspended sentence. The jury's verdict was 'not guilty.'

While such cases illustrate the independence of the jurors from the judiciary, it gives rise to criticism that juries are too easily swayed by emotional factors or advocacy. It is also felt that juries should not be allowed to pronounce on sentence which many believe is a matter for the specialist, and should not be subject to any prejudices or emotions of the jury.

On the other hand, the prevailing view appears to be that the jury system, on balance, is beneficial in that the layman, untramelled by legal professionalism, often applies commonsense and by ignoring strict legal rules renders justice more humane. There is also the argument that since justice is designed to protect the individual citizen, in a democratic society, the citizen should have a say in the enforcing of justice.

Appendix 2. 'Crimes Passionnels'

(*See para 32*)

As a general rule, the excuse that the accused acted while his passions were aroused does not amount to a defence to a criminal charge. The oft quoted exception to this rule is contained in Article 324 of the Penal Code which states 'It is a valid defence for a husband charged with the murder of his wife and her paramour if it is proved that the murder was committed at the very instant he surprised them committing the act of adultery in the marital home'. Apart from this exception, the defence that the accused acted in the heat of passion, should only serve to mitigate sentence and not as an answer to the charge. However French juries regularly ignore the provisions of the law in taking a sympathetic approach to 'crimes passionnels'.

In the case of Léone Bouvier (Cour d'assises de Maine et Loire, 1953) the accused was charged with the premeditated murder of her lover, Émile Clenet. Bouvier, who came from an appallingly poor background and was very plain in appearance, became Clenet's mistress in 1951, when she was aged twenty-one years. In due course, she became pregnant, whereupon Clenet, not only refused to marry her, but insisted she have an abortion, which resulted in her prolonged illness and ultimate dismissal from her job. Clenet took every opportunity to humiliate her and eventually parted company with her abruptly on 15th January 1952. Bouvier became exceedingly distraught and was seen several times looking in gunsmith's windows. On 17th February she purchased a .22 pistol. She met Clenet by chance and arranged a further meeting for 27th February. When Clenet appeared, he said he was emigrating and never had any intention of marrying her. Although he continued to mock her, he eventually consented to a farewell embrace, in the course of which Bouvier shot him in the head. She immediately sought sanctuary in a convent. There could be no doubt that such a course had been in her mind since 15th January (no mention having been made of purchasing the gun for the purpose of suicide). When asked at the trial why she had killed Clenet, she replied 'I loved him'. Despite the evidence, the jury found her guilty of murder, but not of premeditation, thus saving her from execution.

A more striking example is the case of Yvonne Chevallier (Cour d'assises de Rheims 1951), accused of the murder of her husband. There was no dispute that the accused had shot her husband five times, using a pistol. The shooting took place in the bedroom of their home and between the fourth and fifth shots the accused emerged to ask a maid to tend to the accused's four year old son who wanted to know what was happening in the bedroom. It appeared that the accused acted out of jealousy for her husband's mistress (who was not present at the time of the crime). The mistress gave evidence at the trial openly admitting her liaison with the accused's husband. The jury returned a verdict of not guilty.

A third example of the jury's attitude to a 'crime passionnel' is the case of Jean Berdold (quoted in Appendix 1).

Appendix 3. Plaintes

(See para 39)

The following are typical examples of 'plaintes' received by the procureur de la République at Paris from private individuals.

(1) The complainer writes that he was a passenger in a motor car which was involved in an accident seven days previously; he suffered minor injuries involving one day's loss of work, and damage to his clothing; he wishes to lodge a formal complaint against 'whoever was responsible for the accident', no person being specified by the complainer; he also wishes to make a civil claim against any person who may be prosecuted.

(2) The complainer writes that he was injured in a road accident ten months previously and has been receiving medical treatment ever since; he requests the procureur to prosecute the person (unspecified) who caused the accident—no further details being given.

(3) The complainer writes that some unknown person is continually telephoning him during the night; when he answers the phone, the caller hangs up; he wishes the procureur to take steps to stop this nuisance.

(4) The complainer writes that his child aged four years was assaulted by a neighbour's wife nine months previously; the child sustained injuries necessitating thirty-five days treatment in hospital; a list of witnesses to the incident and a copy medical report from the hospital are enclosed; no explanation is given for the delay in reporting the assault; he requests that the neighbour's wife be prosecuted.

(5) The complainer writes that a neighbour had come into her (the complainer's) home ten days previously and assaulted her and her husband; no further details are given; she requests the procureur to prosecute the neighbour for assault.

(6) The complainer writes that some unknown person tried to set fire to the door of his office three days previously; he requests the procureur to make investigations and prosecute whoever was responsible.

(7) The complainer writes that she has received anonymous letters of 'an insulting nature'; photocopies are enclosed; she suspects a neighbour of being responsible; she requests the procureur to make inquiries.

(8) The complainer writes that he was playing football three weeks previously in a 'cup-tie match'; in the course of the match, a spectator rushed onto the field and assaulted him; he requests the procureur to prosecute the spectator, no further details being given.

(9) The complainer writes that her husband threatened her and assaulted her four days previously, she sustained bruising but did not require medical attention; she wants the procureur to prosecute her husband.

(10) The complainer, who at the time is detained in prison, writes to say that he was assaulted by a prison officer three months previously; a very full account of the assault is given together with the names of potential witnesses; he requests the procureur to prosecute the prison officer.

Excluded from the above examples are 'plaintes' which are accompanied by full witness statements and a great wealth of detail. Also excluded are 'plaintes' of an eccentric nature, those which have not even a remote connection with criminal law, and those complaining of an incident (usually a road accident) occurring several years previously.

The procureur in sending 'plaintes' to the police for investigation will accompany them with a 'soit transmis', of which there are two styles. The undernoted style usually instructs the police to make inquiries ('enquête preliminaire') and may or may not give further precise instructions.

TRIBUNAL

DE GRANDE INSTANCE

DE PARIS

PARQUET

DU

PROCUREUR DE LA RÉPUBLIQUE

N°_____

A renvoyer avec la réponse
et les pièces jointes

SOIT TRANSMIS

à Monsieur le

Procureur de la République

Directeur de la police judiciaire

Commissaire de police

Commandant de section de gendarmerie

Maire

Directeur de la maison d'arrêt

à_____

en ayant l'honneur de le prier de bien vouloir

Le _____

LE PROCUREUR DE LA RÉPUBLIQUE

Imp. Adm. Melun — Cello. 2591-1970

n° 105 (Paris)

The following alternative style is used when the procureur wishes to give more detailed instructions:

TRIBUNAL
DE GRANDE INSTANCE
DE PARIS
——

PARQUET
du
PROCUREUR DE LA RÉPUBLIQUE
——

N° ....

— ▣ —

SOIT TRANSMIS

à Monsieur le

Procureur de la République

Directeur de la police judiciaire

Commissaire de police

Commandant de Compagnie de gendarmerie

Maire

Directeur de la maison d'arrêt

....

à ....

A renvoyer avec la réponse
et les pièces jointes

qui paraît compétent,

aux fins demandées,

après objet .... rempli,

pour exécution,

pour faire préciser l'objet de la demande,

pour recevoir la plainte par procès-verbal,

pour renseignements et avis,

pour enquête,

pour audition de ....

pour — notification — remise — contre récépissé à me faire parvenir,

en ayant l'honneur de le prier de bien vouloir

Le ....

Le Procureur de la République,

When, after investigating the 'plainte', the procureur decides not to institute criminal proceedings, he will instruct the police to notify the complainer of his decision, often using the following form:

TRIBUNAL
DE GRANDE INSTANCE
de PARIS
––––––

PARQUET
du
PROCUREUR DE LA REPUBLIQUE
––––––

N° ....

●●

à renvoyer avec la réponse
et les pièces jointes

AVIS DE CLASSEMENT
––––––

SOIT TRANSMIS

à Monsieur le
Procureur de la République
Directeur de la Police Judiciaire
Commissaire de Police
Commandant de Compagnie de Gendarmerie

....

a ....

en ayant l'honneur de le prier de bien vouloir faire connaître au plaignant ....

....

— qu'après enquête mon Parquet n'estime pas qu'il y a lieu de poursuivre d'office,

— que sa réclamation étant d'ordre purement civil ne saurait motiver l'intervention du Parquet,

....

....

En conséquence, sa plainte est classée sans suite à mon Parquet sous le numéro ci-dessus indiqué.

Le plaignant a la faculté, soit de poursuivre lui-même devant la juridiction civile ou pénale compétente, soit de demander l'ouverture d'une information en se constituant partie civile devant M. le Juge d'instruction, qui fixera le montant de la consignation à effectuer au greffe pour couvrir l'avance des frais de cette information. En cas d'indigence ou d'insuffisance de ses ressources, il peut demander le bénéfice de l'assistance judiciaire.

L'attention du plaignant sera appelée sur les conséquences que pourrait entraîner pour lui une constitution de partie civile insuffisamment motivée ou injustifiée (art. 91 du Code de procédure pénale).

Le ....

LE PROCUREUR DE LA RÉPUBLIQUE,

Imp. Adm Melun — C.2865-1970

n°111 (Paris)

Appendix 4. Sudden Deaths

(See para 43)

The procureur de la République has the responsibility of investigating all sudden, unexpected or suspicious deaths. If there is a question of foul play, the procureur may request a juge d'instruction to make the inquiry, but in most instances the procureur himself will retain the responsibility only requesting intervention by a juge d'instruction after the initial steps have been taken and foul play apparent. Even if there is no evidence of foul play, the procureur always has the option of requesting a juge d'instruction to inquire into a death. This is called an 'information pour recherche'. Should the cause of death be obvious, and if there is no question of criminal proceedings—for example suicide by hanging—the procureur will normally instruct a doctor to make a visual examination of the body, without the necessity of a post mortem dissection. He may instruct such action informally and need not use the 'Requisition aux fins d'autotopsie' (see infra). The following are typical examples of deaths reported to the procureur, and the action taken:

(1) *Fatal road accident*—a female pedestrian aged sixty-nine years walked across the street without looking to see if there was any traffic; she was knocked down by a motor cyclist, receiving injuries from which she died the following day; the motor cyclist told the police he braked and swerved to avoid her, but was unable to avoid colliding with her; the only independent witness confirmed the statement of the motor cyclist, absolving him from all blame; the procureur did not order a post mortem, but released the body for burial, having decided to take no further proceedings; he notified the relatives of the deceased about his decision, and advised them what steps they could take to institute criminal proceedings if they were dissatisfied with his decision (the relatives having lodged a 'plainte' against the motor cyclist).

(2) *Fatal road accident*—the driver of a car overtook a slower car and in so doing struck it, went out of control and crashed into a tree; the driver of the overtaking car was killed; the driver of the slower car said he observed the overtaking car in his mirror and could give no explanation for the collision; no other witnesses were traced; the procureur did not order a post mortem and released the body for burial; he decided that no further proceedings should be taken unless he received a formal 'plainte' from deceased's relatives giving further evidence, in which case he would reconsider his decision.

(3) *Suicide*—Body of a male, aged fifty-seven years was found hanging from

a rope tied to a beam in his own house; the body was found by deceased's daughter; there was no evidence of foul play, but clear indications that the deceased had stood on a chair then stepped off; the deceased had a history of mental illness and depression; the procureur arranged for a doctor to make a visual examination of the body, but did not order a post mortem dissection; the procureur decided that no further proceedings should be taken; this decision was made without interviewing deceased's widow, as she had already been questioned by the police; the procureur's attitude was that it would be heartless to interview her a second time, and if she was not satisfied with his decision, she must take the initiative of coming to see him.

(4) *Suicide or accident*—A student aged twenty-two years was found hanging from a rope attached to a hook in the room where he lodged alone; his hands were tied behind his back, but an examination of the knot showed it could easily be self-tied; he was wearing female clothing; the procureur ordered a post mortem dissection of the body, which confirmed that death was due to hanging; the post mortem also revealed that the deceased was accustomed to perverted sexual practices; literature in his room appeared to confirm this; the single doctor who conducted the post mortem gave the opinion that the deceased while engaging in sexually devious conduct had attempted to partially choke himself; the 'experiment' went wrong and he died—death therefore probably being accidental rather than suicidal; there was no evidence of interference by a third party; the procureur decided that no further proceedings should be taken and sent a copy of the doctor's report to the deceased's relatives on their request.

It should be noted that in none of the above cases was there any evidence of murder.

For an example of the form used by the procureur instructing a post mortem dissection (Requisition aux fins d'autotopsie) see over.

PARQUET
DU
TRIBUNAL
DE GRANDE INSTANCE
de PARIS

Réquisition aux fins d'autopsie

LE PROCUREUR DE LA RÉPUBLIQUE
PRÈS LE TRIBUNAL DE GRANDE INSTANCE DE PARIS

Vu l'enquête suivie : ....
....

pour ....
....

par ....
....

Vu l'article .... du Code de procédure pénale :

Vu la nécessité de faire constater d'urgence les circonstances et les causes de la mort de :

Requiert M ....
aux fins de procéder à l'autopsie complète du cadavre déposé à l'institut médico-légal, pour établir les circonstances et les causes de la mort et rechercher tous indices de crime ou délit;

Procéder à la description détaillée du cadavre. Faire procéder à tout examen radioscopique qui apparaîtrait utile à la manifestation de la vérité et, éventuellement, à des prises de clichés radiographiques ou photographiques;

Saisir et placer sous scellés tout projectile ou autre objet qui serait découvert dans le corps. Prélever un échantillon du sang et, en cas de nécessité, les viscères.

Desdites opérations il sera dressé un rapport qui sera transmis par ledit expert après en avoir affirmé le contenu sincère et véritable.

Fait à Paris, le .... *19*...........

LE PROCUREUR DE LA RÉPUBLIQUE,

N° 406

Appendix 5. 'L'Enquête Flagrante' —Examination of accused persons by the procureur de la République

(*See para* 47)

When the accused is brought in custody before the procureur at the end of the period of 'garde à vue', the procureur is handed the police information giving the details of the offence. He normally starts his examination by confirming the accused's personal particulars before turning to the offence itself. The following gives a resumé of some examinations made by the procureur in Paris. The extracts are restricted to the part dealing with the offence, and it must be noted that as each procureur will have his own personal style, all such examinations need not follow this pattern closely.

(1) Male accused aged 25 years—charged with vagabondage. The procureur questioned the accused closely about his address and means of support. The accused insisted that he had a job and a fixed place of abode, but that the police had not believed him. He produced documents to support his claim. After a detailed cross examination, the procureur stated he believed the accused.
Decision: no further proceedings, accused to be released forthwith.

(2) Male accused aged 41 years—charged with failing to pay a taxi fare after the driver had taken him to his destination.

> *Question* 'Did you take the taxi and tell the driver to take you to a particular address?'
> *Answer* 'Yes'.
> *Question* 'Do you agree that you refused to pay the fare?'
> *Answer* 'Yes, but I had no money and had to get home'.
> *Decision*: liberate accused to be cited to court at a later date.

(3) Male accused aged 25 years—charged with being found in Paris after being ordered to leave following a previous conviction.

> *Question* 'Do you admit the previous conviction?'
> *Answer* 'Yes'.
> *Question* 'Do you agree you were ordered to leave Paris?'
> *Answer* 'Yes'.
> *Question* 'Do you agree you were found in Paris last night and arrested there?'
> *Answer* 'Yes'.
> *Question* 'Did you have any legal or justifiable reason for returning to Paris in defiance of the court order?'
> *Answer* 'I wanted to see my friend'.
> *Decision*: Detain accused and place before the court using 'Flagrant Délit' procedure.

(4) Male accused aged 19 years—charged with theft of a motor cycle.

Question 'Did you steal this motor cycle?'
Answer 'Yes'
Question 'When?'
Answer 'About ten minutes before my arrest'
Question 'Why did you steal it?'
Answer 'To visit my girl friend'
Decision: detain accused and place before the court using 'Flagrant Délit' procedure.

(5) Four male accused all aged between 21 and 25 years—charged with theft of a brief case from a car; all were brought in together and questioned in the presence of each other; the accused numbers 1 and 3 admitted the theft, numbers 2 and 4 denied it.

Question (to 2 and 4 jointly) 'But you were in the company of the other two?'
Answer (by No. 2) 'But they already had the case before we met them. We did not know it was stolen'
Question 'But two policemen say they saw the four of you together before the theft was committed'
Answer (by No. 4) 'That's not true'
Question (to 1 and 3 jointly) 'Were the other two in your company when you stole the case?'
Nos. 1 and 3 refused to answer.
Decision: Detain all four accused and place before the court using 'Flagrant Délit' procedure; cite the two policemen as witnesses for the trial.

(6) Male accused aged 56 years—charged with loitering in a cellar with intent to steal.

Question 'Do you admit the charge?'
Answer 'I deny it'
Question 'Do you admit being in the cellar?'
Answer 'Yes, but I went there out of curiosity, not to steal'
Question 'Is that all you have to say? No one will believe that. You can make your explanation in court'
Decision: Detain accused and place before the court using 'Flagrant Délit' procedure.

(7) Male accused aged 31 years—charged with theft of cloth from a shop.

Question 'Do you admit the charge?'
Answer 'I deny stealing the cloth. I found it lying on the floor of the shop'
Question 'But shops don't put items they are going to sell on the floor?'
Answer 'I found it on the floor. I did not steal it'
Question 'Well, if that's your only explanation it will be recorded. Are you working?'
Answer 'No'
Question 'Why not? When did you last work?'
Answer 'I had an accident three months ago and have not worked since'
Decision: Detain accused and place before the court using 'Flagrant Délit' procedure.

(8) Male accused aged 23 years—charged with theft of a motor cycle.

Question 'Why did you steal this motor cycle ?'
Answer 'To visit my girl friend'
Question 'According to the police you have been taking drugs'
Answer 'Yes. A few months ago I underwent psychiatric treatment for this'
Question 'What drugs did you take and how ?'
Answer 'I smoked cannabis'

Decision: Bring accused before a juge d'instruction immediately (so that the accused's background could be more fully investigated)

(9) Male accused aged 28 years—charged with theft of cigarettes from a café.

Question 'Did you steal the cigarettes from the café ?'
Answer 'No. I was never even in the café'
Question 'Well listen to what a witness says'—the procureur then read a witness statement in full in which the witness states that the accused entered the café and stole a box containing cartons of cigarettes—'Is this true ?'
Answer 'I was never in the café'
Question 'The police found you in possession of the cigarettes'
Answer 'I found the box of cigarettes in a street near the café'
Question 'It appears from the police information that you were banned from Paris following a previous conviction. Is this true ?'
Answer 'No'
Question 'Well it seems to me further inquiries will have to be made. Have you anything else to say ?'
Answer 'No'

Decision: Bring accused before a juge d'instruction immediately (so that full inquiries can be made).

(10) Male accused aged 28 years—charged with theft of a car; the accused had told the police he stole the car to use it for spare parts for his own; the car was recovered partly dismantled, in the accused's possession.

After verifying the accused's personal particulars, the procureur asked no further questions.

Decision: Bring accused before a juge d'instruction immediately (to make full inquiry).

(11) Male accused aged 44 years—charged with drunk driving. When questioning the accused about his personal particulars, the procureur came to the conclusion that the accused had no fixed place of abode.

Question 'You admit driving the car ?'
Answer 'Yes'
Question 'Were you given a breathalyser test which proved positive ?
Answer 'Yes'

Decision: Bring accused before a juge d'instruction immediately (proceedings could not be taken until the result of a blood alcohol analysis was made known. This would take about fifteen days. In the interim the procureur was not willing that the accused should be liberated for citing—the usual procedure—as he had no fixed place of abode. By bringing him before a juge d'instruction, the latter could exercise his discretion and order the accused be detained in custody until the result of the blood/alcohol analysis was known).

Appendix 6. Confrontation

(*See para 62*)

The following is not a record of an actual confrontation (in view of the strict rules concerning the secrecy of proceedings before a juge d'instruction) but is based on one.

The facts of the case as elicited by the juge so far were that in May 1970 Mr. A., Mrs. A. and Mr. B. went to a café owned by the accused. All of them except Mrs. A. had criminal records, although the accused had not been in trouble for 15 years. Shortly after their arrival the police came to the café and requested Mr. A., Mrs. A. and Mr. B. to accompany them—the reasons for this request not being entirely clear. Mr. A., Mrs. A. and Mr. B. left with the police who questioned them for an hour and released them, whereupon Mr. A., Mrs. A. and Mr. B. returned to the café, blaming the accused for the incident. This the accused denied, but Mr. A., Mrs. A. and Mr. B. remained in the café ordering wine (which Mr. A. confided to his companions he was not going to pay for). An argument developed between Mr. A. and the accused—the witnesses giving different versions of the argument—but all were agreed that the accused drew out a gun, shot and killed Mr. A., and shot at Mr. B. four times, missing him each time.

The accused was charged with murdering Mr. A.

Mrs. A. had lodged a claim as 'partie civile'.

On the afternoon arranged by the juge for the confrontation, he commenced by examining Mr. B. alone, having already done so on a previous occasion. Having confirmed Mr. B.'s particulars, the juge put him on oath and asked him to give his evidence. Mr. B. proceeded to do so, saying that when they all returned to the café, there was no argument between Mr. A. and the accused, and that the accused suddenly drew a gun, shot and wounded Mr. A., fired at him (Mr. B.) then again shot Mr. A., this second shot killing him. The juge interrupted to ask if Mr. A. and the witness were armed—as the accused had alleged this—but Mr. B. denied this. The juge asked Mr. B. if, prior to the shooting, there had been an argument between Mr. A. and the accused, in the course of which Mr. A. struck the accused. The juge read out several witnesses statements to this effect. Mr. B. denied this had taken place, despite vigorous questioning by the juge. The juge asked 'Well, why should the accused shoot Mr. A.?', to which Mr. B. replied 'I've often wondered that myself.'

The juge then ordered that the accused (and his lawyer) and Mrs. A. as partie civile (and her lawyer) be brought in. When this was done, the juge having explained that he wished to discuss the events of the night of the offence in more detail, then read to the accused the statement made by Mrs. A. to him (the juge). As he did so, he verified the statement with Mrs. A. In this statement, Mrs. A. admitted that her husband had argued with the accused, but as she had left to go to the toilet, she could not give too much detail.

The juge asked the accused to comment on Mrs. A.'s statement. The accused then said that when Mr. A., Mrs. A. and Mr. B. returned to the café they ordered some wine and that shortly afterwards Mr. A. began insulting him, accusing him of being a homosexual, threatened him with violence and struck him several times; Mr. A. then threatened to kill him, whereupon Mr. B. intervened and suggested to him (the accused) that if he gave Mr. A. 2000 francs, Mr. A. might calm down and forget the incident. At this point Mr. A. put his hand inside his pocket and the accused thought he was armed. In view of this and Mr. A.'s threat to kill him, the accused pulled out a gun and fired one shot at Mr. A. Mr. B. then rushed at him (the accused) whereupon he fired at Mr. B. in panic, missing him. He (the accused) had taken the gun from a drawer where it had lain for years, and put it in his pocket at the start of the argument.

The juge then asked Mr. B. to comment on the accused's evidence, which Mr. B. then disagreed with vehemently. In particular, he denied that there was any argument, any blows, any mention of money and reiterated that the accused fired first at Mr. A., then at him, then again at Mr. A. hitting Mr. A. both times.

The juge then asked Mrs. A. if she could give more detail. Mrs. A. said that there was a struggle between Mr. A. and the accused just before the shooting and that the accused fired a shot at Mr. A. After that there were further shots but she was too confused to notice much detail. As she had been absent from the table for a few minutes prior to the struggle she could not say if any remark was made about 2000 francs.

The juge then dictated all the above in narrative form to his clerk who typed it as dictated. All the parties agree that the juge's narrative accurately recorded what they had said.

The juge then told Mr. B. 'Our purpose here is to find the truth. Cast aside any thought of malice or vengeance . . .' and began to question Mr. B. with some force concerning the remark about the 2000 francs. Mr. B. eventually admitted that there had been a struggle between Mr. A. and the accused, and that Mr. A. had struck the accused. Finally Mr. B. admitted that he had made the remark concerning the 2000 francs

At this point the juge dictated Mr B.'s further statement in narrative form to his clerk. He read the narrative over to Mr. B. to ask if it accurately recorded what he had said. Mr. B. denied that he had admitted making the remark concerning the 2000 francs, whereupon the juge insisted that he had admitted the remark. The lawyers for the accused and the 'partie civile' intervened to support the juge and Mr. B. eventually admitted that he had told the juge he had made the remark and it was true to say he had made the remark on the night in question.

The juge then asked the accused about the number and order of the shots, and asked him to re-enact the scene, which the accused did, confirming his earlier evidence. The juge then asked Mrs. A. if she could give more detail, but she said she was unable to do so.

The juge then asked Mr. B. about the shots, and Mr. B. confirmed his earlier version of this, accusing the accused of lying. At this, the accused, who was very emotionally disturbed, interrupted the proceedings by shouting at Mr. B. and calling him a liar. The juge warned the accused about his conduct and told him to keep quiet and not to interrupt again. The accused's lawyer also attempted to calm him down.

The juge turned to Mr. B. again and told him that the post mortem showed that Mr. A. had only been hit once, and that the ballistic expert had demonstrated that the angle of the shot was consistent with the accused's version of the incident. The juge then asked Mr. B. to re-enact the scene, but he was unable to do so in the manner described by his earlier evidence. Mr. B. then said that he must have been mistaken, and that the accused's version must be accurate. He could only account for his mistake as being due to the intense emotion he was suffering from at the time of the shooting.

The juge then said he had no further questions to ask but inquired if the lawyers representing the accused and Mrs. A. had any. Mrs. A.'s lawyer suggested two questions which the juge directed Mr. B. to answer. These questions and answers were noted verbatim, the effect being to show that Mr. B. had been lying about an earlier incident on the night of the crime.

After the juge had completed dictating everything else in narrative form, and after Mr. B. and the accused agreed that the narrative accurately recorded what they had said, the juge, the accused and Mr. B. signed each page of the record.

The duration of the confrontation was four hours. Its effect was to discredit Mr. B. as a credible witness and to confirm the accused's version of the main facts of the offence.

Appendix 7. Trials in the Tribunal Correctionnel

(*See para* 77)

While the conduct of a trial in the tribunal correctionnel will depend on the attitude and personal style of each president, and also on the pressure of business affecting a particular court, the following are typical examples. In none of them is exhaustive detail given, but the main features are mentioned. It should be remembered that the president will have made a study of the 'dossier' or police report prior to the trial itself. While the following cases are taken from different courts sitting on different days, taken together they might constitute a typical afternoon's work for the court, commencing at 1.30 p.m. and ending 5 p.m. The president will dictate the order in which the trials will be taken, the session usually commencing with cases deferred for verdict and sentence. Obviously cases of greater complexity would last much longer.

(1) Male accused aged 24 years: charged with being in possession of 4 grains of cannabis and attempting to sell the same: the accused was a first offender; he had been detained in custody for five months awaiting trial, while a juge d'instruction investigated the case.

The trial commenced with the accused answering to his name and the president questioning him about his background; he was single, unemployed and had no previous convictions. The president then told the accused the details of the charges and narrated the facts of the case from the dossier. He then examined the accused:

President: 'Do you deny being in possession of 4 grains of cannabis?'
Accused: 'No, but I did not try to sell them'
President: 'But the police saw you speaking to two young students'
Accused: 'The students stopped me to ask the way. I did not know them'
President: 'But they say you offered to sell them cannabis'
Accused: 'This is not true'
President: 'You have been taking drugs for five years? By what method?'
Accused: 'I have been smoking cannabis for five years'
President: 'The police say they saw you showing two packets to the students. On your arrest it was found that the packets contained cannabis'
Accused: 'This is not true'
President: 'When they were interviewed by the police, the students said they were looking for someone to sell them drugs, that they met you and you agreed to sell them some. You were discussing the price and at that point the police intervened'
Accused: 'That is not true'

President: 'So the police and the other witnesses are lying? Do you still maintain you were not attempting to sell the drugs?'

Accused: 'Yes'

President: 'The students gave the same evidence to the police, to the juge d'instruction and when they were confronted with you by the juge d'instruction'

Accused: 'They were lying'

There were no questions suggested by the procureur or the defence lawyer and no witnesses gave evidence. The procureur addressed the court suggesting that the court treat the offence as being serious and the sentence should include expelling the accused from Paris (the scene of the offence). The defence lawyer admitted the accused's guilt with regard to possessing the drugs. With regard to the attempted sale, he argued why the accused should be acquitted, but if the court convicted, he urged several matters which should mitigate the penalty.

The court adjourned for a few minutes. When it resumed, the president read the court's judgment stating which facts the court held proved and the relevant statutory provisions. The accused was convicted of both charges, and sentenced to ten months imprisonment (having spent five months in prison awaiting trial, the accused would have a further five months to serve).

(2) Male accused aged 23 years: charged that while acting along with four other persons, he assaulted a night club owner by cutting him on the face with a razor, then discharged several revolver shots through the closed door of the night club; the accused had been liberated while an investigation was made by a juge d'instruction. The trial commenced with the accused coming forward in answer to his name and the president questioning him about his background. He was married with three children; he was employed as a school teacher and had an excellent record; his spare time activities included assisting in clubs for under-privileged children and similar youth work; he had never been convicted before. His four co-accused had all been dealt with for the above charges, all being sent to prison. A. for twelve months, B. for twelve months, C. for six months and D. for four months. All five accused were negroes.

The president told the accused the details of the charges and began to narrate the facts of the case. On the evening prior to the offence A. had gone to the night club with a female companion and had been forcibly ejected after an argument with the owner. On the night of the offence A. was in the company of B., C. and D. in a café when the accused arrived there.

President: 'How did you come to be in the café?'

Accused: 'Purely by chance'

President: 'How did you come to be in the company of the others?'

Accused: 'I know A. slightly as we used to belong to the same sports club. After a chat he asked me to give him a lift in my car. He said he had some business to attend to but I did not know what it was'

President: (after reading aloud the statements of B., C. and D., which confirmed the accused's evidence) 'What happened next?'

Accused: 'A. directed me towards this night club. On arrival there, A. and the other three went inside and asked me to wait. They said they would only be a few minutes. I waited in the car. A few minutes later A. and the other three came running out of the club'

President:	'Did you hear revolver shots?'
Accused:	'Yes'
President:	'In his statement to the juge d'instruction, A. said . . . (The president then quoted A.'s statement verbatim. The effect was that A. alleged the accused had a revolver in the car, the accused took it out and the accused fired three or four shots through the closed door of the night club) . . .' 'Is this true?'
Accused:	'No, definitely not. One of the others fired. I don't know which one. When I heard the shots I was trembling with fright'
President:	'But A. in his statement was quite explicit that you had the revolver. I will read it to you again . . . (the president read A.'s statement for a second time) . . . .'What do you say?'
Accused:	'That is completely false. I never had the revolver'

There were no questions suggested by the procureur or the defence lawyer, and no witnesses gave evidence. The procureur addressed the court reviewing the evidence both for and against the accused, and concluded that he personally believed the accused. He left the question of verdict and sentence with the court, having no recommendations to make. The defence lawyer moved for an acquittal. In the course of his address he compared the character of the accused with that of the other four accused, drawing on facts from the dossier.

The court adjourned for a few minutes. When it resumed, the president read the court's judgement stating which facts the court held proved and the relevant statutory provisions. The accused was convicted of both charges and sentenced to six months imprisonment, the sentence being suspended.

(3) Male accused aged 26 years: charged with theft of kitchen utensils and a jacket; driving without insurance, driving licence and registration book for the car; the accused had no previous convictions; he had been liberated by the procureur following his arrest and detention by 'garde à vué'; the police had made the pre-trial inquiries.

The trial commenced with the accused coming forward in answer to his name and the president questioning him about his background; he was married but had no children; he had no previous convictions. The president then told the accused the details of the charges and narrated the facts of the case as contained in the police report. He then examined the accused.

President:	'Were you driving this motor car when the police had occasion to stop it?'
Accused:	'Yes'
President:	'The police asked you to produce your driving licence and other documents, then found the stolen property in the car. You were interviewed by the police, but refused to say anything other than you thought the car was insured. What have you to say now?'
Accused:	'Nothing'
President:	'What is your explanation for driving without insurance?'
Accused:	'I thought the car was insured. It was when I bought it'
President:	'I will read a statement which the previous owner gave to the police . . . (the president then read the statement in which the previous owner said he told the accused the insurance would be cancelled

when the car changed ownership) . . . . 'What have you to say to that?'

Accused: 'Nothing'

President: 'Have you no explanation to give concerning the other charges? Is there nothing you wish to say?'

Accused: 'No, nothing'

There were no questions suggested by the procureur or defence lawyer and no witnesses gave evidence. The procureur addressed the court suggesting that the accused be convicted of all charges and disqualified from driving for a lengthy period. The defence lawyer gave the accused's explanation, being the first occasion when this had been given. The accused had bought the car twenty-one days before the offence and as he was allowed fifteen days within which to obtain a registration book, this offence was minimal. With regard to the insurance, the previous owner had lied to the police, having told the accused the insurance would be transferred to his name. The accused's driving licence had merely expired. The property found in the accused's possession was for the most part of little value, all being broken or damaged and having been taken by the accused as scrap. The jacket had been inadvertently left in the car by a passenger and the accused had failed to return it to the owner. The court adjourned for a few minutes. When it resumed the president read the court's judgment stating the facts the court held proved and the relevant statutory provisions. The accused was convicted of all charges and sentenced to four months imprisonment (suspended) and a fine of 1000 francs: he was also disqualified from driving.

(4) Male accused aged 31 years: charged with taking away a motor vehicle without the owner's consent, driving under the influence of alcohol, and causing a road accident whereby two persons in another car were injured; the accused was a first offender; the offences had been investigated by a juge d'instruction; the accused had been detained in custody for a few weeks then liberated. The trial commenced with the accused coming forward in answer to his name. One of the injured parties came forward and intimated that he was a 'partie civile', but the other injured party who had entered such an appearance before the juge d'instruction was not present. The president then questioned the accused about his background, told the accused the details of the charges and narrated the facts of the case from the dossier. He then examined the accused.

President: 'Do you admit you were the driver of the car?'

Accused: 'Yes'

President: 'Were you employed by the owners of the car, and did you take the car without their consent?'

Accused: 'Yes'

President: 'Were you driving at 70 kilometers per hour . . . (President described the accident as contained in the witnesses' statements) . . . Is this true?'

Accused: 'Yes'

President: 'You had been drinking more than you usually do? Do you accept the results of the blood/alcohol analysis?'

Accused: 'Yes'

President: 'Why did you take the car without consent?'

Accused: 'I had been drinking'
President: 'Do you realise you caused a serious accident?'
Accused: 'Yes'

There were no questions suggested by the procureur or defence lawyer or 'partie civile' and no witnesses gave evidence. The 'partie civile' who was not legally represented was invited by the president to address the court. He replied that he merely wished to be awarded the damages and expenses detailed in the 'dossier'. At this stage a representative of the Social Security Ministry stepped forward and asked that expenses be awarded against the accused and in favour of the Ministry in respect of compensation paid by public funds to the two injured parties by way of injury benefits etc. The procureur addressed the court merely saying that the offences merited several months imprisonment and suspension of the accused's driving licence. The defence laywer dealt with both the criminal and the civil case at great length. In mitigation he stated that the accused had been driving for ten years without an accident and on the night of the offence he had met some friends who pressed him to drink more than his usual amount.

The court adjourned for a few minutes. When it resumed the president read the court's judgement stating which facts the court held proved and the relevant statutory provisions. The accused was convicted on all charges. He was sentenced to one year's imprisonment (suspended) plus a fine of 1000 francs. He was disqualified from driving for five years. He was ordered to meet the civil claims of both injured parties and the Social Security Ministry in full.

(5) Male accused aged 20 years: charged with being in possession of a stolen vehicle, failing to stop for a police signal, knocking down and injuring a police officer, colliding with a motor cycle driven by a second police officer, injuring him also; the accused was a first offender, he had been detained in custody for twelve months while the charges were investigated by a juge d'instruction. The trial commenced with the accused answering to his name. A lawyer representing one of the policemen entered appearance as 'partie civile'. The president questioned the accused about his background. He then told the accused the details of the charges and narrated the facts from the dossier. The accused was given a 'lift' in a car which the driver then told him was stolen. The driver then stopped the vehicle and left it. The accused drove off in the vehicle. A policeman requested him to stop for a routine road check, the time being 3 a.m. The accused instead of stopping, drove the car directly at the policeman, knocking him down and injuring him. The policeman summoned assistance by radio and a police motor cyclist on seeing the car gave chase. The accused drove the car into a cul-de-sac, then reversed into the police motor cyclist causing him to sustain minor injuries. The president then examined the accused. The examination was very lengthy and the following is only a brief excerpt.

President: 'Did you see the policeman signalling you to stop?'
Accused: 'No'
President: 'But the street was well lit, there was no other traffic and the policeman was in front of the car'
Accused: 'I did not see any signal. I only saw someone in front of the car. I did not even know it was a policeman.
President: 'But he was in uniform. How can you say you did not know he was a

206

policeman? You had better be completely frank with me. I am far from satisfied that you are telling the truth. Did you drive the car deliberately at the policeman?'

Accused: 'No. I meant to brake, but I put my foot on the wrong pedal'

President: 'And when you reversed into the second policeman, was that deliberate?'

Accused: 'No. I put my foot on the wrong pedal again'

President: 'And by mistake, put the car into reverse gear? Are you trying to make a fool of me?'

Accused: 'No. I am telling the truth'

President: 'The first policeman says you steered the car towards him'

Accused: 'He is lying'

The president then examined the accused with great force and vigour, quoting witness statements verbatim etc. At the conclusion, none of the parties to the case suggested further questions.

The president then examined three police witnesses, two of whom were the injured policemen. The procureur suggested that the president ask the first policeman how long he was off duty as a result of the accident. The president put the question, the answer being two months. No other questions were suggested.

The lawyer for the 'partie civile' (the first injured policeman) addressed the court. He demanded a conviction, using most vehement terms . . . 'I would have no hesitation in demanding the guillotine had either of these policemen been killed and it seems to me that only the guillotine is appropriate for this scoundrel'. The procureur addressed the court merely asking the court to convict the accused but making no reference to sentence. The defence lawyer dealing with both the criminal and civil aspects of the case, while not denying the basic facts pointed out that the accused was short sighted. He had requested the juge d'instruction to grant an 'expertise' to prove this, but the juge had refused. He did, however, have medical certificates which were produced. The incidents were caused mainly by the accused's short sighted condition, panic and lack of driving experience.

The court adjourned for fifteen minutes. When it resumed, the president read the court's judgement stating which facts the court held proved and the relevant statutory provisions. The accused was convicted of all charges and sentenced to six years imprisonment (which in view of his period in custody awaiting trial meant that the accused still had five years to serve. The accused was disqualified from holding a driving licence and ordered to pay the civil claim in full.

At this point a lady (believed to be the mother of the accused) made her way from the public benches and began to shout at the president. He ordered her to be removed from court which was forcibly done by two police officers.

(6) Male accused aged 27 years—charged with theft of a handbag; the accused was an alcoholic who had received medical and psychiatric treatment for alcoholism; he had no previous convictions; he had been detained in custody for five months awaiting trial while a juge d'instruction investigated the case, the most important aspect of which was the accused's background. He had been examined by several experts on the orders of the juge d'instruction. The trial commenced with the accused answering his name and the president questioning him about his background, which was examined in great detail. The president then told the accused the details of the charge and narrated the facts of the case from the dossier. The accused had approached a teenage girl from behind and snatched her handbag

from her hand; it contained nothing but a pair of spectacles. The girl was not injured. The president then examined the accused.

President: 'What have you to say?'
Accused: 'I regret what I did'
President: 'Have you anything else to say?'
Accused: 'No'

There were no questions suggested by the procureur or defence lawyer, and no witnesses gave evidence. The procureur addressed the court merely saying that the accused is obviously guilty, but had already spent five months in prison. The defence lawyer made a brief plea in mitigation.

The president without adjourning the court, consulted the other two judges briefly (the conversation being private). He then read the court's judgement stating the facts the court held proved and the relevant statutory provisions. The accused was convicted and sentenced to five months imprisonment (which in view of the period spent in custody awaiting trial, meant that the accused would be released forthwith).

(7) Five male accused all aged between 25-30 years. The charges were theft, being in possession of stolen property, uttering forged cheques from a stolen cheque book—making thirty charges in all. Each accused was only involved in some of the charges, and either had no previous convictions, or convictions for minor road traffic offences. One of the accused who was involved only in one charge had been released prior to the trial, but the other four had been detained in custody for sixteen months while the case was investigated by a juge d'instruction.

The trial commenced with the four accused in custody answering to their names; the fifth accused was not present, so the president ordered a separation of his trial and fixed a new diet therefor in ten weeks time. He ordered that the fifth accused be re-cited to the new diet of trial. None of the parties was asked his views about the separation of trials, and none objected. The president then questioned each of the four accused about his background, told him of the details of the charges against him and narrated the facts very briefly from the 'dossier'. He then examined each accused in turn, in most instances merely asking the accused if he admitted the charges against him. The procureur and the defence lawyers had no questions to suggest. At this point a man walked forward from the public benches saying that he was a 'partie civile'. The president then examined him briefly, the man having been defrauded of 25 francs by means of a forged cheque. He wished repayment of the 25 francs. Neither the procureur nor the defence lawyer suggested any questions. No further witnesses gave evidence. The 'partie civile' addressed the court in person and asked for an award of 25 francs. The procureur then made a very brief address mainly giving his views about the sentences that should be passed on each accused. The defending lawyer, who acted for all four accused, ignored the civil claim. He said that none of the accused had ever sought to deny his guilt. He gave references as to character and discussed other mitigating factors, stressing that the accused had already spent sixteen months in prison awaiting trial and that while there was a large number of charges, the financial sums involved were paltry.

The court adjourned for thirty minutes. When it resumed, the president read the court's judgement stating which facts the court held proved and the relevant statutory provisions. Each of the four accused was convicted, three of them being sentenced to three years' imprisonment, half of the sentence to be suspended (in effect since they had spent sixteen months in custody, they would require to spend a further two months in prison). The fourth accused was sentenced to four years' imprisonment (of which he had already 'served' sixteen months). The accused involved in the charge where there was a claim by the 'partie civile', were ordered to make restitution of the 25 francs claimed.

(8) Male accused aged 35 years: charged with causing death by careless, negligent or dangerous driving of a motor vehicle, and driving under the influence of alcohol: the case had been investigated by a juge d'instruction and the accused had not been detained in custody awaiting trial.

The trial commenced with the accused answering to his name and the president questioning him about his background. The president then noticed a flaw in the citation ordering the accused to appear. The accused said he had not received the citation, but knew about the trial and the details of the charge. The president asked the accused if he was appearing voluntarily, to which the accused answered that he was. The president then told the accused the details of the charges and narrated the facts of the case from the 'dossier'. In so doing he quoted several witness statements verbatim and gave the results of the post mortem dissection on the deceased and the accused's blood/alcohol analysis. The basic facts were that the accused, while driving a motor car under the influence of alcohol, knocked down and killed a pedestrian who was crossing the road. There was only one eye witness to the accident (who had not been cited to give evidence). The president then examined the accused, by asking him 'What have you to say?' The accused commenced by saying he had been driving for ten years without an accident, whereupon the president interrupted to ask him full details about his driving record. The accused then continued with his narrative to the effect that the pedestrian stepped out from behind a stationary vehicle in front of his car which was only a few metres away. The president again interrupted to say that this did not correspond with the brake marks left on the road by the accused's vehicle which showed he had started to brake some distance from the point of impact. The accused refused to comment on the brake marks. The president invited the accused to approach the bench and explain his evidence in relation to a sketch plan of the accident. The accused did so, and the president asked him to indicate where the stationary vehicle had been as it was not shown on the map and had not been seen by the police when they arrived at the scene of the accident. The accused could not explain this. The president then finally asked the accused 'Do you recognise your fault?' to which the accused replied 'Yes, but only to a very limited extent'.

The procureur, 'partie civile' (heirs of the deceased) and defence lawyer had no questions to suggest. The president then examined the only witness who had been cited, namely a police officer who had arrived at the scene of the accident and drawn the sketch plan. The questions mainly concerned the brake marks on the road and the absence of any stationary vehicle as referred to by the accused. None of the parties suggested any questions to put to this witness.

The lawyer for the 'partie civile' addressed the court, and while moving for a conviction, was mainly concerned with the civil aspects of the case. The procureur made a very brief address suggesting the accused be convicted, but saying nothing about sentence. The defence lawyer dealing with the criminal aspect of the case addressed the court at great length, moving for an acquittal on the charge of causing death by reckless or careless driving. He produced a letter to the effect that the accused was normally a very careful driver. A second defence lawyer then addressed the court, and while also requesting an acquittal, the bulk of his address was concerned with arguments as to why the accused should not be held liable to meet the civil claim.

The president announced that the court would adjourn the case for fourteen days when the court's judgment would be given. The accused could continue to remain at liberty.

(9) Male accused aged 25 years: charged with theft. Before the trial commenced, the accused's lawyer moved that the trial be adjourned to a later date as a second accused was also involved in the charge. The second accused was not before the court as the case quoad him had been sent to a juge d'instruction, the second accused having a history of mental illness. The reason for the adjournment was to allow both accused to be tried at the same time.

The procureur did not object to the defence request The lawyer for the 'partie civile' who was present, was not asked for his views, but did not object.

The president adjourned the case for 4 weeks.

(10) Male accused aged 22 years: charged with being found in possession of hashish; he had one previous conviction for forgery; the case was investigated by a juge d'instruction who had liberated the accused awaiting trial. The trial commenced with the accused's name being called, but the accused failed to appear. The president questioned the 'huissier' concerning the citation of the accused to court, and examined the execution of service of the citation. Having satisfied himself that the accused had been properly cited, the president announced that the trial would proceed in his absence.

The president then gave a very brief resumé of the accused's background and the facts of the case from the 'dossier'. The amount of hashish involved was very small. The president then read verbatim the statement made by the accused to the juge d'instruction in which the accused admitted being in possession of the drug which was intended for his own personal use.

There being no witnesses, the procureur formally asked the court to convict and sentence the accused 'according to the law'.

The president, without adjourning the court, held a brief private consultation with the other two judges, then gave the court's judgement stating which facts the court held proved and the relevant statutory provisions. The accused was convicted and sentenced to four months imprisonment.

(11) Male accused aged 45 years: charged with driving offences. The case had not been investigated by a juge d'instruction, but only by the police. The accused had been cited to attend court, but when the case called, he failed to answer to his name. The president questioned the 'huissier' about the citation and examined the execution of service thereof.

After a brief consultation with the two other judges, and without obtaining the views of the procureur, the president announced that although the accused had been properly cited, the case would be adjourned for three weeks, the accused to be re-cited to attend the adjourned hearing.

Appendix 8. Excerpts from Trials in the Cour d'assises

(See para 89)

The following are excerpts from trials in the Cour d'assises de Paris in 1972.

(1) Attempted theft and attempted murder

The accused who was a male aged 29 years concealed himself in a department store near its closing hour; when everyone had left, he went to a cash register on the fifth floor, which he had previously noted had been full; while the accused was attempting to open the cash register, a security guard came by chance to the fifth floor; the accused concealed himself and as the guard passed him, the accused leapt out and stabbed the guard in the back; the guard sustained serious injury and his life was only saved by major surgery; the accused admitted planning the theft one week previously, and admitted taking the knife with him for this purpose—both these admissions being made during his examination by the juge d'instruction.

The security guard had entered the subsequent proceedings as 'partie civile', as had the Social Security Ministry.

The trial opened in the usual way (as described in para 89 etc.), the prosecution objecting to one juror and the defence objecting to two. The defence 'avocat' intimated the presence of a witness of whom no notification had been given and who had not been cited. She was the mother of the accused and has been in hospital from before the time of the offence until the day before the trial. She could speak to the character of the accused, but not to the facts of the case. None of the parties objected, so the president allowed her to leave the court with the other witnesses.

The president began his examination of the accused by asking him about his background. Most of this was done by leading questions—'You were born at . . . ?' 'Your parents were . . . ?' etc. The accused was asked about his birth, schooling, parents, brothers and sisters (including their present whereabouts and characters); work record (which included references by his employers—e.g.—'Your third employer said you were given to moods and not amenable to discipline—is this true?'). Having quoted what various such people said about the accused, and asked the accused to comment thereon, the president then asked the accused details of his previous convictions, of which there were several. The president asked the procureur général and the 'avocats' for the accused and 'parties civiles' if they had any questions—no one had any.

The president then examined the accused about the offence itself. Where he thought the evidence was not in dispute, he used leading questions, but otherwise only used such questions where he thought it necessary, viz:

President: 'Did you have a knife with you?'
Accused: 'Yes'

President:	'Where did you get it?'
Accused:	'I've had it for years'
President:	'Why did you take it with you?'
Accused:	'I don't know. Perhaps in case I was attacked'
President:	'Would you please explain why you told the juge d'instruction that you took the knife in case anyone caught you committing the theft. That differs from what you say today'
Accused:	'Probably what I told the juge d'instruction was the correct answer'

The president examined the accused in full about all the details of both charges, quoting verbatim from statements made by witnesses to the juge d'instruction. At the conclusion of the examination none of the parties had questions to put to the accused.

The president then examined the first witness who was the injured security guard. As 'partie civile' he did not take the oath. The examination concerned only the criminal aspects of the case and did not touch on the civil claim. At the conclusion of his examination, the president allowed the 'avocat' for the accused to question the witness as to the accused's sobriety at the time of the offence. The general tenor of the witness's answers was that the accused had been drinking, but was well aware of his actions.

The president then examined an expert witness, being a psychiatrist who had examined the accused on the instructions of the juge d'instruction. He gave a detailed report, the effect of which was that the accused showed no signs of mental illness. The president then examined two further experts concerning the accused's state with regard to alcohol at the time of the offence, a sample of the accused's blood having been given a blood/alcohol analysis on his arrest shortly after committing the offence. Both experts gave the opinion, that while the accused was under the influence of alcohol, this was not such as to render him drunk and incapable or to make him unaware of his actions. The defence 'avocat', with the permission of the president was allowed to cross-examine both witnesses direct and at great length.

The president then examined the remaining witnesses—the store manager, a shop assistant and the police witnesses. None of the parties had any questions to put to these witnesses. The president then called the accused's mother. Since no one objected to her being examined, the president proceeded to do so, the witness not giving evidence on oath (as a relative of the accused). Her evidence basically consisted of an account of the accused's childhood and upbringing. She concluded by making a very emotional plea to give the accused a chance and not to send him to prison.

The president then adjourned the court for thirty minutes and on its resumption, invited the parties to address the court, which they did as follows:

'*Avocat*' for Social Security Ministry (partie civile)'

'The accused is guilty of the offence, but as he has spent more than twelve months in prison awaiting trial, the court might consider that punishment is enough'. The Social Security Ministry had entered appearance as 'partie civile' to recover from the accused the sums of money it had expended as sickness benefit to the security guard. If the accused were released, he could find a job and make repayment from his earnings.

'*Avocat*' for the Security Guard (partie 'civile')

The guard had entered appearance as 'partie civile' in order to claim damages from the accused. The guard had suffered greatly having spent several months in hospital and still having occasional pain. He had to give up his job, but constantly thought of his former colleagues exposed to risks of violence of this nature—and such crimes were on the increase. The guard was not acting out of vengeance, but the accused must meet the due consequences of his criminal act. The accused's claim that he was under the influence of drink was not borne out by the expert evidence. The accused should and must be convicted.

Procureur

The accused had never led a satisfactory life. At the age of twelve years he was in trouble with the police for theft; at the age of thirteen years he was placed in detention; nine years ago he was sentenced to one month's imprisonment for theft. Other members of the accused's family were honest and hardworking and there was no reason for the accused to be otherwise, except for his basic bad character. When he married, his wife might have reformed him but 'I read in the dossier that he beat her regularly' (Note—No mention had been made of this fact before). With regard to the offence, it was clearly premeditated. The accused carried a weapon and admitted planning the offence prior to its commission. The expert evidence dealt with his alcoholic condition. 'I also noted from the dossier that each time he was questioned, the accused continually increased the amount of alcohol he claimed to have consumed' (Note—No mention had been made of this fact before). The court must consider all other persons working as security guards, policemen etc. often subjected to attacks of this nature, and far too often being killed. 'We are living in an age of violence. If the aggressor knows that such acts will surely be followed by severe penalties, this may help to suppress such violence.' This offence was deliberate and premeditated—'If you were to find that there were no mitigating features, the penalty for this case is death. I do not ask for the death sentence, but I ask you to impose a penalty of ten year's imprisonment.'

'Avocat' for the Defence

'When this case was debated before the chambre d'accusation, the prosecution said they were not persisting in their allegation of premeditation. I am therefore most surprised to hear them emphasising this point today.' The last time the accused was in trouble was nine years ago. Since then he has settled down and been in regular employment. Most of his employers spoke well of him. He came to settle in Paris some months prior to the offence. He tried to find a job without success and expended all his savings. In this situation he became subject to fits of depression and began drinking excessively (Note—No evidence had been led to this effect). On the day of the crime he had consumed two bottles of white wine and several glasses of cognac. He was not so drunk that he did not know what he was doing, but he was not in a normal state. He took the knife, went to the shop and concealed himself. Almost on instinct he jumped on the guard and stabbed him. He later told the juge d'instruction—'I did not want to hurt him, I'm sorry.' Since that date, while in prison, he sent the guard all the small sums of money he received from his wife intended to buy small personal comforts in prison. He recognised he had committed a serious crime but 'I know this man. I have visited him every week over the past fifteen months. He is not an evil man. He could be saved, but not if you impose the sentence suggested by the prosecution. He is a young man who has gone astray but is not lost.'

The president then asked the accused if he had anything he wished to say. The accused said, 'I'm sorry for what I did. I ask the guard's forgivenness . . .' (at this point the accused burst into tears and became incoherent.

The president then told the jury their duty was to decide the case depending on whether they were thoroughly convinced etc. (see para 93) but did not read out the questions. The court then retired. When it resumed about one hour later, the president informed the accused that he had been convicted of both charges by majority but that since mitigating circumstances existed, the penalty would be seven years' imprisonment. (A copy of the list of questions and the answers thereto is annexed. This copy was made available after the trial). The first question asked if the accused was guilty of the attempted theft. On being answered in the affirmative succeeding questions dealt with factors which by French law act as aggravations to theft—viz. was the accused carrying a weapon, was the offence committed at night, was the place where the theft was committed inhabited. The next question asked if the accused was guilty of the attempted murder of the guard. On being answered in the affirmative, the following question asked if the attempt was made in furtherance of theft, which is an aggravation under French law. The final question asked if there were mitigating factors (unspecified) in the accused's favour.

After the president informed the accused briefly of his rights should he wish to appeal, the court adjourned, then reconvened without the jury, to consider the civil issues. The accused remained in the dock.

The avocat for the Social Security Ministry presented details of the benefits paid to the injured guard, and moved the court to order the accused to make repayment in full.

The avocat for the injured guard gave details of his claim at great length—the guard was permanently scarred, his health was permanently ruined, he had had to give up sports, change his job etc., etc. He had suffered great pain. He therefore claimed damages amounting to X francs.

The defence avocat accepted the claim by the Social Security Ministry. With regard to the claim by the injured guard, he accepted some items but not others. He then argued at great length why this claim should be abated.

The procureur did not address the court, which adjourned for ten minutes. On resuming, it ordered the accused to make repayment to the Social Security Ministry in full and to pay an amount to the injured guard slightly less than he had claimed.

COUR D'ASSISES DE PARIS

Audience du 28 avril 1972

DECLARATION DE LA COUR ET DU JURY

dans le procès contre le nomné PARIAT Jean Claude

Questions:

PARIAT Jean Claude accusé ici présent est-il coupable d'avoir à Paris, le 27 aout 1970 en tous cas sur le territoire français et depuis moins de dix ans, tenté de soustraire frauduleusement une certaine somme d'argent au préjudice des Ets 'Printemps Nation' ladite tentative manifestée par un commencement d'exécution n'ayant été suspendue ou n'ayant manqué son effet que par des circonstances indépendantes de la volonté dudit PARIAT?

Réponse: Oui à la majorité de 8 voix au moins.

Question:

Aggravations: Ladite tentative de soustraction frauduleuse ci-dessus spécifiée a-t-elle été commise:

(1) le coupable étant porteur d'une arme apparente ou cachée?

Réponse: Oui à la majorité de 8 voix au moins.

Question: La nuit?

Réponse: Oui à la majorité de 8 voix au moins.

Question: dans un lieu habité ou servant à l'habitation?

Réponse: Oui à la majorité de 8 voix au moins.

Question: Ledit PARIAT Jean Claude est-il coupable d'avoir à Paris, le 27 aôut 1970, en tous cas sur le territoire français et depuis moins de dix ans, tenté de donner volontairement la mort au sieur PONCE Claude, ladite tentative manifestée par un commencement d'exécution n'ayant été suspendue ou n'ayant manqué son effet que par des circonstances indépendantes de la volonté dudit PARIAT Jean Claude:

Réponse: Oui à la majorité de 8 voix au moins.

Aggravation:

Question: Ladite tentative d'homicide volontaire ci-dessus spécifiée a-t-elle précédé, accompagné ou suivi ladite tentative de soustraction fraudeleuse ci-dessus spécifiée?

Réponse: Oui à la majorité de 8 voix au moins.

Question: existe-t-il des circonstances atténuantes en faveur de l'accusé?

Réponse: oui

Fait en Cour d'Assises au PALAIS DE JUSTICE à Paris

le 28 avril 1972

Signatures

En conséquence de la déclaration qui précède, la Cour et le Jury réunis, après en avoir délibéré ensemble sans désemparer conformément à la loi, decident à la majorité absolue de condamner PARIAT Jean Claude à la peine de sept années de réclusion criminelle.

Signatures.

(2) Attempted Murder

The accused who was a male aged 22 years was charged with the attempted murder of his brother-in-law by stabbing him with a knife and throwing him over a railway bridge.

The victim, who was married to the accused's sister frequently beat his wife severely; she frequently left him to live in the parental home, where he invariably followed her, and created a scene; on one occasion he beat her cruelly until she agreed to have intercourse with him; he was an alcoholic; his wife lived in a state of real terror of him and had instituted divorce proceedings. On the day of the offence, the accused saw his brother-in-law loitering about outside his wife's place of employment, obviously waiting for his wife. The accused went into the factory and told his sister of this. She became terrified and begged her brother (the accused) to rescue her.

The accused approached his brother-in-law, who was so drunk that he was unsteady on his feet, and persuaded him to accompany him. The accused then led him to a railway bridge where he asked him to stop molesting his (the accused's) sister. When his brother-in-law refused, the accused with no prior warning drew out a knife and stabbed him several times in the back. He then threw his brother-in-law over the bridge to the railway lines below. Fortunately a passerby rescued him and after a period of intensive care in hospital, he survived. The accused told his sister what he had done, then gave himself up to the police.

The trial opened in the usual way. After the jury had been ballotted, the 'huissier' read out the names of the witnesses, and it was learned that the accused's brother-in-law (the victim) was not present. The president asked the procureur and the avocat for the accused if the trial could proceed in the absence of this witness, and both agreed that it could. The brother-in-law had not entered appearance as 'partie civile'. Apart from him, there were no eye witnesses to the offence.

The clerk of court then read the remit from the chambre d'accusation, which when giving a summary of the facts stated that the accused had never sought to deny the facts of the case.

The president began his examination of the accused by considering his background. Most of this was done in the form of leading questions, tracing the accused's life from birth until the day of the offence. The opinions of various persons were quoted, viz. 'Your school report says you were calm, friendly but not too intelligent.' 'One employer says you were careful, hardworking and he was sorry to lose you; another says that you were a really good worker.' The accused was asked to comment on these opinions. The accused had no previous convictions. After this part of the examination was concluded and neither of the parties had any questions to put, the president said that to understand the accused's behaviour, it was necessary to consider the way of life of the victim of the offence. The president then read a life history of the victim, from time to time quoting verbatim from witness statements in the 'dossier', and asking the accused to comment thereon. The effect was to show that the victim was an alcoholic and of a violent character, especially towards his wife. The president then examined the accused on all aspects of the offence, using leading questions if he thought the matter was not in dispute, viz.:

President: 'Did you have any weapon?'
Accused: 'I was carrying a knife in my pocket'
President: 'Why?'
Accused: 'Because I was afraid of my brother-in-law'
President: 'Why were you afraid? Had he ever assaulted you before?'
Accused: ———— No answer

Later in the examination the following questions and answers were made:
President: 'So you and your brother-in-law were on the bridge over the railway. What happened next?'

Accused:	'I am not sure how it all started'
President:	'Did you tell the juge d'instruction that you asked your brother-in-law to leave your sister alone and he refused?'
Accused:	'Yes'
President:	'Well was that how it started?'
Accused:	'Yes'

In the course of the examination of the accused by the president, the procureur occasionally interrupted to put a question to the accused, and the defence 'avocat' suggested several questions which the president instructed the accused to answer. At the conclusion of the examination, neither party had any further questions.

The president then examined the witnesses, one of whom was the accused's sister (i.e. the wife of the victim) and who was not put on oath because of her relationship to the accused. Each witness was told 'Please tell us what you know of this affair,' and then gave his evidence in narrative form. Occasionally the president, procureur and defence 'avocat' interrupted the narrative to ask questions (the president always instructing that these questions should be answered), but in general all questions were deferred until the end of the witness's narrative. One of the witnesses was a psychiatrist who had examined the accused on the orders of the juge d'instruction. He referred frequently to a paper in his possession (presumably a copy of his report which would be contained in the 'dossier') but which was not lodged as evidence. The psychiatrist stated that the accused showed no signs of mental illness or abnormality. The court adjourned for thirty minutes after the last witness had been examined.

When it resumed, the procureur addressed the court. After giving a resumé of the facts of the case, he gave his view that the victim had obviously lost all interest in the case as he had not even bothered to attend the trial, despite being properly cited. The accused was not really an evil person—'I suggest you sentence him to five years' imprisonment. Should the defence suggest this sentence be suspended, I have no comment to make. Alternatively you may consider imposing a sentence of nine months' imprisonment, being the time the accused has spent in custody awaiting trial' (Note—this would mean the immediate release of the accused).

The defence 'avocat' stressed the good character of the accused contrasting it with the brutality of the victim. The accused only acted to protect his sister—'I acknowledge he committed this act and must be convicted, but you can be merciful in your sentence.' At the conclusion of this address, the president asked the accused in person if he had anything to say. The accused said nothing, but wept.

After the president addressed the jury, telling them to decide according to whether they were thoroughly convinced etc., the court retired, the questions not having been read aloud. When the court re-convened fifteen minutes later, the president announced that the accused had been unanimously convicted and was sentenced to five years' imprisonment, the sentence to be suspended.

(3) Murder

Male accused aged 37 and a female accused aged 29 were both charged with murder. The female accused who was the mistress of the male accused, was also the mistress of the victim of the offence, who was unaware of her attachment to the male accused. On the night of the offence, both accused went to the victim's house, the male accused hiding outside. The female accused was admitted, and later excusing herself for a minute, she opened the door, allowing the male accused to enter, unknown to the victim. The male accused hid in the bathroom. The female accused then suggested to the victim that they have sexual intercourse, knowing that the victim would probably go to the bathroom first. When the victim went there, the male accused stabbed him several times, killing him. The female accused, while later protesting that she thought the male accused had only intended to stun the victim, then assisted the male accused to ransack the victim's house, robbery being the motive for the attack. Later both accused were found in possession of some of the victim's clothing.

When both accused were subsequently interviewed by the juge d'instruction separately and in confrontation with each other, both gave different versions of the offence, each accusing the other of lying. The version given by the female accused was as above. The male accused maintained he had never been present at the scene of the crime and knew nothing about it. He was only involved in so far as on the following day the female accused had given him some male clothing, which admittedly he suspected must have been stolen. He alleged that the murder had been committed by the female accused and another unknown accomplice. The female accused had only implicated him to protect this unknown accomplice.

The trial opened in the usual way, and the president commenced by examining the female accused, starting with her background. She had one conviction for prostitution five years ago and was an epileptic. Apart from that, there was nothing of note about her background. The president then examined her about the facts of the case, most questions taking the form of 'what happened next?'. He then questioned her with force and vigour concerning the statement by her co-accused, quoting the statement verbatim and occasionally asking the male accused to verify if the statement correctly recorded his evidence. The president suggested to the female accused that she was lying and the male accused was telling the truth. Despite this very lengthy and exacting examination, the female accused refused to change her evidence. No questions were suggested by the procureur, the accused's own 'avocat' or the 'avocat' for the male accused.

The president then examined the male accused, starting with his background. This included a reference by an employer to the effect that while the accused was a good worker, he was resentful of authority and prone to violent outbursts. When considering the accused's health record, he quoted a report from a sanatorium, to the effect that while in the sanatorium the accused had often displayed a violent temper. The accused refused to comment on these remarks, but when the president asked him to comment on a statement by a former girl friend that the accused was violent, brutal and jealous, having attacked her viciously on several occasions without reason, the accused's comment was —'Well, more or less.' The president asked the accused if his wife was in the process of divorcing him, and when the accused denied this, the president said 'Well you told the juge d'instruction a divorce was pending. What are we supposed to believe?' He was then questioned about his previous convictions, which included several for assault. In one of the incidents, the accused had been arrested on a charge of assault, but the procureur de la République had not proceeded with the case. The president asked several questions about this. At the conclusion of this part of the examination, the president said 'It may fairly be said that you were a good worker, but prone to a bad temper and bouts of unreasonable and brutal violence. Do you agree?' The accused said he did.

As none of the parties had any questions to put, the president then examined the accused with regard to the offence. Some parts of the examination were conducted by leading questions by saying 'I do not think you are contesting these details.' With regard to the main facts of the case, the president allowed the accused to give his evidence in his own words, after which he questioned him very forcefully, quoting verbatim the statements and prior evidence of his co-accused, and also quoting statements made by witnesses to the juge d'instruction. Throughout this part of the examination, the accused either said the co-accused and other witnesses were lying, or else he refused to comment or answer the questions.

The president then questioned both accused jointly, but both refused to change their evidence.

No questions were put by the procureur or the defence 'avocats'.

The president then examined the witnesses, most of whom spoke to formal matters, or the actings of both accused after the offence. The male accused was unable to produce any witnesses to provide him with an alibi.

At the conclusion of the trial, both accused were convicted.

Appendix 9. Sudden Deaths

(*See para 165*)

In Scotland, the procurator fiscal has a duty to investigate all sudden, unexpected or suspicious deaths, all of which must be reported to him. He alone has this power, there being no other official or judicial inquiry (except as noted below). In particular there is no coroner's inquest as in England. The procurator fiscal must make an immediate inquiry as to the cause of death, and while he may avail himself of whatever assistance the police afford, he has the sole responsibility for the inquiry.

No precise definition is given as to what constitutes a sudden, unexpected or suspicious death as each case depends on the circumstances. The following examples merely typify the more common categories of deaths reported, but should not be taken as an exhaustive list: deaths directly resulting from violence or injury (including murder, criminal violence, road accidents, industrial accidents, fires, drowning etc.) regardless of whether the injury was caused deliberately or by accident; deaths indirectly resulting from violence or injury—i.e. where the injury itself did not have fatal consequences but gave rise to a further condition which led to the death (a common example being death due to broncho-pneumonia following on a fractured femur in an elderly person); deaths which might have been caused directly or indirectly by the actings of a third party (including deaths in the course of or following a surgical operation for which a general or local anaesthetic was administered); suspected suicides; deaths where the cause is unknown or uncertain; all cases of persons found dead; and generally any death that was sudden or unexpected. The word 'suspicious' must be interpreted in its widest sense and not restricted to instances where there is clear evidence of criminal behaviour; any circumstances where negligence might be suspected, or even where there is merely some unusual feature may be classed for this purpose as 'suspicious.' In brief, while it is an over-simplification to state that *all* deaths must be reported to the procurator fiscal unless clearly caused by old age or some known medical condition, such a rule is not far from the truth.

A death may be reported to the procurator fiscal by anyone, but the commonest sources are the police, the medical profession and hospitals, registrars of births, marriages and deaths, and occasionally private individuals. The police usually learn of the death from a relative or some other witness, and having made a brief investigation, they submit a report to the procurator fiscal within twenty-four hours of the occurrence. In a case such as a man suddenly dropping dead as a result of a coronary thrombosis, the report will often be in the form of a summary of the facts, but in other instances the police will normally submit the statements taken from the witnesses.

The medical profession and hospitals usually report deaths to the procurator fiscal by telephone although this is sometimes done by the doctor coming to see him. Except for 'anaesthetic deaths,'[1] the procurator fiscal will then usually instruct the police to make inquiry and submit a report to him, although such a course is not obligatory.

By arrangement, registrars report to the procurator fiscal any uncertified death, any death which was caused by an accident arising out of the use of a vehicle, or which was caused by an aircraft or rail accident, any death arising out of industrial employment, any death due to poisoning, any death where the circumstances appear to indicate suicide, any death where there are indications that it occurred under an anaesthetic, any death resulting from an accident, any death caused by neglect, any death caused by drowning, fire or explosion, and numerous other categories of death. Since all deaths require by law to be registered, this arrangement ensures that the procurator fiscal will be informed of all such deaths, whether or not he has already learned of them from another source.

Private individuals occasionally report deaths directly to the procurator fiscal. This usually only arises when the individual is of the opinion that the death resulted from negligence or lack of treatment on the part of a third party, or where the individual thinks that the circumstances surrounding the death should be inquired into.

When the procurator fiscal is informed of a death, he must take immediate action to satisfy himself as to the cause and to decide what further steps, if any, should be taken. The body may not be buried (or cremated) without the express consent of the procurator fiscal, and since in Scotland burials usually take place within three or four days of the death, the need for immediate action is apparent to avoid unnecessary distress to the next of kin.

Where the cause of death is obvious and has been certified by a medical practitioner, and where there is no evidence of fault on the part of a third party, the procurator fiscal on receiving the police report will usually release the body for burial and take no further steps except to send a formal intimation to the registrar. If in such circumstances the death has been due to suicide, the procurator fiscal will normally interview the next of kin at a later stage. It sometimes happens that a doctor has examined the body, and while reasonably certain of the cause of death, is unwilling to certify the cause because he lacks background information. Since this is usually contained in the police report, the procurator fiscal may discuss the case with the doctor who may then decide to issue a death certificate after he has been acquainted of the full facts of the case. The responsibility for doing so lies with the doctor. In theory should he refuse to issue a death certificate and should the procurator fiscal decide that no further inquiry is necessary, the latter may still allow the body to be buried. In practice, however, it is doubtful if any procurator fiscal would follow this course. Another situation which frequently arises in this class of deaths is where the doctor is satisfied as to the general cause of death, but would like to have a post mortem dissection for specific medical reasons. In such cases the procurator fiscal will usually release the body for burial, but arrange with the doctor that should a private post mortem dissection be performed (with the consent of the relatives), the doctor will inform him of the

---

[1] In anaesthetic deaths the procurator fiscal receives a written report from the doctors involved and thereafter instructs a post mortem dissection by an independent medical practitioner.

results of the post mortem. A procurator fiscal will not normally order a post mortem dissection merely because the cause of death, in the medical sense, is unexplained, if extrinsic circumstances sufficiently explain the cause of death in the popular sense, unless of course there is a suspicion of criminality or negligence.

Where the cause of death is not obvious or certified, or where there are suspicious circumstances, evidence of negligence or criminal conduct, the procurator fiscal will order a medical expert to perform a post mortem dissection of the body. Before doing so, the procurator fiscal should obtain a formal warrant from the sheriff authorising the dissection. Such warrants are granted as a matter of routine by the sheriff who is only required to append his signature to the document. The consent of the relatives of the deceased is not required. While a sheriff's warrant may be dispensed with, this is never done in view of the ease with which one is obtained. If a warrant is urgently required outwith normal working hours, or on a public holiday, the procurator fiscal will usually send a police officer to the sheriff's house in order to obtain the necessary signature. When a death occurs in one district as a result of an accident in another, the procurator fiscal in whose district the accident occurred is responsible for the investigation. He will obtain a post mortem warrant from his own sheriff and the sheriff in whose district the death actually occurred will grant a warrant of concurrence.

When the procurator fiscal decides to instruct a post mortem dissection, he must further decide whether the dissection should be performed by one or two medical practititoners. Where there is a possibility of criminal proceedings being taken against some person or persons consequent to a death, and it is necessary to prove the fact and cause of death, the procurator fiscal will order two medical practitioners to act in view of the need for corroborated evidence at any subsequent trial. Occasionally the procurator fiscal may be generally satisfied that only one doctor is required although having some slight doubt on the matter. He will then instruct the doctor to proceed with the post mortem, but to stop immediately if he finds any unexplained or suspicious circumstances, so that a second doctor can be brought into the case. When he orders a post mortem dissection, the procurator fiscal must also ensure that the body is properly identified to the medical practitioner by two witnesses. When the body can not be identified, the procurator fiscal will instruct that it be photographed and finger-printed prior to the dissection.

In certain instances the procurator fiscal will require to give specific instructions as to what steps are to be taken before, during or after the post mortem. These may include the taking of samples of blood for analysis and alcohol content, the taking of specimens of head and pubic hair, nail scrapings, finger-prints, samples of dirt, dust etc., photographing of specific wounds, marks or part of the body, the examination of wounds in relation to particular weapons or other objects, in cases of manual strangulation an examination for finger-prints on the surface of the body etc., etc.—all depending on the circumstances of each case. He may also order that the entire body, or specific parts thereof be subjected to an x-ray examination prior to the dissection. This is usually done as a matter of routine where the 'battered baby syndrome' is suspected, but otherwise it will depend on the circumstances of the case, or sometimes on the x-ray facilities that are available.

The procurator fiscal may also order that parts of the body be retained, or subjected to expert analysis and for this purpose may instruct any expert in any field. In general, then, he must take all steps to ensure that the cause of death is properly ascertained and capable of proof. With regard to the question of proof, should the death be the subject of a criminal trial, the reports of the doctors and experts, together with any parts of the body retained as evidence will be made available to the defence for examination before the trial in the usual way. Where an accused has already been arrested prior to the post mortem dissection, some procurators fiscal will notify the defence lawyer of the forthcoming dissection so that the accused may nominate a medical expert to be present as an observer.

When the post mortem has been concluded and no further examination is necessary, or in deaths where no post mortem has been instructed, the procurator fiscal, as above noted, will release the body for burial. Where cremation is desired, such consent must be given in writing, and while the procurator fiscal may grant such consent of his own accord, he usually requires medical certificates from two doctors as to the cause of death (unless, of course, he has instructed a post mortem and has obtained the result thereof). For all cremations it is necessary to have the consent of a medical referee, although the consent of the procurator fiscal dispenses with this. Thus it occasionally happens that a death which has not been reported to the procurator fiscal will be notified to him by a medical referee who is not prepared to consent to cremation. In theory, the procurator fiscal can always refuse to allow the body to be cremated and insist that it be buried instead, so that if need be, at a later date it could be exhumed and re-examined. In practice such a situation never arises as the procurator fiscal will ensure that all necessary examinations are performed before the body is released.

Whether or not there is a post mortem dissection, if the procurator fiscal is satisfied with the evidence which he receives from the police, he may close his inquiry. If, however, the case has special features or he thinks further inquiry is desireable, he may make such inquiry himself by precognoscing witnesses. He must always adopt this course if the death falls within the following classes—which he must also report to Crown Counsel—namely: where there are suspicious circumstances; where the death was caused by an accident arising out of the use of a motor vehicle; where the circumstances point to suicide; where the death occurred in circumstances the continuance of which or possible recurrence of which is prejudicial to the health and safety of the public; where death occurred in industrial employment, or in any prison or police cell; where the death was directly or indirectly connected with the actions of a third party; where any desire has been expressed that a public inquiry should be held or where the procurator fiscal is of the opinion that such an inquiry should be held; and various other types of death about which the Lord Advocate has given specific instructions.

When he is investigating a death, the procurator fiscal is particularly interested in investigating any evidence of criminal conduct, negligence or circumstances liable to be injurious to the public. The number of witnesses precognosced depends on the case, but invariably the next of kin will be interviewed to ascertain whether or not they wish a public inquiry. The witnesses are cited to attend the procurator fiscal's office and all the interviews are in private. All information obtained is confidential and may not be communicated to third parties without the previous consent of Crown Counsel. At the end of the inquiry the results are not made public. As a result the whole proceedings are secret, a fact which is often appreciated by the next of kin especially where the death was suicidal or accompanied by other distressing circumstances. Where, however, the next of kin are not satisfied with the procurator fiscal's inquiry, or wish the results made public they may request that a public inquiry be held. In reporting this request to Crown Counsel, the procurator fiscal must also express his own views thereon. Occasionally the next of kin may request a public inquiry for the improper motive of having the evidence recorded on oath and thus forming the basis of a future civil claim. Instead of requesting an inquiry, it is always open to the relatives to institute private inquiries, but these would usually prove unsatisfactory. Occasionally a procurator fiscal may suggest to Crown Counsel that a public inquiry be held, even where the next of kin does not wish one, or is opposed to one.

Fatal Accident Inquiries
Under the Fatal Accidents Inquiry (Scotland) Act 1895, a public inquiry must be held in all cases of death of any person, whether employers or employed, engaged in any industrial employment or occupation in Scotland due or reasonably believed to be due to accident occurring in the course of such employment or occupation. In addition to this particular class of deaths, the Fatal Accidents and Sudden Deaths Inquiry (Scotland) Act 1906 authorises the Lord Advocate 'whenever it appears to him to be expedient in the public interest to direct a public inquiry into such death and the circumstances thereof be held.' It is under this latter provision that the relatives may request or the procurator fiscal recommend that a public inquiry be held, the Lord Advocate having a complete discretion in the matter.

The form of the inquiry is the same whether it is held under the 1895 Act or the 1906 Act. It is held before a sheriff and a jury of seven laymen. Jurors who are related in any way to any of the parties involved are usually excluded. Where more than one inquiry is being held on the same day, the same jury usually deals with all the inquiries. The Crown is represented by the procurator fiscal, although in inquiries of major importance an advocate depute or even the Solicitor General may act. Prior to the inquiry, notices are inserted in the newspapers and specific intimation is given to the next of kin, and other interested parties. Such intimation is also given to any individual who may possibly be held responsible for the death.

The inquiry commences with the jury being selected and sworn. The sheriff clerk then reads a very brief resumé of the facts, after which the procurator fiscal calls witnesses to give evidence. As in criminal trials, each witness is examined by the procurator fiscal, then by any interested parties, then re-examined by the procurator fiscal. When the procurator fiscal has called his last witness, the interested parties may call any further witnesses. Since however, the proceedings take the form of a judicial inquiry and not a criminal trial, it is not left to the parties to present opposing sides of the case, and the rules of evidence are not so strictly followed. Where there are reasonable grounds for believing that criminal proceedings may eventually follow against a certain individual who is called as a witness, the procurator fiscal must ensure that he is warned by the sheriff that he need not answer 'any question tending to show that he is guilty of any crime or offence.' Further no question should be asked of him by the procurator fiscal tending to incriminate him. The witness should merely be told that he may make any statement he desires in regard to the facts and circumstances of the case. Should a criminal trial afterwards take place and these precautions have been duly followed, the evidence given by the witness at the inquiry is competent evidence against him at the criminal trial. Despite this ruling, there is nothing to prevent one of the parties at the inquiry attempting to question the witness at length.

At the conclusion of the evidence the procurator fiscal and the parties may address the jury, but this is seldom done. The sheriff usually makes a brief address, then the jury considers its verdict. This is frequently done without retiring and a formal verdict is often returned. During the hearing of the evidence, a juror may ask any questions from any of the witnesses. When giving its verdict, the jury may add any recommendations which it thinks appropriate. The entire proceedings are recorded by a shorthand writer and any interested party may request a copy of his extended shorthand notes.

Where it is known that criminal proceedings are to be taken, the criminal trial will be held before any public inquiry, since failure to do so would allow the evidence to be published in advance of the trial, with a risk of prejudice to the accused. It usually follows that where there has been such a trial, it is pointless to hold a subsequent public inquiry. Furthermore since deaths arising from industrial accidents usually give rise to civil actions which explore the issue in greater depth, the public inquiry into this type of death merely acts as a brief preliminary to the civil action.

Because of these factors it is sometimes argued that Fatal Accident Inquiries have little purpose and should be abolished. They do, however, provide a valuable means of publicly investigating deaths which have given rise to public disquiet, or where the relatives are not satisfied that the circumstances surrounding the death have been adequately made known. For these reasons, it is all the more important that a verdict be given by a jury consisting of members of the public.

The number of deaths investigated by procurators fiscal in 1971 was 8,320 and in 220 instances, Fatal Accident Inquiries were held.

Appendix 10. The Hearing of Additional Evidence on Appeal

See para 231)

In the case of H.M. Advocate v Temple (1971) the accused was convicted on indictment in the sheriff court, the verdict of the jury being by majority. The accused then presented an application to the High Court for leave to appeal, asking the court's permission to lead further evidence for the purpose of determining whether there had been a miscarriage of justice. A defence of alibi had been presented at the trial, and evidence led in support of it, but the accused had been identified by two Crown witnesses, and in convicting him, the jury obviously rejected the alibi. The evidence which the accused wished to lead on appeal was further evidence in support of his alibi. This evidence could have been led at the original trial.

The court refused the application for leave to appeal, Lord Justice General Clyde stating . . . '. . . before the court will allow such witnesses to give evidence, it must be satisfied that the verdict of the trial was a miscarriage of justice. The court (i.e. the Appeal Court) cannot re-try the case, but it may allow additional evidence to be led if it considers that the new evidence it is proposed to lead would, had it been before the jury at the trial, have led it to reach a different verdict. The test is not whether we think the jury might have done so but whether we are reasonably satisfied that the jury would have done so.' Since evidence of alibi had been led at the trial and rejected by the jury, Lord Clyde was obviously satisfied that the jury's verdict would not have been different even if the jury had heard the additional evidence.

Section 16 of the Criminal Appeal (Scotland) Act 1926 entitles the Secretary of State for Scotland when considering the exercise of the prerogative of mercy in relation to a conviction on indictment, to refer the whole case to the appeal court for determination, or to refer any point arising to the appeal court for their opinion (See paragraph 230). Whether or not either of these courses is followed depends on the discretion of the Secretary of State for Scotland. In the case of Temple, when the application for leave to appeal was rejected, the accused applied to the Secretary of State to exercise his prerogative. In terms of Section 16, the Secretary of State requested the Appeal Court to hear the additional evidence. The court appointed one of its judges (Lord Avonside) to do so. After he had heard the additional evidence, Lord Avonside reported to the Appeal Court who in turn reported to the Secretary of State for Scotland. Both these reports were confidential. The Secretary of State after considering the report, refused to exercise the prerogative of mercy.

It is sometimes suggested that the law be changed to enable the Appeal Court to order a re-trial in cases such as the above. One body of legal opinion is against

226

such a change and may be summed up in a report issued by the Council of the Law Society of Scotland in the following terms: 'A system of re-trials necessarily involves that the jury's verdict may be displaced by the verdict of another jury, or perhaps even a series of juries. It therefore introduces a further element of uncertainty into the judicial process which, apart from its effects on the accused, may throw out of focus the whole decision making procedure as it affects judge, jury, counsel—and perhaps all the participants. It necessarily involves delay. It puts a premium on incompetence by giving the badly represented the opportunity of a second chance before a jury.

It is not unusual for an appeal to succeed on the grounds of a mere technicality. Often the Appeal Court express their reluctance on quashing a conviction. If, in such a case, the court had power to order a re-trial, this might be thought to violate the principle that once the accused has 'tholed his assize' he should not be proceeded against a second time. It is thought that the prosecuting authorities would be slow to seek such powers, and that there is no public demand for it. But such a system which allowed re-trial only on the presentation of fresh evidence for the defence might be thought curiously one-sided and tending to favour only the accused.

Finally, it is the Council's view that a system of re-trials would lead to a spate of hopeless appeals. Every solicitor has had experience of an accused who complains after his conviction because some shred of useless evidence was not led before the jury, or some totally discreditable witness, likely to do more harm than good, was not adduced on his behalf. With the prospect of 'another go at the jury' or before a different sheriff, as the prize, every disappointed prisoner would importune his solicitor to appeal for a new trial.

For these reasons . . . such an unpromising procedure should be resorted to only if it can be shown that our present procedure is seriously defective in the sense that it is likely to lead to injustice. The Council would reject any such allegation. Our present procedure allows the Appeal Court to admit new evidence, and enables the court, if satisfied by such evidence, to substitute its opinion for that of the jury and quash the conviction. Certainly the test imposed by the court is a severe one. It will not admit the evidence merely on the view that if it had been led before the jury it might have resulted in an acquittal. The court must be reasonably satisfied that it *would* have resulted in an acquittal. The fact that there is no reported case (i.e. since 1926) of a conviction being quashed because of new evidence does not seem . . . to show that their approach is unduly stringent; on the contrary, it seems . . . inconceivable that the standard should be less exacting. . . . If the Appeal Court can be satisfied that fresh evidence—and in Temple's case it was not fresh evidence that was offered but additional evidence—can be adduced which would have resulted in an acquittal, the conviction falls to be quashed, and the Council therefore see no point in introducing the complication of a re-trial.'

Such an opinion as the above, however, provides no solution to the situation where the accused is acquitted because of some mere technicality in procedure, which could be rectified if there was a re-trial. The Appeal Court sometimes answers this problem by the way in which it interprets the law—hence, for example, when dealing with driving while under the influence of alcohol, the law prescribes that the accused must be asked by a policeman in uniform to provide a specimen of breath in a device approved by the Secretary of State for Scotland. In one case where the prosecutor forgot to prove that the policeman was in uniform, the

Appeal Court held that all policemen may be taken to be in uniform unless the contrary is proved; in another case where the prosecutor led no evidence to the effect that the device had been approved by the Secretary of State for Scotland, the Appeal Court held that such devices were so approved. It may be questioned if the correcting of minor procedural errors by means of such interpretation of the law would be followed if a system of re-trial were allowed.

Bibliography

In English

Renton and Brown's Criminal Procedure According to the Law of Scotland:
Third Edition.
The Law of Evidence in Scotland *by Allan Grierson Walker and Norman Macdonald
Lockhart Walker.*
The Criminal Law of Scotland *by Gerald H. Gordon.*
The Criminal Law of Scotland *by Sir J. H. A. Macdonald:* Fifth Edition.
The Parliament House Book.
The Scottish Legal System *by David M. Walker.*
Preliminary Investigations of Criminal Offences: *A Report by 'Justice'* 1960.
The Prosecution Process in England and Wales: *A Report by 'Justice'* 1970.
Report of Working Party on Public Prosecutions 1971 *by Her Majesty's Stationery
Office* cmd. 554.
Observations by the Council of the Law Society of Scotland on Questions submitted
by the Committee on Criminal Procedure under the Chairmanship of Lord
Thomson.
Criminal Justice (Scotland) Act 1949.
Summary Jurisdiction (Scotland) Act 1954.
Criminal Justice (Scotland) Act 1963.
The French Legal System *by René David and Henry P. de Vries.*
The Role of the Prosecutor in French Criminal Trials *by Robert Vouin.* The
American Journal of Comparative Law, Volume 18, 1970.
The Administration of Criminal Justice in France. An Introductory Analysis *by
George W. Pugh.* The Comparative Study of the Administration of Justice,
Illinois 1962.
L'instruction criminelle *by A. E. Anton.* The American Journal of Comparative
Law. Volume 9, No. 3. 1960.

In French

Traité de Droit Pénal et de Criminologie *par Pierre Bouzat et Jean Pinatel* 1963.
Traité de Droit Criminel *par Roger Merle et André Vitu* 1967.
Compte Général de l'administration de la Justice Criminelle etc. Annee 1969 *par
le Ministére de la Justice.*
Quelques Aspects de la Procédure Pénale Française *par P. A. Pageaud, Procureur
de la République, près le Tribunal de Grande Instance de Paris.*

Code Pénal *par Librairie Dalloz* 1970-71.

Code de Procédure Pénale *par Librairie Dalloz* 1970-71.

Le Nouveau Visage de la Magistrature *par George Verpraet*.

Les Avoués près la Cour de Paris 1968.

Droit Pénal et Procédure Pénale *par Vouin et Léauté* 1960.

Droit Pénal Général et Procédure Pénale *par Stephani et Levasseur* 1959.

Practique criminelle des cours et tribunaux: droit pénal *par F. Hélie* 6th edition 1954.

Dictionnaire formulaire des parquets et de la police judiciaire *par G. Poittevin* 1950-54.

Le Ministerè public en matière répressive et civile et l'exercice de l'action publique *par Rousselet et Patin* 3rd edition 1953.

L'accès à la Magistrature par le Centre Nationale d'Etudes Judiciares.

Le Ministere Public *par Michele-Laure Rassat*.

Note: In addition, information was obtained from legal journals, law reports and periodicals both in English and in French; text books to which occasional reference was made have been omitted. Much of the information foɪ France was gathered by observing and working with French 'magistrats' and officials in courts and offices in France, and for Scotland by ten years service in the Procurator Fiscal service.

Printed in Scotland for Her Majesty's Stationery Office by McCorquodale (Scotland) Ltd., Glasgow.   Dd 954101/3319 K8 9/75